Applications and Approaches to Object-Oriented Software Design:

Emerging Research and Opportunities

Zeynep Altan
Beykent University, Turkey

A volume in the Advances in
Systems Analysis, Software
Engineering, and High Performance
Computing (ASASEHPC) Book Series

Published in the United States of America by
    IGI Global
    Engineering Science Reference (an imprint of IGI Global)
    701 E. Chocolate Avenue
    Hershey PA, USA 17033
    Tel: 717-533-8845
    Fax: 717-533-8661
    E-mail: cust@igi-global.com
    Web site: http://www.igi-global.com

Library of Congress Cataloging-in-Publication Data

Names: Altan, Zeynep, 1958- editor.
Title: Applications and approaches to object oriented software design : emerging research and opportunities / Zeynep Altan, editor.
Description: Hershey, PA : Engineering Science Reference, an imprint of IGI Global, [2020] | Includes bibliographical references and index. | Summary: "This book explores applications and approaches to object-oriented software design"-- Provided by publisher.
Identifiers: LCCN 2019037020 (print) | LCCN 2019037021 (ebook) | ISBN 9781799821427 (hardcover) | ISBN 9781799821434 (paperback) | ISBN 9781799821441 (ebook)
Subjects: LCSH: Object-oriented programming (Computer science) | Application software.
Classification: LCC QA76.64 .A628 2020 (print) | LCC QA76.64 (ebook) | DDC 005.1/17--dc23
LC record available at https://lccn.loc.gov/2019037020
LC ebook record available at https://lccn.loc.gov/2019037021

This book is published in the IGI Global book series Advances in Systems Analysis, Software Engineering, and High Performance Computing (ASASEHPC) (ISSN: 2327-3453; eISSN: 2327-3461)

Advances in Systems Analysis, Software Engineering, and High Performance Computing (ASASEHPC) Book Series

ISSN:2327-3453
EISSN:2327-3461

Editor-in-Chief: Vijayan Sugumaran, Oakland University, USA

MISSION

The theory and practice of computing applications and distributed systems has emerged as one of the key areas of research driving innovations in business, engineering, and science. The fields of software engineering, systems analysis, and high performance computing offer a wide range of applications and solutions in solving computational problems for any modern organization.

The **Advances in Systems Analysis, Software Engineering, and High Performance Computing (ASASEHPC) Book Series** brings together research in the areas of distributed computing, systems and software engineering, high performance computing, and service science. This collection of publications is useful for academics, researchers, and practitioners seeking the latest practices and knowledge in this field.

COVERAGE

- Virtual Data Systems
- Computer Graphics
- Human-Computer Interaction
- Software Engineering
- Engineering Environments
- Storage Systems
- Enterprise Information Systems
- Parallel Architectures
- Network Management
- Distributed Cloud Computing

IGI Global is currently accepting manuscripts for publication within this series. To submit a proposal for a volume in this series, please contact our Acquisition Editors at Acquisitions@igi-global.com or visit: http://www.igi-global.com/publish/.

Titles in this Series

For a list of additional titles in this series, please visit:
https://www.igi-global.com/book-series/advances-systems-analysis-software-engineering/73689

Fundamental and Supportive Technologies for 5G Mobile Networks
Sherine Mohamed Abd El-Kader (Electronics Research Institute, Egypt) and Hanan Hussein
(Electronics Research Institut, Egypt)
Information Science Reference • © 2020 • 360pp • H/C (ISBN: 9781799811527) • US
$225.00

Deep Learning Techniques and Optimization Strategies in Big Data Analytics
J. Joshua Thomas (KDU Penang University College, Malaysia) Pinar Karagoz (Middle
East Technical University, Turkey) B. Bazeer Ahamed (Balaji Institute of Technology and
Science, Warangal, India) and Pandian Vasant (Universiti Teknologi PETRONAS, Malaysia)
Engineering Science Reference • © 2020 • 355pp • H/C (ISBN: 9781799811923) • US
$245.00

Formal and Adaptive Methods for Automation of Parallel Programs Construction Emerging
Research and Opportunities
Anatoliy Doroshenko (National Academy of Sciences of Ukraine, Ukraine) and Olena
Yatsenko (National Academy of Sciences of Ukraine, Ukraine)
Engineering Science Reference • © 2020 • 195pp • H/C (ISBN: 9781522593843) • US
$195.00

Crowdsourcing and Probabilistic Decision-Making in Software Engineering Emerging
Research and Opportunities
Varun Gupta (University of Beira Interior, Covilha, Portugal)
Engineering Science Reference • © 2020 • 182pp • H/C (ISBN: 9781522596592) • US
$200.00

Metrics and Models for Evaluating the Quality and Effectiveness of ERP Software
Geoffrey Muchiri Muketha (Murang'a University of Technology, Kenya) and Elyjoy Muthoni
Micheni (Technical University of Kenya, Kenya)
Engineering Science Reference • © 2020 • 391pp • H/C (ISBN: 9781522576785) • US
$225.00

For an entire list of titles in this series, please visit:
https://www.igi-global.com/book-series/advances-systems-analysis-software-engineering/73689

701 East Chocolate Avenue, Hershey, PA 17033, USA
Tel: 717-533-8845 x100 • Fax: 717-533-8661
E-Mail: cust@igi-global.com • www.igi-global.com

Table of Contents

Section 3
A Real-World Application on Internet of Things

Preface

Software has been part of professional life since the 1960s and has made calculations easier. The beginning of these initiatives dates back to German Schickard, the inventor of the first mechanical calculator to work with gears and wheels in the 17th century and Pascal (1642), the inventor of the first commercial calculator. With the start of the industrial revolution in Europe in the 18th century, the model designed by Jacquard was developed to operate the weaving looms made the most important contribution of mechanics to the calculation; this discovery has also paved the way for today's electronic world. Babbage's Analytical Machine, which was able to make strong calculations in different number systems in the late 19th century, was developed using Jaguard's weaving looms. This machine was defined as a general-purpose machine with the ability to read/write data and make comparisons, and this resulted in the first programmable machinery concept. In the same years, Hollerith's commercial machine will later be named as IBM (International Business Machines).

Considering these developments, it would not be right to exclude the NATO conference, where software engineering was first used as a term and as the milestone of the east of software engineering. In fact, by going back even further, Gödel's incompleteness theorem and Shannon's information theory should also be examined as scientific problems. Abstract mathematics, which is used for the implementation of these problems and for the analysis and design of today's many complex real-world problems, is also the sub-discipline of software engineering.

After the first NATO conferences in 1968 and 1969, it has been started to search how the software to be developed would be a high-quality product. The software developed in the 1970s was customer-oriented. With an article published in 1970 (Royce, 1970), the first software development methodology, the waterfall model, was formally published. This model, which was later implemented (Bell & Thayer, 1976), has been the pioneer of iterative (Royce, 1987) incremental and spiral (Boehm, 1988) software development models and today's contemporary development approaches according to changing needs in information systems modeling. In those years, overcoming the software lifecycle crisis was the most important quality criterion. The term quality was used for the first time at the NATO 1968 conference and this meant difficulties in completing growing software problems on time and with the determined budget. Although the aim of the developed product was to realize all the requirements in time and in the budget, this could happen at a very low rate for various reasons.

Software applications developed in the 1980s turned towards shared responsibility and customer satisfaction consideration. Languages for object concept starting with Simula language (Nygaard, 1978); languages such as Ada (Booch, 1983), C ++ (Stroustrup, 1986), Smalltalk (Goldberg & Robson, 1983) and Eiffel (Meyeri 1988) laid the foundations of object modeling in the 80s. It had never been used until Booch first mentioned the term object-oriented design in 1982 in an article (Booch, 1982). In fact, procedure-oriented development methods have started this process step by step over time. In the end, the number of object-oriented design methods that combine data and methods with cohesive units and classes has increased (Lorensen, 1986; Jacobson, 1987; Wirfs-Brock et al., 1990; Rumbaugh et al., 1991; Booch,1991) and the use of unified modeling language (UML) (Booch et al.,1999) that models these systems has become widespread. This design technique, called object-oriented software engineering, has been used in modeling real-world problems since those years and is also an irreplaceable part of today's software development methodologies.

CHALLENGES AND MODERN SOLUTIONS

In the requirements, analysis and design stages of software development lifecycle models, visual analysis is performed at successive levels and the problem is prepared for implementation. The fact that the shared responsibility, which was the quality criterion of software products developed in the 1980s, continues by expanding its scope; the visualizations of the problem in the abstract analysis have great importance. The worst-case scenario for the quality of the software is the problems detected by the user (customer). As long as any small problem is not solved, it causes more problems. Therefore, shared responsibility has been important since the time it was taken as an assessment criterion in determining the quality and it grows in importance every day. Brooks, known as one of the leaders (pioneers) of software engineering, stresses in his famous article No Silver Budget (Brooks, 1987) that the difficulties in fulfilling the quality criteria cannot be overcome by object-oriented programming languages or the rule-based programming languages of artificial intelligence applications while solving the complex software problems of those years. According to Brook, it is important to achieve the solution of the problem at the end of good design. And this happens when designers who do their job well choose a suitable development method for the problem and perform a strong conceptual analysis. As we can see, the history of taking the human factor as a criterion for a highly qualified software product dates back to the 80s.

With the problems becoming more complicated in the 1990s, the scope of quality was expanded. For example, security has turned from mathematical vulnerability into cryptography as a non-functional issue. While security-focused more on protecting the database in those years, today, many security vulnerabilities can be seen at any time at the end of the faults in the software. Therefore, the software test is rapidly becoming the main problem of the software industry. Today, the web aims to reach more users in a competitive environment as now being an indispensable deployment platform. Enterprise applications are that more users can access large programs that are quite comprehensive. In addition, embedded software is becoming more ubiquitous day by day. Open-source codes are increasingly meeting the expectations of software developers. All this means that giving security much more importance as a non-functional issue requires developers to have more knowledge about testing. Agile processes also oblige (force) both testers and developers to test better. The fact that high testability components give more confidence is not enough. The testability of low testability components should also be increased to reduce the risk. And this requires a good risk analysis.

Developed in a complex and tightly linked open eco-system, contemporary software systems have placed software ethics to the first place in quality assessments. As the developed systems grow and become more open every day, an increasingly large amount of data is intricately linked, and safety in relationships begins to be questioned. Social embedding of software in developed systems requires software engineers to evaluate ethical concerns in much greater detail. These are defined as non-functional requirements. For example, as a service-oriented software engineering application on peer-to-peer (P2P) networks; a malicious, undesired application that has never been encountered before can be detected automatically with the integration of different analysis techniques. Criteria for determining the ethical issues of software engineering have started to take shape in recent years. Although Ethical automation toolkits have started to be seen as a new application of data science, it is clear that the ethics of automating everything will be questioned more and more over time. In small-scale studies, it is possible to decide on ethical requirements by using the abstract, comprehend and communicative infrastructure of conceptual models. Just as in determining software requirements, specific ethical tools for specific problems can be designed with interviews and surveys made with communities. Thus, even if the risk taken by such an application is not reduced by 100% it will still prevent misusing of the application.

In summary, the concept of quality, which is the most important measurement of the software product, was about how to achieve software maintainability in the early stages of software engineering. As factors with customer satisfaction;

providing the needs for the decision to continue using the software, the simplicity of the product usability and the speed of the software were important. While the cost, timely delivery, and reliability of the product were important quality criteria for management; the number of bugs in the software was the fundamental constraint that developers had to set to ensure reliability needs.

For the quality criteria that must be included in the documentation of software, functional specifications that describe what to do for the solution are determined first. Then, the quality plan that shows the quality attributes to be defined for the implementation and how these attributes will be assured is prepared. In the final stage, the project management plan is required. A project management plan can be given as timing, dependencies, and resource requirements.

The software metric, which is one of the factors determining the quality of software, is a quantifiable measurement of the quality criteria of the problem to be solved. The software metrics may not always give the desired result. A few of these situations are that the relationship between quality criteria and metric values doesn't give the intended results, some criteria cannot be measured, or there are no tested metrics. Another problem is the difficulty in estimating some metrics since they are associated with more than one criterion. In addition to all these disadvantages, software metrics can bring additional costs to the project. Therefore, a predetermined quality model should be chosen according to the structure of the product to be developed for quality metrics classified with 3P as a process, product, and project, and it should be aimed to meet the criteria for this model. This formal process, called software quality assurance, makes evaluations and documentations related to the targeted criteria of the product developed during software development life circle. (Boehm et al., 1978; Grady, 1992; McCall et al., 1977). In software quality standards studies, which started 10 years after software engineering was accepted as a separate discipline, new technologies such as computational grids have started to be used as problems become more complex, and more advanced object-oriented modeling techniques have been implemented (Czajkowski et al., 2001).

Coupling is a software metric as quality measurement and it defines how closely the software modules are linked together. This concept was first introduced in the 1960s as the foundations of structural design, formulated in an article in 1974 and later turned into a book as the basis of structural design (Yourdan & Constantine, 1979). This feature, which dates back to the birth of software engineering, has become the cornerstone of large-scale distributed event-based applications with the 21st century. Coupling's downgraded grid computing has been the solution environment for many real-world problems. Service-oriented architecture has started to be used by the business community in applications and has pioneered the large-scale distributed applications of the next 10 years. Interactions of software agents providing loose coupling are defined to create both functional and non-functional requirements in today's applications by creating a service-oriented architecture. The notification of web service at the design stage of the life cycle is realized with object-oriented design techniques and a single responsibility principle that provides loose coupling and high cohesion. The aim of the design in web service projects is not only to obtain solutions with high availability and efficiency but also to choose the most appropriate technologies to the characteristics of the infrastructure to be used. Many libraries and standards are used for this. Thus, the infrastructure becomes easier to understand and use, and its portability increases. In summary, technologies to be used to achieve the desired performance level of the application should be selected very carefully. Large-scale web service applications using the event-based approach aim to meet performance requirements by reducing coupling. The specifications of the security and reliable messaging standards of a highly decoupled web service system are also important (Kowalewski, et al., 2008).

Service computing provides flexible computing architectures to support modern service industry. With the spread of cloud computing, cloud infrastructures have been developed to provide stronger functionality in services. Both the number of services and service users are increasing rapidly. Therefore, data generation has also been huge with the data come from mobile devices, user social networks, and large-scale service-oriented systems. Large-scale service-oriented systems are required instead of traditional infrastructures to solve the current problems. As the scalability and complexity of distributed systems increase, cloud computing systems have been required as large-scale distributed systems. This structure includes a large number of interactions between service components. It may also cause the performance problems. Trace logs provide valuable information to find the cause of performance problems. Furthermore, a dynamic environment forces to be built reliable service-oriented systems. Therefore, software fault tolerance is an important approach to build reliable systems. It is achieved by employing functionally equivalent components. Since distributed systems include a number of service components, the service environment is highly dynamic. Hence, dynamic service migration is in need by moving the service from one physical machine to another at runtime as in many commercial cloud platforms.

Finally, with the transformation to the digital environments in the industrial sector and the transition from the industrial economy to the service economy, it is necessary to modernize the solution methodologies of complex real-world problems in order to implement technological developments.

ORGANIZATION OF THE BOOK

The book is organized into three sections under the titles of "Power of Science and Technology on the Software Products", "Some Matters on Object-Oriented Design and Architecture", and "A Real-World Application on Internet of Things". The first article that constitutes the first chapter describes the effects of science, especially abstract mathematics and physics, technology and also as a very important factor humans, in the development of electronic devices from the past to the future. In the second section, there are six chapters. Although the subject of the book has been extensively studied in the literature, the researchers of this chapter have clarified object-oriented design problems that are commonly encountered in the solution of today's real-world problems. In addition, for the detailed design of the software problem, they examined the architectures used in today's products comparatively. Another topic of this stage is the software metrics of which was analyzed in a different chapter. The third section includes a chapter which explains an Internet of Things application in detail beginning from the specification of requirements to the development of design phases, and finally to the implementation of the product.

A brief description of each of the chapters follows:

Section 1: Power of Science and Technology on the Software Products

Chapter 1 starts with the statement that the first NATO Conference hold in 1968 has shaped the future of the computer and software world, and continues by explaining the contributions of abstract mathematics and physics to present day and the future. The effects of information theory to the first computers progressed with the Neumann architecture as modern computers, and in the last decades computers have begun to be designed with quantum information. Not only science but also technological advances have contributed to all of these improvements. On the other hand, abstract mathematics has great impression on solving complex real world problems. If the studies of Shannon, Gödel, Turing and others were absent, it would be impossible to talk about digital transformation.

Section 2: Some Matters on Object-Oriented Design and Architecture

Chapter 2 highlights the integrations problems of applications in distributed information systems. For the solution, it is important to achieve the lowest coupling while ensuring the least interoperability requirements between the applications. In other words, the changeability has to be kept in minimum, but applications have to be able to interact effectively to supply the dependency attribute. This is a way of merging the applications with exact interoperability. Compliance and conformance concepts allow an application to replace by another without breaking the service, or to remain in service while a variant serves additional clients.

Chapter 3 states that there are inconsistencies in the definitions of many architectural methods and applications in the literature and analyzes the fundamental concepts of object such as MOF, MDA, PIM, MVC, BCE. The researcher designs a consistent system as a Model Driven Engineering approach that enabled the unambiguous determination of the responsibility of components of these patterns. Consecutive model elements beginning from CIM, through PIM to the PSM form has been established by using UML and BSMN notations.

Chapter 4 deals with various aspects of service oriented software architecture patterns in big data systems. Microservice architecture and serverless computing are examples of transferring from monolithic systems to service oriented architecture. Microservice architecture, as an efficient platform for data intensive applications in Internet of Things environments, implements the technology independently and heterogeneously. Differently with the widespread use of cloud platforms, cloud programming models and adoption of cloud technologies plays crucial role in the progress of serverless computing. In addition to many advantages of these architectures, both have some issues according to each other and to other architectures.

Chapter 5 clarifies the concepts, architectures, technologies and techniques associated with big data processing. Firstly, it has been expressed data generation, data storage and data processing stages in detail which constitute the big data life cycle. Later, chapter elaborates six different big data analytics techniques. Lastly, Apache Hadoop which has been developed for software safety, distributed environments and scalable software projects is described. The chapter will be a guide to the researchers who is willing to work in this field.

Chapter 6 investigates the RESTful web services and their behaviors in terms of object-oriented principles. Before the clarification of RESTfull service thoroughly, the comparison of this service with big web services has done according to four basic properties of services, and big web services have been explained briefly. Then, the chapter illustrates how a RESTfull service is developed step by step and demonstrates the general and technical differences between big and RESTfull services. Anyone who reads this chapter will clarify the ambiguities about the choice of which service is more appropriate for her project.

Chapter 7 clarifies the importance of software metrics in software engineering concept. The chapter takes into account different and most popular object-oriented software metrics and some software testing tools. When a new metric is added to a software product, it brings a new problem together, therefore the choice of software testing tools are also substantial for the development team.

Section 3: A Real-World Application on Internet of Things

Chapter 8 presents the development of a mobile and web application utilizing new technologies to collect and distribute blood bags between blood banks and hospitals in order to enhance the healthcare sector. The development team has categorized the application based on main stakeholders as the hospital sub-system, the blood bank and campaign sub-systems, and the donator sub-system. One of advantages of this system is the friends or family members are informed in case of any emergency case. The developed application is open to perform automatic notification with more detailed Internet of Things technologies such as the use of wearable devices.

REFERENCES

Boehm, B. W. (1988). A spiral model of software development and enhancement. *IEEE Computer*, *21*(5), 61–72. doi:10.1109/2.59

Boehm, B. W., Brow, J. R., Lipow, M., McLeod, G., & Merritt, M. (1978). *Characteristics of software quality*. North Holland Publishing.

Booch, G. (1982). Object oriented design. *ACM SIGAda Ada Letters*, *1*(3), 64–76. doi:10.1145/989791.989795

Booch, G. (1983). *Software engineering with Ada*. Benjamin Cummings.

Booch, G. (1991). *Object-oriented design with applications*. Redwood City, CA: Benjamin/Cummings.

Booch, G., Rumbaugh, J., & Jacobson, I. (1999). *The unified modeling language user guide*. Reading, MA: Addison-Wesley.

Brooks, F. (1987). No silver bullet: essence and accidents of software engineering. *Proceedings of International Federation for Information Processing*, 1069-1076.

Czajkowski, K., Fitzgerald, S., Foster, I., & Kesselman, C. (2001). Grid information services for distributed resource sharing. *Proceedings of the Tenth IEEE International Symposium on High-Performance Distributed Computing*. 10.1109/HPDC.2001.945188

Goldberg, A., & Robson, D. (1983). *Smalltalk-80: The language and its implementation*. Reading, MA: Addison-Wesley.

Grady, R. B. (1992). *Practical software metrics for project management and process improvement*. Prentice Hall.

Henderson-Sellers, B., & Edwards, J. M. (1990). The object oriented systems life cycle. *Communications of the ACM, 33*(9), 142–159. doi:10.1145/83880.84529

Jacobson, I. (1987). Object Oriented Development in an Industrial Environment. *ACM SIGPLAN Notices, 22*(12), 183–191. doi:10.1145/38807.38824

Kowalewski, B., Bubak, M., & Balis, B. (2008). An event-based approach to reducing coupling in large-scale applications. *Computational Science. International Conference on Computational Science ICCS 2008*. 10.1007/978-3-540-69389-5_41

Lorensen, W. (1986). *Object-oriented design*. CRD Software Engineering Guidelines, General Electric Co.

McCall, J. A., Richards, P. K., & Walters, G. F. (1977). *Factors in software quality, RADC TR-77-369*. Rome Air Development Center.

Meyer, B. (1988). *Object-oriented software construction*. Englewood Cliffs, NJ: Prentice-Hall.

Nygaard, K., & Dahl, O.-J. (1978). The development of the SIMULA languages. In History of Programming Languages, (pp. 439-480). ACM Digital Library. doi:10.1145/800025.808391

Royce, W. W. (1987). Managing the development of large software systems. *Proceedings of the 9th International Conference on Software Engineering*, 328-338.

Rumbaugh, J., Blaha, M., Premerlani, W., Eddy, F., & Lorensen, W. (1991). *Object-oriented modeling and design*. Englewood Cliffs, NJ: Prentice Hall.

Stroustrup, B. (1986). *The C++ programming language*. Reading, MA: Addison-Wesley.

Thomas, E., & Thayer, T. A. (1976). Software requirements: are they really a problem? In *Proceedings of the 2nd International Conference on Software Engineering*. IEEE Computer Society Press.

Winston, R. (1970). Managing the development of large software systems. *Proceedings of IEEE WESCON, 26*, 1–9.

Wirfs-Brock, R., Wilkerson, B., & Wiener, L. (1990). *Designing object-oriented software*. Englewood Cliffs, NJ: Prentice Hall.

Yourdon, E., & Constantine, L. L. (1979). *Structured design: fundamentals of a discipline of computer program and systems design*. Prentice-Hall.

Section 1
Power of Science and Technology on the Software Products

Chapter 1
The Role of Science, Technology, and the Individual on the Way of Software Systems Since 1968

Zeynep Altan
iD https://orcid.org/0000-0002-0383-9261
Beykent University, Turkey

ABSTRACT

The NATO conference held in Garmisch in 1968 was on the future of the computer and software world, and it presented the process of realization of what has been talked about in those dates to the present day. This chapter also examines the development of software systems since 1968, depending on the technological developments. The contribution of mathematics and physics to the development of information systems was explained in chronological order by comparing the possibilities of yesterday and today. Complementary contributions of science and technology have been evaluated in the evolutionary and revolutionary developments ranging from the definition of information theory in 1948 to teleportation. It can clearly be seen that discrete mathematics directly affects the improvements in computer science. This review study clearly shows that it would not be possible to talk about digital transformation and quantum computation if the discoveries of Shannon, Turing and Neumann, and the studies of other scientists before them did not exist.

DOI: 10.4018/978-1-7998-2142-7.ch001

INTRODUCTION

At the NATO conference in Garmisch in 1968, the future of the computer and software world was dealt with. The arguments at the sessions were in preparation for today's digital world. The conference was held for two consecutive years and software engineering was recognized as an independent discipline. One of the editors of the meeting booklets of today's software infrastructure, Randel (2018) evaluated fifty years of software engineering. The paper summarizes the development of software engineering as a new discipline. The transfer of conference reports to an electronic platform in 2001 (McClure, 2001) informed the IT industry about the conversations held at the conferences and confirmed that all progress in information technologies and the software sector aligned with previous experiences.

The roles of science, technology, and human beings are all entwined when examined in the context of software engineering. Although all engineering disciplines utilize these three parameters, software engineering differs from others. The resulting software product in this discipline is abstract and is the product or a portion of the product that must entirely be completed. However, in civil engineering, for example, it is possible to open a bridge before the side roads are completed. This example should not be confused with the delivery of the software product to the user in parts. No matter how small a software product is, it is a stand-alone product and must be delivered to the user in a fully operational state. Examples can be increased for all other engineering fields that offer tangible, concrete products. Therefore, software engineering is different from other engineering disciplines because customer satisfaction is most prominent; the software needs to meet the needs of the user. This puts the human factor in the first three criteria. Today's rapidly changing software products require developers to work closely with the customer. In this context, the evaluations of satisfaction and performance for software engineers and software developers are indispensable criteria for this engineering discipline. In fact, the quality of the work performed in most labor sectors has been measured psychologically by scientific studies for a long time. There are many models investigating the relationship between the pleasure of the working environment and quitting the working, and intention not to work. While the intention of a software engineer or a product developer to quit their job is an important risk factor for the company, doing the job willingly is a positive appraisal for the business. In fact, the degree to which an organization's employees are satisfied with the working conditions and the working environment is an indication of how much that organization attaches importance to its employees.

In the first fifty years of software engineering, and by changing over from hardware engineering to software development processes, new techniques were developed and tools were used to deal with the complexity problem. During the evolution of software engineering, advanced engineering principles and complicated mathematical foundations have been applied to solve more complex software problems. While the effectiveness of the developed product was important in the early applications of software engineering, the accuracy and usability of the result (i.e., software) became more substantial as the problems became more complex. Therefore, the contribution of individuals on the product had to increase. Complex, real-world problems led to the development of reusable products, and new development tools and methods have emerged as a result. However, since these tools solve increasingly complex problems and are designed according to the scope of human capabilities, the success in producing solutions with today's new technologies will guide the solution of complex systems in the future. Therefore, the integration of software engineering with system engineering and the cognitive psychology highlighted by human factors have important roles in overcoming the problems of today's engineering world. On the other hand, it is also necessary to consider the extent to which it is appropriate to use technological developments and important revolutions in solving current and future problems. Many of the negative conditions that can be caused by the modern world, especially security, are important issues that engineers must consider.

The technological advances of the 60s and 70s made significant contributions to the development of the software sector and it continued to develop in the 80s in cooperation with the software industry. Technology-driven software products that were effective in the 90s have transformed into a business world that uses technology as a focus today. The improvement of software engineering projects through the success stories of the past have always moved this new discipline forward. It is reported in the Standish Reports that similar, previously completed software projects have been utilized in many software projects. Furthermore, if there had been no major changes in the past in software technologies, it would have been impossible to imagine future of software applications.

Becoming an independent discipline in 1968 stemmed from prior scientific studies. Later, these studies were applied in the software field. In the 1950s, the people who focused on solving a software problem were either mathematicians or engineers who specialized in hardware. In this context, the problems were focused on the military, scientific calculations, and space research. The software development processes of the problems were being developed in the computing capacity of the computers of that time and under the guidance of hardware engineering. This is clear from the fact that the hourly cost of room-sized computers was 300 times higher than the cost of the engineer working on the system. However, it should be remembered that the system that solved the problems were also the first application of sequential waterfall models in the 70s. The solution from the 60s focused on developing the software product as the antithesis of the 50s. Thus, many software applications have changed from hardware intensive to human-intensive. Since human-computer interaction issues have become more significant than the strict engineering rules applied in software projects, the projects have been evaluated from a psychological perspective.

Since the software does not wear out like hardware, the maintainability concept of software was measured differently from the maintenance evaluation of the previous period. During this period, the human factor had been an effective parameter for planning and determining the cost of untouched software products. In the 70s, this factor made the solution difficult even though the problem was not very complex. Because the quality of software would become the focus of the product, the determination of this abstract concept would become more difficult. The prominence of the product to be developed led to the rapid development of programming languages. However, the languages used in software development in those years were not developed according to any software standard. NATO Conferences gave software engineering a formal structure that started in the 70s. Software products were being developed based on a software development methodology so that it was possible to work on large software projects. These large software projects were the first examples of today's digital world. Almost all design and programming principles of today's applications were created in this period. The software products of this era were compute-intensive. Further technological improvements were required to implement more data-intensive applications. These would constitute the electronic world of the 21st century.

In the 80s, the scalability of the products began to rise. The most important principle of the 80s was productivity. The specification of the software development standards was one of the main reasons for the increase in product productivity. Software development standards were examples of software products developed in the following periods.

Other important criteria for productivity are the usage of software tools, the realization of the environment configurations, and the integration of them; together, they developed software products on a global scale. Utilizing the abstract mathematics theories, formal software development principles have contributed significant effort to the improved productivity of software products. With the support of knowledge-based approaches, advanced software development environments have resulted in the first expert system applications. As the scope of the problems widened, the complexity of the software that would challenge the productivity solutions have appeared. Since the early 00s, new software development approximations have continuously been designing. They resolve the disadvantages seen in the previous projects and continue updating the methods to solve real-world problems.

Conceptualization and visualization in the solutions to problems are guided by the reuse of software as an important solution approach in the later periods of the software discipline and became one of the basic parameters in increasing productivity. With the spread of the Internet, distributed software engineering applications have increased worldwide. Further, with the combination of software departments of many companies on an international scale, some problems such as communication difficulties, timetable issues, infrastructure deficiencies, and documentation mismatches have occurred. As an outcome of technological developments and improvements in software applications, it has been seen that today's global projects could easily overcome these obstacles. Concurrent software applications of distributed software development methodology have strongly contributed to the transformation of open-source software development.

Returning back to the 90s, human-computer interaction has found its place in the computer world and usability has become an important criteria for product development. Thus, the focus was on the group developing the product rather than the performance of the individuals. This approach constitutes the agile software development methods of the 00s. It was also the beginning of rapid changes in information technologies due to globalization.

The remainder of the chapter is organized chronologically. The next section describes the birth of the first computers and the advances from the calculations performed with the existing computers to the future of the calculations, namely quantum computing. Then, the indispensable contribution of logic to the evolutionary development of technology and applications is discussed, and the study continues by discussing the evolutionary developments and revolutionary innovations. The ongoing study concludes with a general assessment of the human factor in successful software products.

COMPUTERS AND COMPUTING FROM THE PAST TO THE FUTURE

First Computers and Information Theory

George Stibitz developed the electrical digital computer that could compute complex numbers in 1937 and is considered one of the fathers of the first modern computers (Saxson, 1995). With Stibitz, Boolean logic was used for the first time in electronic world applications (Ceruzzi, 2012). At Bell Labs, where he was also a researcher, he designed computer circuits with adding, subtracting, and storing operations. Stibitz did not know that Konrad Zuse, in Berlin, was working on the same subject; but he was aware that Claude Shannon had designed binary relay circuits using symbolic logic in his doctorate study at MIT (Collins, 2002). These studies were carried out independently of each other in the same years and are the first examples of modern-day computers. Shannon also studied coding theorems, which is one of the concepts of information.

The general definition of information theory is the quantification, storage, and communication of information. In 1948, Shannon developed a general system that would form the basis of communication theory by enabling the transmission of information by signals, just as in today's data compression. A transmitter described by the system provided the appropriate signal and processed the message from the source throughout the channel. The entropy value of the source calculated by the noiseless channel coding theorem measured the optimal compression of incoming messages (Shannon, 1948). The capacity of a channel measured the speed of maximum transmission of the information at a certain noise level with the noisy channel coding theorem (Shannon & Weaver, 1949). Error-correcting codes, a fundamental principle of Shannon's information theory, were obtained after these theoretical studies and are still valid in boosting the transmissions of today's modems.

In the 1980s, modems carried out data transmission via telephone lines with a maximum speed of 9.6 kilobits per second. In those years, the need to increase the speed of data transmission meant that there were a large number of errors in the data. If Shannon had not developed information theory, there would have been no rapid data transmission, not enough space on disks, and no Internet world would emerge. The definition of Shannon entropy is the measurement of the information in the message in bits, while the Shannon limit is the information that can be sent with zero error at maximum speed (Lombardi, Holik & Vanni, 2016a). This can be explained using the following example: if a 3-bit message is transmitted 3 times, the receiver will receive 9 bits. But, the correct 3 bits will be sent with the error correction code. When the noisy status of the channel increases, more information will be needed to meet the errors. Shannon's studies have shown that the longer the code, the more accurate the message will be. Today, every device used has an error-correction function.

Today's Computers and Neumann Architecture

Developments in the field of electronics, along with the Von Neumann architecture (O'Connor & Robertson, 2003), were led by Moore's law (Moore, 1965). Moore expressed the need to integrate the circuit design with a greater number of components. Therefore, Moore, the father of semiconductor components, should be mentioned together with Neumann, the father of computers. In 1975, computers were generated by squeezing 65,000 components in a single silicon chip where the unit cost was reduced by taking advantage of Moore's law (Thackray et al. 2015). This was the beginning of many technological developments striving to meet the need for intensive data processing from integrated circuits to the present day. Computations made in the technological conditions of those days were performed at a much lower cost due to the lower power consumption than in previous years and with a higher performance where power densities increased dramatically. With the introduction of silicon chips, the era of low-efficiency hardware was over. By 1989, with the 486 processor, the transistor number rose to 1.4 million.

Increases in today's computer capacities in the last quarter of the 20th century enabled the development of product configurations; therefore, certain large computer manufacturers focused on platform-oriented products. The transformation into an all-encompassing architecture with a general-purpose processor has spawned the concept of reconfigurable computing. To meet the calculation need, operating systems that perform multi-task management, resource management, and time-sharing were developed. In these systems, global data transmission is realized according to tasks defined by making graph partitioning. Scientists think that the correction in the error-correction functions of devices will lead to the improvement in much more effective techniques with quantum information. In other words, if information carriage in problem-solving and data processing is a quantum system instead of a binary system, the problem of error correction will be eliminated. It is claimed that data transmission will be much more secure than today's technology (Lombardi, Holik & Vanni, 2016b). The binary structure of the computer architecture still in use also performs protection with entanglement systems, providing security by processing only slightly more knowledge. In today's computer systems, error corrections perform automatic communication with self-integration instead of the combination of different devices that are required in older applications. In other words, computer scientists are constantly designing more efficient algorithms to prevent traditional computers from lagging behind in the race.

Recently, requirements for new processor configurations for companies using data-intensive, powerful machine learning techniques such as deep learning have been rapidly increasing. Even today's supercomputers are forced to update their calculations on a machine with the same capacity. Still, 3D chips continue to improve processor performance. Another solution to the computing power of machines has been the migration of data centers to a single computation entity. Cloud services offer fairly cheap and easy alternatives, called in-house software. Despite these developments, the question of how to produce more powerful hardware that is compatible with complex data science, analytics applications, and self-learning systems is already one of the major problems of the processor manufacturers.

Quantum Information Theory and Quantum Computers

Quantum technology is rapidly improving, though it is controversial whether quantum computers will close the gap between classic and quantum computers. In companies using information technology, hardware capacities are constantly being increased, but this is not enough. Although large-scale quantum processors are very expensive today, quantum theory and algorithms will be the hardware infrastructures of future generations of computers, and the huge information of the future will be easily processed with these processors. Nations equipped with high technology are in a race to achieve supremacy in quantum computing, and huge systems have quantum computer requirements. The IBM Q System is the first quantum computer created in laboratories with quantum researchers and is preparing to serve the scientific and business world (Lardinois, 2019; Vincent, 2019). Despite being designed for commercial purposes, it is reported that this computer is not yet ready for widespread use. Google, on the other hand, claims that they have quantum supremacy and have a quantum computer with one million processors. Google's studies on artificial intelligence (AI) continue with powerful chips growing at an exponential speed relative to those in use (Hartnett, 2019).

Returning to how this radical quantum technology transformation began in information technology, it was claimed in 1999 that Shannon's knowledge was incompatible with the quantum context (Brukner & Zeilinger, 1999). When information storage, processing, and transmission were realized with quantum information theory according to the laws of quantum physics, no powerful computer operating with classical information technology would have access to this computational power that evolved at an exponential speed. Quantum bits (qubits) are the two states of a classical data bit, in which the transistor on the chip has two different voltage forms (Neilsen & Chuang, 2010). In other words, qubit symbolizes the state of a bit in a 2-dimensional vector space as 0 or 1. Qubit has the same characteristics as bits if it is single-way. Any qubit state space has a permanently expanding schedule. It is possible to summarize the existent application areas of quantum computing with the following titles:

1. Sophisticated modeling of financial services,
2. Research in medicine and pharmacy, simulations on biomedical,
3. Supply chain logistics applications in which billions of trillions of operations are Performed per person, where existing optimization problems will be insufficient for the Solution,
4. Applications that contain huge information in which exponentially faster data analysis is performed, in other words, machine learning.

One of the biggest changes in the Internet is that cloud computing made data computing power much more important as a revolution of the 21st century. In sum, quantum information theory studies continue to increase in three subjects depending on the field of application: super dense coding, quantum teleportation, and quantum computation (Wilde, 2019).

THE CONTRIBUTION OF LOGIC IN THE EVOLUTION OF MACHINES AND SOFTWARE TECHNOLOGY

Decision Problem and Computation Theory

Kurt Gödel's incompleteness theorem has made significant contributions to computer science and the modern-day computer world (Raattkaine, 2015). The Turing machine was a machine that called everything that has been calculated computable. This was Hilbert's solution, who was a famous decision and problem-solver in mathematics. Turing developed the Turing Machine to answer the following question, which Hilbert asked in 1928:

How can a general algorithm be written so that any mathematician can solve any mathematical expression?

This machine, with which Turing proved that a machine that can calculate everything, put an end to the famous decision problems of mathematics, suggested by Hilbert. Alan Turing's paper on computable numbers is proof that he is the principal originator of modern computers (Turing, 1936). Hilbert described the axiomatic formalization of systems before the solution of the decision problem with a number of formulas, and Turing also designed his famous abstract machine with axioms in formal terms. As a universal computational device where any algorithm is solved, the Turing machine performs calculations using the sequence of symbols found in an infinite tape. The number of states used to solve the problem is finite and the right end of the tape is limited to the operations that the computer can perform at once.

John von Neumann, who worked on the incompleteness theorem during the same period as Turing, solved this theory and described the infrastructure of computer architecture that has been in use since the 1940s. This solution represents the basis of modern-day architecture as Von Neumann Architecture was designed concretely with an input device, control mechanism, memory and output device, and the processing of the expressed system used in the solution of the incompleteness problem (Istrail & Marcus, 2013).

The English physicist Deutsch pioneered a new computing system by asking the following question aimed at Turing's theory:

Is there a single (universal) computing device that can effectively simulate any other physical system? (Deutsch, 1985)

In addition to physics, the graph theory, which is an important subfield of discrete mathematics, has been used in solving both hardware and software problems of systems. An example of this can be given from circuit design: a VLSI (Very Large Scale Integration) design is the algorithm of a multilevel graph partition (Karypis & Kumar, 1998). An implementation of this is the realization of a highly qualified hypergraph partitioning in a short time is in the design of telephone networks.

Ontology and Semantic Technologies

Since the perception and reasoning of knowledge are different in various people, it is natural to encounter communication difficulties. With the emergence of different terminologies, the data that refers to the same concept may not be able to connect different storing devices. When there is a huge amount of data using different terminology, ontology is a good technology that can solve this problem.

Ontology is the formal depiction of a shared conceptualization (Borst, 1997). The most important advantage of using ontologies is the symbolization and sharing of knowledge with the vocabulary used. In short, ontology acts as a format provider for information exchange, enables interoperability, reuses information, and integrates knowledge with automated verification. Thus, the machine's readability and operation can be more easily understood. The concept of lattice (described as Galois lattice) had important applications in data mining; it is a partial ranking system symbolized by the Hasse diagram (Berry & Sigayret, 2004), and it is the indispensable of ontology. Ontology languages such as OWL have also been developed based on description logic. OWL (Web Ontology Language) is widely used in many applications for representing and reasoning processes, planning and recognizing AI (Gil, 2005), modeling business processes (OMG, 2011), in web services, and for recognizing human behavior (Rodriguez, 2014). Different conceptualizations between systems exist, and different terminologies and meanings can be shared using ontology. The integration of ontologies is achieved if the relations between two or more ontology concepts are deduced in the solutions of real-world problems. Thus, the realization of heterogeneous data applications in distributed systems through ontology is a success of green information technology (Binder & Suri, 2009). In sum, the negative impact of information technology operations is minimized in computers and in every product related to computers at every stage from design to product manufacturing.

The main problems in the industry can be summarized as semantic interoperability, ubiquitous computing, enterprise integration, and business convergence. Mobile computing has been an integral part of daily life in the last five years. Mobile application developers are increasingly utilizing the benefits of semantic technologies in sharing, reusing knowledge, and knowledge decoupling. The wisdom of developed applications comes from the measure of new knowledge extracted from the inferred information (i.e. semantic reasoning). But, purpose-specific, standardized, and unambiguous data prepared with semantic technology imitates human logic by using simpler algorithms. Much simpler algorithms are used in operations using big data, and these algorithms attempt to imitate human memory.

Solving the Problems with Inference Rules

As mobile platforms became more widespread, ontology-based reasoning became indispensable and using semantic data became prevalent. The conceptual solution of many problems with uncertainty in this symbolization is generalized with probabilistic description logic. As description logic is determined in standardizing decision problems in big problems, the usage of finite automata has also been seen. Mobile devices on different platforms have established their own semantic APIs (Application Program Interface) using description logic with the improvement of semantic web technology. For example, description logics defined for health care and life sciences (e.g., tourism and augmented reality) have been realized with different ontology languages. Further, the solution for many real-world problems can easily be transformed into applications with influence diagrams (Borgida et al., 2019).

A classic example of influence diagrams used in many studies is the problem of deciding whether to go to a weekend picnic by looking at weather forecasts. To automatically transform the inference rules on mobile applications between platforms, rules defined in different languages need to be transformed syntactically (i.e., from Java to Swift) because such definitions play an important role in the performance evaluation between APIs (An et al., 2018). Another example of a transformation between APIs of two different platforms is for Java and C# (Nguyen et al., 2014). The success criterion of the transformation between platforms is determined by defining the unambiguous grammar used by the intermediate representations of each API. The possibility of a duplicate solution from the code with intermediate representations (e.g., the occurrence of condition before and at the end of the loop) is out of the question.

Such ambiguity problems are eliminated by defining the formal representations of grammar rules with multiple statements. In addition, the syntactic tree may be designed in such a way that intermediate representations do not allow expressions to be nested and the source code is normalized. Even though these features seem to be commonplace, they are important criteria that allow the solution of the problem to be transformed into code as clean code.

Toward Quantum Computing

Since computer theory was developed so rapidly, computer scientists were looking for a new universal computer; they frequently expressed the possible contribution of physics in universal computers and the changes to the laws of physics (Feynmann,

1982). With the exact simulations of quantum physics, computers were intended to operate in complete harmony with nature. According to the researchers, this was only possible in a finite volume of space and time and therefore, a finite number of logical operations could be fully analyzed. These studies reveal that quantum computing has been built on Turing's legacy.

The main goal of simulation studies, which have been going on since the 80s, is that when a large physical system is fully simulated, the boundary value of exponentially growing computers in power will drop. In this context, incomplete physical knowledge and its conversion into practice are still being studied with great effort. Additionally, the speed of continually renewed computer processors in the last fifty years according to Moore's law (e.g., the logarithmic increase in the number of transistors on chips in every two years) has begun to slow down in the second half of the 2010s. It is expected that this slowdown will be fixed in the 2020s and computers that operate quantum computing with qubit chips whose prototype studies continue, will commercially begin to be implemented (Health, 2018). But, despite the theoretical quantum teleportation studies that began in 1993 and developed rapidly (Bennett et al., 1993), the transmission of an unknown qubit state to another location in the early 2000s still had not succeeded. The studies of those years drew attention to the concept of entanglement and teleportation and scientifically laid the foundations for the computer world by stating that information will not be copied, just as it is today.

Teleportation, which took place in 2017 between entangled photons in a 1200 km distance between China and Tibet, was an application of the new technology studies (Messier, 2019). This Chinese experiment has been the longest quantum teleportation phenomenon ever made. The explanation by the scientists confirms that the experiments depending on Einstein's statement "spooky action at a distance" told in 1948 (Musser, 2015) continue to increase the speed.

Numbers Theory and Cybersecurity

As quantum computers have enormous power in computing, it is envisaged that it will solve the problem of cybersecurity as well. The security studies, which began entirely intuitively, evolved from ad-hoc designs from the 1980s to a methodology whose principals were determined. These methodologies were determined as (1) a mathematical problem that had not yet been solved for any security problem was selected and (2) whether the solution to this problem provides the targeted confidence was investigated. Numbers theory has been the biggest contributor to solving these problems. The basis of today's encryption, cryptography and cybersecurity theorems are also based on numbers theory. When the first studies on numbers theory were investigated, Pythagoras who lived in Ancient Greek in 600 BC was found. In 300

BC, Euclid's work on this subject was seen in converting the mathematics of that period into deductive science. Further, the Sumerians (2500 BC) had studies on number systems and the Babylonians (2000 BC) had mathematical tables written on tablets before these two Greek scientists (Ore, 1948). The theory of numbers, the fundamental theorem of arithmetic, has found its application in many important and critical issues today, thanks to the mathematicians and scientists who have followed the important inventions of prehistory.

TRACES OF THE NATO CONFERENCES IN CONTEMPORARY SOFTWARE PRODUCTS

Software Engineering in 1968 and Agile Manifesto

The concept of a software crisis, defined by Bauer in 1968 at the NATO Conference, revealed that programs were not sufficient in solving problems using computers and in the control of solutions. Therefore, it was suggested that software engineering should be used as a term (Bauer, 1987). This meant that the software product that was developed was not successful for different reasons. The developments in the software world from the 50s to the beginning of the 70s generally followed the technological evolutions in the first, second, and third-generation computers. Looking at NATO conferences (Buxton & Randell, 1969; Naur & Randell, 1968), Ercoli (1968) addressed the cost of very large operating systems per instruction in his talk. Harr, on the other hand, emphasized the importance of developing the operating system according to a scheduling algorithm for quality as user requirements change. D'Agapeyeff asked questions about whether a single operating system would be sufficient for a computer, and whether a computer made up of a single framework could meet the requirements of different users. Lampson made additions to Harr's opinion at the conference in 1969 and said that systems should be designed as open-ended so that they could be expanded to meet changing requirements. All of these talks were the predictions of the development stages of hardware systems described in the previous chapter.

Another speaker at the conferences, Dijkstra, said that as the problems become complicated, the need for the distribution of knowledge would be inevitable and this would lead to incorrect coding of the problem. In addition, as it is impossible to determine the quality of the product being developed, he argued that the design process and implementation must be interpenetrated. The views advocated in those years still remain valid today. It is no coincidence that the importance (and to some extent necessity) of formal representations of solving software problems was mentioned before the 70s. It is possible to see the role of conceptualization in the progress of computing and the computer world as much as possible in the previous sections. Dijkstra advocated for:

Complexity controlled by the hierarchical ordering of function and variability explained the solutions to the software crisis in his book (Dijkstra, 1976).

Royce (1970) proposed the waterfall method to solve large-scale problems and laid the foundations for the new methodologies in software/system development. The waterfall method requires documentation at each stage before moving from one development stage to another in the product because the output of the previous stage is the input of the next stage. Dijkstra (1968) explained the necessity of documentation for successful software in his speech:

I have a point with respect to the fact that people are willing to write programs and fail to make the documentation afterward... I would suggest that the reason why many programmers experience the making of predocumentation as an additional burden, instead of a tool, is that whatever predocumentation he produces can never be used mechanically.

The Agile Manifesto (2001) was published by 17 computer scientists in Utah (Beck, 2001). Even though contemporary methods are based on the manifesto have been used in many software products to emphasize that documentation is not necessary and focus on the importance of the software operating in small parts instead, this has not been the case. Soon after the manifesto's applications began to appear, the importance of documentation in a software project was understood, and it was concluded that documentation should be added to new product development approaches.

Dijkstra had another speech at the conference that formed the second of the four key principles of the Agile Manifesto where decisions on the future of software development were made. In this session, he stated that communication between groups will make the flow of negative information easier and this will also positively reflect the development of the product. He also described software developers as manufacturers and stated that it was not right to blame them for each problem. The message jointly given by other speakers in this session was that the software system should be a product that is acceptable to all users. This view is fundamental for today's service-based architecture in the software industry. When associated with the manifesto, the third principle is encountered as customer collaboration.

Software Engineering in 1968 and Service Contracts

Software developers, called manufacturers at that time, would lose money and time by collecting false data on the product to be developed and should plan accordingly. Randell foresaw further and asked users to demand safeguards with contracts due to the rapid increase in the size of the problems. Until the manifesto, contract negotiations were made between the user and the developer that contained the entire product to be developed. These later were transformed into the contract of the software piece to be developed. Randell's speech at the 1968 conference is a reminder of today's service contracts as the agreement between a remote service and a service consumer. The inbound and outbound data organized in the contract format illustrates the foresight at the NATO conference because it said the operation of the data would be complicated in the future. In today's application, the data used in the contract is decided in the planning stage and could be XML (Extensible Markup Language), JSON (JavaScript Object Notation), Java Object, etc., and the solutions are compatible with the work produced. Service contracts have an important function in problem-solving and are prepared either as service-based or consumer-driven contracts. The only difference between these contracts is collaboration. While you get to be the sole owner of the contract in the first, the latter has a close relationship between the service and the service consumer. Remote access protocols in Internet applications such as REST or SOAP operate according to the service-based contract principle (Flander, 2009; Richards, 2015). While service-based contracts can be modified by the owner regardless of requirements, this type of contract requires that the consumer complies with the rules. Thus, while healthy solutions are offered to complicated problems, challenging conditions also arise. This is one of the hidden parameters of the software crisis that was first discussed in 1968 and continues to exist even as complex, real-world problems are solved.

Even though the importance of the compiler was emphasized by many speakers of the first NATO conference due to complex problems, could d'Agapeyeff's following question be a prediction of the reduction of today's health system's electronic solution to the mobile platforms?

An example of the kind of software system I am talking about is putting all the applications in a hospital on a computer, whereby you get a whole set of people to use the machine. This kind of system is very sensitive to weaknesses in the software, particular as regards the inability to maintain the system and to extend it freely.

At the time, d'Agapeyeff was designing the bridge between the assembler and compiler by putting middleware between the application program and the control program. d'Agapeyeff's speech describes the real-world problems of today, in which the inference rules are explained with description logic.

Software Crisis and Chaos Reports

Chaos reports have been published regularly since 1994 by the Standish Group and have the same levels of complex problems. The lean software sector of the earlier years has developed over time and has spread across industries such as banking, financial, government, healthcare, manufacturing, retail, services, telecom, and others; time overrun in the projects has increased from 50% to 100% (Jensen, 2014; Mulder, 1994). The changes in project size, along with time-out in chaos demographics have also resulted in cost overrun and the limited rate of the performance of the target/scope. Thus, the evaluation criteria in the software projects beginning in 1994 underwent changes according to the conditions of the period, including the region where the products were developed. Despite this, the rates of successful, challenged, failed projects have not changed much since the 2000s. This is due to the systematic development of methods realized with technological advances since the adoption of software engineering as a separate discipline. Successful projects that were 16% in 1994 rose to 29% in 2004. This value is also the rate of successful projects in the Standish Group statistics from 2015. The success rates of software projects between these years (2004–2015) have increased to 39%. An important reason for this increase is that the executive IT managers at the Standish Group asked project participants about three different statistical results used to solve the problems. Also, the concept of software project management gained great importance. The Software Capability Maturity Model (CMM) was developed by the Software Engineering Institute (SEI) as a standard and started to be implemented in the government and industry sector in 1991. The importance given to standards and project management can be a reason for the increased success of software projects. Continuous improvements by SEI were renamed as CMMI Developers and changed the standard that provided a combination of software and system engineering disciplines. Other process-improvement methods such as ISO 9000, Six Sigma, and Agile also contribute to institutes' timely delivery of service and software products with lower cost and higher quality.

FROM EVOLUTION TO REVOLUTION

21st Century Software Products

In the early 2000s, software development and management processes of sectors such as traffic and tourism, banking, automotive, industry and trade, telecommunication and media, and insurance on issues such as e-commerce, sales and support, order processing and supply chain were called industrial software engineering products. Large-scale software projects that began to be developed in those years included independent modules/components and were designed with architectures using cross-sectional functions. Tool generating and code fragments were also important in these projects. Effort, measured as person-years on an industrial scale suddenly rose up to hundreds of times. Accordingly, code lines reached into the millions in accordance with the size of the problems. With the start of the 2000s, software problems changed from individual solutions to team solutions. Thus, organizations' communication, management, and quality assurance requirements changed. New technological developments and new perspectives on project solutions are the main reasons for the increased success rates of software products developed between 2005 and 2015.

Evolutionary developments and revolutionary changes in the software world have influenced the solutions to complex, real-world problems. On the improvement of software and systems, the usage of mouse, the World Wide Web (WWW) and MapReduce can be considered successively as a revolution. Software products before the 2000s did not focus on the changing needs of customers, and the necessary changes were taking place very slowly. The efficiency of the product developed focused on the choice of priorities. But, by the 2000s, it was decided that the strategic outlook needed to be changed. This was an evolution that aimed to make the developed product have better value compared to its competitors. Since the scope of the problems were gradually expanding, solutions that focused on the direct satisfaction of users needed to be found. This intelligent evolutionary process that continues slowly is similar to the change of the hereditary characteristics of an organism population from one generation to the other in biology.

The evolution process that was slow, reliable, and continuous turned into a revolution in terms of time and the direction of the requirements. The concept of Industry 4.0 is an example of the transformation from evolution to revolution; there is never enough time for developing the product at the end of the improvement cycles in the modern business world. Thus, problems are solved by taking too many risks. Instead of waiting patiently for the evolution of product development, change was accelerated by speculating revolutionary ideas. In some cases, the importance of the problem and the scale of changes needed on the old system made the implementation of new ideas much more effective because it left old concepts behind. Producing the expected results in the process of quick transformation to Industry 4.0 must be controlled; otherwise, the harms the system might face could exceed the benefits. An answer to the question, "Could an incompleteness in quantum mechanics lead to the next scientific revolution?" (Siegel, 2019) might be this: by rapidly ensuring cybersecurity and safety, cranking the cryptography can occur very quickly in many protected networks (Herman, 2019).

Digital Transformation

The revolutionary opportunities of many Internet of Things (IoT) applications such as driverless cars, smart grids, 5G, and cyber and space satellites pose challenges to the dream of switching to quantum computers. Today's computers will never reach the targeted intelligence with the current technology because the current architecture is a structure that can perform logical reasoning on only a programmed idea-collection, so it cannot produce revolutionary ideas. Industry 4.0 (Kagermann, 2013) focused on automation, innovation, data, cyber-physical systems, processes, and people. Robotics, cloud computing, and the evolutions in operational technology are examples of the Industrial Internet of Things (IIoT). IIoT is a new computer term that refers to the processing of information technology with operational technology. IDC (International Data Corporation) announced in 2011 that big data/analytics, mobile, cloud, and social technology applications underwent a transformation called third platform technologies. This transformation brought a more modern look to the software world than the second platform technologies (i.e., personal computers, local area networks, and Internet and client-server architectures).

The history of using a large number of different applications by different users can be summarized as follows: tens of thousands of applications have been used by hundreds of millions of users in mainframe terminals since the second half of the 80s, while with client-server architecture, tens of thousands of applications have been popularized by hundreds of millions user in the 2010s. The goal of the 2020s has started to be realized in the form of smart intelligent solutions. Mobile broadband, big data/analytics, social business, cloud services, mobile devices, and apps will be used by billions of users is already an indispensable part of everyday life.

At the end of 2019, the cost of digital transformation is expected to reach $1.7 trillion on a world scale (Avanade, 2018). The world's major companies use intelligence apps extensively and aim to increase customer experience by doing big data analytics. Banking, health care, insurance, and manufacturing, for example, are the leading sectors where the third platform is used. The banking sector highlights customer experiments in its analysis to support more customers. For example, by collecting data through call centers, they raise the quality criteria of the service. Although such assessments increase the cost of the sector, the goal is to maximize the service by estimating the degree of nervousness and satisfaction from the customer's tone of the voice and the words they choose through AI applications. Health care services enable a detailed diagnosis of diseases and the monitoring of patients with intelligent solutions. Insurance companies perform intelligent enterprise with machine learning and predictive analytics methods through a widespread network, repairing the organization's losses. Retail chains no longer consider geographic distribution and demographic diversity in sales and market strategies. Rather, the focus is to make online transactions attractive to the customer by means of intellectual corrections that are revolutionary in nature. In addition, information from the user's in-store experiences is measured to include the customer in the service performed and thus the collaboration factor is brought to the fore.

Third Platform

The third platform is part of the technology system and the evolution of Web 2.0. In an increasing number of industrial products, meaning inference is made using new mobile technologies and their communication with each other using AI. This new structure plays an active role in the purchasing process, people's interactions with each other, shaping work environments, and all kinds of behaviors in daily life. With the emergence of this platform, cloud technology reduces the price of many components and the place of IoT in daily life will become more robust.

The third platform deals with what can be done with it as well as being a technology. In this context, it will take some time for the social, human, and business transformations to take place. Before explaining how business transformations take place, many existing projects that use applications such as Customer relationship Management (CRM) and Enterprise Resource Planning (ERP) have been developed to meet the needs of a single industry, or even a single customer, which increases the complexity of today's problems. However, with the third platform, business processes are simplified. Agility is now provided by receiving a standard application from the cloud and transforming it into compliance with industry-specific requirements. Here, a function of business transformation is to accelerate the transformation and ensure that those who use smart technologies are aware of the innovations and adapt to the system. Digital realization follows new technology's constant advancement such as AI, automation, IoT, and virtual reality/augmented reality.

Manufacturing signifies a revolution in the service area with digital transformation. The customer in the IT sector looks to pay no more than they would use instead of having the whole product. The manufacturer will benefit from the third platform with this business model change and will be able to complete the work at a lower cost by informing the customer in advance how to meet their requirements. By using the same product many times with different customers, the manufacturers will be more profitable.

HUMAN CONTRIBUTION

Previous studies that evaluate human satisfaction date back to the 40s. The development of electronic computers in 1941 and computers with stored programs in 1949 were the starting point for AI research. Newell and Simon (1956) took the first steps of modern AI with the computer program Logic Theorist. Being the pioneers of AI and cognitive science studies, Newell and Simon (1972) envisioned emotion directly in their theoretical research. Their first collaborative work on AI aimed to understand human problem solving, and they asked questions in three different categories related to the emotional experience:

1. What happened?
2. What can I do about it?
3. What did I do and what were the results of my actions? (Stein and et al., 1993).

Thus, the expression of the role of emotions in determining goal-oriented behaviors with talks was classified as event-based emotions (Bagozzi et al., 1998). This was also the person's affective reactions to events that are likely to occur.

Emotional Experiences

The importance of emotional experiences in achieving the goals of the members in a software team has been increasing (Graziotin et al., 2018). The first examples of this were Extreme Programming (XP) applications (Auer, 2002; Beck, 1999). From the agile programming processes used for the first time in 1996, XP highlighted user stories with other agile product development features. As it is known, these are the criteria for the acceptance tests made by the user after the release of the product. This has brought a new perspective to software product development. In XP, the goal is an efficient (positive) release planning where the implementation time of each user story has been optimally determined. Thus, team members working in the pairing structure who concentrate on the target are drawn to a very intensive and stressful environment. In some cases, index cards are used to determine user requirements, while some user stories can be identified with a custom-built documentation tool. No matter which path is chosen to ensure the requirements, the contribution of the goal-directed emotions is important for the success of the developed product (Cao & Park, 2017).

Another principle of XP modeling and the values derived from them is refactoring. Because this process creates an environment with high tension, an individual's emotions are important for strong refactoring (Fowler, 2019). For example, according to a user story, refactoring may not be required, but developers definitely want to refactor. The opposite is also possible. While developers do not recommend refactoring, refactoring can be included in the user story.

In an article examining three different real-world problems, the problems of the teams during the pairing were evaluated and similar feedback was received (Robinson & Sharp, 2005). This shows that social interactions are inherent in the principle of pairing. These are critical in the continuous integration of code to generate communication in the context of the next release.

The three important criteria of traditional software projects that use classic development models are cost, time, and scope (i.e. quality balance). In agile projects, the goal is to implement the release. This is because the established objective may change based on environmental conditions. It is possible for project managers to make unrealistic decisions when they aim to meet customer requirements. When the teams are forced to work cohesively, developers with different levels of knowledge can make decisions based on their emotional experience. Different developer behaviors and decision-makers cause the software product to succeed/fail, just as it did in the 70s. Thus, the goals of developing an on-time, cost-effective, and quality software product are transformed into successful product parts so the team can quickly respond to changes in user/customer requirements.

Goal-Directed Emotions

In today's software engineering studies, agile software development teams play an important role in deciding goal directed emotions. Teamwork is the first criterion of the agile approach because it increases the pressure between team members and creates difficulties in managing a large number of stakeholders (Mc Hugh et al., 2012). In modern agile approaches, the customer is also part of the system developed as a stakeholder. Therefore, it is argued that users are perfect in themselves, while the task of ensuring this is in the development team. Team members carry different emotions with different appraisals. When the objective is reached during the operation, the member is happy. If it is not possible to correct any event that does not meet the determined purpose, this makes the whole team unhappy. Depending on the flow of the event, they may decide to change or maintain the current situation with the experienced emotions by the developer. Enacting objective behaviors by monitoring them is not only used in developing the product but also in planning the product and solving the problem (Stein et al., 1993). Another view is that emotional experience can be determined by inaccurate reports because representations of the events enable the understanding of the cognitive effects.

Affective agile design (Pieroni et al., 2017) has been proposed as a reflection of the principle of affective computing (Picard, 1995). This interdisciplinary field consisting of computer science, psychology, and cognitive science interprets and evaluates human effects in solving the software problem. Italy's largest telecommunication service provider Fastweb launched a digital transformation project in 2016 and used agile methodology for the project. The developers used affective agile design as a new agile model, and they defined user stories on the sprint scale (Pieroni et al., 2018). The evaluation of emotional feedback in the project, where many criteria of agile approach were applied, was realized by investigating whether the implementation of the sprints responded to user requirements in different releases.

To determine the expectations of team members developing different tasks in agile projects, Yu and Petter (2014) utilized shared mental models theory to describe the interactions with each other. This means that human-agent teams effect the success of the project with goal directed emotions. For example, the developer's high cognitive performance has a positive impact on the project, giving an important component of creativity. Here, the relationship between specific moods in the individual's particular working conditions and their creativity is evaluated. A positive relationship naturally leads to innovation. Moreover, the criteria that hinder creativity in any project are individual or organizational must be distinguished. In summary, innovation and the agile methods required for innovation mean the implementation of successful software products together with the creativity of the happy developers. The result of high productivity also means high code quality.

Studies on the happiness/unhappiness of people in the work environment are increasing in the software industry. Graziotin et al. (2014) have investigated the behavioral effects of software engineering on the software product by evaluating human aspects and happiness situations according to the developer's experiences (Graziotin et al., 2014). They found that emotion and core affect are important not only in software product development but also in interface design. Emotions are increasingly placed among the qualitative criteria of research in many studies. Russell (2009) explored problems such as culture, language, emotional behavior, and coherence (i.e., the subjects of emotion theory for software developers) and labeled them unhappiness. Thus, the conclusion of a person's neurophysiological condition in the form of happiness/unhappiness in the working environment is caused by positive/negative factors around the person. Today's agile-based software product development methods are also consistent with Russell's views. The time problem of the software product developed in small parts never ends. No matter how small the part of the product is developed, there will always be problems during delivery to the customer. Teamwork means that the person is constantly nervous. The responsibility of the entire team in agile work will put the individual in the race.

All of these can also be evaluated from the perspective of possible negative effects of the product developed as a result of the unhappiness of the people. Graziotin et al. (2017) conducted a quantitative analysis of unhappiness factors using not only data from software developers but also answers to questions from researchers and students from the GitHub archive. Personal results affecting the performance of the developed product were expressed as low cognitive performance, as low motivation, as inadequacy, and irregularity. On the other hand, process-oriented results were summarized as low productivity, low code quality, and as a complete cancellation of the written results. Various unhappiness indicators such as mental anxiety may cause team members to withdraw from the project and this would delay, or even end the project.

CONCLUSION

As in Boehm's (2006) keynote speech at ICSE, this study naturally follows a Hegelian approach. When the success stories of the past are not utilized, it is difficult to reveal future products. However, benefiting from existing success stories does not mean that the target will be successful. This is why software engineering is a complex discipline and its problems are very difficult to solve. In his speech, Boehm adopts the definition of "engineering" as:

The application of science and mathematics by which the properties of software are made useful to people.

Boehm's new definition of the word "engineering" in his speech has obligated this chapter to start with the explanation of the information technology concept. With the birth of electronic computers in the 50s, the contribution of computing to applications was labeled as information theory. In the 1970s, the impact of information theory on software products has been applied to many phases of the software life cycle as measurements. Although many of the measurements at that period were not empirically validated, they led to each development stage of subsequent software applications. Since measurements are fundamental for high-quality software products, there is a lot of research about this. For example, Horst Zuse (1991) has defined a number of complex software metrics that were unable to be described in the context of the chapter. On the other hand, Konrad Zuse's (Horst's father) main contribution to the computer world was that he invented the first automatically controlled universal computer in 1941 (Zuse, 1999). This machine, which has not been able to be used in public, begun the evolutions in the following decades.

Shannon's Theory was the most fertile theory in the 20th-century, and it was the blueprint of the computer world not only with digital representation but also with data compression (JPEGs, MP3s, and ZIP files). Although there are some points that remain obscure about Shannon's theory, it sheds light on the problems related to the information quantum theory. Additionally, Shor's (1994) algorithm was difficult to solve with existing computers (Coles et al., 2018). This algorithm was exponentially faster at breaking public key encryption than the fastest non-quantum algorithm. It took more than five years to solve this problem with a 5-qubit IBMqx4 quantum computer since no traditional hardware was possible that utilizes the proven quantum speed-up. Everything from 2-qubit quantum computers designed in 1998 by a few universities and IBM to the evolution of the 128-qubit computer announced by the Rigetti Company in 2018 shows the success of quantum physics in the 20th century. Of course, especially Turing, and also Gödel, Neumann, Zuse and many other mathematicians' contributions will never be forgotten in the quantum world of tomorrow. Before Shannon's information theory was inadequate to solve the information-intensive complex problems of the 21st century, Feynman and Manin (1999) argued that in the 80s, quantum computers could perform operations that are out of reach by regular computers. Today, a non-scientific problem, a theory-based algorithmic music composition, has been designed by quantum information (Kirke, 2019). This is a success story of the computer arts world contributing to quantum computing research. Abstract mathematics and physics underlie the evolutionary and revolutionary developments of the computers and complex problems solved by them. Moreover, quantum computing will change cybersecurity because of its speed, security, responsibility, safety, and resistance when compared to traditional computers. The factorization time of mathematically complex large prime numbers will reduce to a matter of seconds. Data transformation with superposition and entanglement will offer information processing benefits such as improved random number generation. But this technology will also arm the hackers.

In software engineering, it is more accurate to evaluate the human criteria starting from undergraduate education. New engineers will shape the next ten to twenty years of research, so education programs need to start preparing students for future trends by using constantly updated course content. Students who learn the importance of lifelong learning will realize the integration of science and technological innovations in the planning of the digital world of the future. Thus, Moore's law, which doubles the computing power of computers every 1.5 years, will have an enormous amount of operating power in 2025.

The increasing need for integrated software and system engineering is important for working groups and individuals during the transfer process from traditional computers to quantum computers. The first rule of developing successful user intensive systems is the importance of continuous learning. Every business model based on user programming and their unprecedented capacities depend on the quality of the individual and on their satisfaction. Since all stakeholders of a developing software product are important, the related person makes risk-based decisions when managing these relationships.

Another important criterion that needs to be evaluated is the kind of methodology to develop for the software product. Software development methods used to solve complex real-world problems must be chosen according to the type of problem to be solved, the structure of the organization, and the capabilities of the product developers. Any agile development methodology (e.g., scrum, crystal, XP, and feature-driven development) can be chosen when the target of the team is to minimize risks. DevOpps deployment methodology is preferred when the strategy is centered on organizational change. This methodology enhances collaboration between the departments responsible for different segments of the development life cycle, such as development, quality assurance, and operations. Rapid application development is a condensed development process that produces a high-quality system with low investment costs. Embracing modern software development practices is what will differentiate one company from the other and to move it forward.

There are many other improvements for the solutions of current and future software problems that were not investigated in this chapter. They will continue to be examined in chronological order with more detailed and broader research.

REFERENCES

Alwen, J. (2018). What is lattice-based cryptography & why should you care. *Wickr*. Retrieved from https://medium.com/cryptoblog/what-is-lattice-based-cryptography-why-should-you-care-dbf9957ab717

An, K., Meng, N., & Tilevich, E. (2018). Automatic inference of translation rules for native cross-platform mobile applications. *Proceedings of ACM MOBILESoft'18*. Retrieved from http://people.cs.vt.edu/~tilevich/papers/inference-translation-mobilesoft2018.pdf

Auer, K. (2002). *Extreme Programming Applied Playing to Win*. The XP Series.

Avanade. (2018). *The intelligent enterprise: It's the way to predict and lead in your market*. Retrieved from https://www.avanade.com/~/media/asset/thinking/intelligent-enterprise-pov.pdf

Bagozzi, R. P., Baumgartner, H., & Pieters, R. (1998). Goal-directed emotions. *Cognition and Emotion*, *12*(1), 1–26. doi:10.1080/026999398379754

Bauer, F. L. (1987). *An Interview with Friedrich L. Bauer*. Retrieved from https://conservancy.umn.edu/bitstream/handle/11299/107106/oh128flb.pdf?sequence=1&isAllowed=y

Beck, K. (1999). *Extreme Programming*. The XP Series. doi:10.1109/TOOLS.1999.779100

Beck, K., Beedle, M., Cockburn, A., Fowler, M., Grenning, J., Schwaber, K., Sutherland, J., & Thomas, D. (2001). *Manifesto for Agile Development*. Retrieved from https://agilemanifesto.org/

Bennett, C. H., Brassard, G., Crépeau, C., Jozsa, R., Peres, A., & Wootters, W. K. (1993). Teleporting an unknown quantum state via dual classical and Einstein-Podolsky-Rosen channels. *Physical Review Letters, 70*(13), 1895–1899. doi:10.1103/PhysRevLett.70.1895 PMID:10053414

Berry, A., & Sigayret, A. (2004). Representing a concept lattice by a graph. *Discrete Applied Mathematics, 144*(1-2), 27–42. doi:10.1016/j.dam.2004.02.016

Binder, W., & Suri, N. (2009). Green computing: Energy consumption optimized service hosting. In *SOFSEM 2009: Theory and Practice of Computer Science* (pp. 117–128). Springer. doi:10.1007/978-3-540-95891-8_14

Boehm, B. (2006). A view of 20th and 21st century software engineering. *International Conference on Software Engineering (ICSE'96),* 12-29. 10.1145/1134285.1134288

Bohr, M. T. (2018). Logic technology scaling to continue Moore's law. *IEEE 2nd Electron Devices Technology and Manufacturing Conference.*

Borgida, A., Toman, D., & Weddel, G. (2019). On special description logics for processes and plans. *DL 2019 International Workshop on Description Logics, 2373.* Retrieved from http://ceur-ws.org/Vol-2373/paper-6.pdf

Borst, W. N. (1997). *Construction of engineering ontologies for knowledge sharing and reuse* (Ph.D. Dissertation). Institute for Telematica and Information Technology, University of Twente.

Brukner, C., & Zeilinger, A. (1999). Operationally invariant information in quantum measurements. *Physical Review Letters, 83*(17), 3354–3357. doi:10.1103/PhysRevLett.83.3354

Buxton, J. N., & Randell, B. (1969). *Software engineering techniques report on a conference*. Sponsored the NATO Science Committee.

Cao, L., & Park, E. H. (2017). Understanding goal directed emotions in agile software development teams. *Emotions in Agile Software Development Team, 24. American Conference on Information System.*

Ceruzzi, P. E. (2012). *A History of Modern Computing*. The MIT Press. doi:10.7551/mitpress/9426.001.0001

Coles, P. J., Eidenbenz, S., Pakin, S., Adedoyin, A., Ambrosiano, J., Anisimov, P., ... (2018). *Quantum Algorithm Implementations for Beginners*. Retrieved from https://arxiv.org/abs/1804.03719

Collins, G. P. (2002). *Claude E. Shannon: Founder of Information Theory*. Retrieved from https://www.scientificamerican.com/article/claude-e-shannon-founder/

Deutsch, D. (1985). Quantum Theory. The Church-Turing Principle and the Universal Quantum Computer. *Proceedings of the Royal Society of London. Series A, Mathematical and Physical Sciences, 400*(1818), 97–117. doi:10.1098/rspa.1985.0070

Dijkstra, E. (1976). *A Discipline of Programming*. Prentice-Hall.

Feynman, R. P. (1982). Simulating physics with computers. *International Journal of Theoretical Physics, 21*(6/7), 467–488. doi:10.1007/BF02650179

Flanders, J. (2009). Service station - More on REST. *MSDN Magazine Block*. Retrieved from https://msdn.microsoft.com/en-us/magazine/dd942839.aspx

Fowler, M. (2019). *Refactoring: Improving the design of existing code*. Addison Wesley.

Gil, Y. (2005). Description logics and planning. *AI Magazine, 26*(2), 73–84.

Graziotin, D., Fagerholm, F., Wang, X., & Abrahamsson, P. (2017). Unhappy developers: Bad for themselves, bad for process, and bad for software product. *Proceedings of the 39th International Conference on Software Engineering Companion (ICSE-C '17)*, 362-364.

Graziotin, D., Fagerholm, F., Wang, X., & Abrahamsson, P. (2018). what happens when software developers are (un)happy? *Journal of Systems and Software, 140*, 32–47. doi:10.1016/j.jss.2018.02.041

Graziotin, D., Wang, X., & Abrahamsson, P. (2014). Software developers, moods, emotions, and performance. *IEEE Software, 31*(4), 12–15. doi:10.1109/MS.2014.94

Hartnett, K. (2019). *A new law to describe quantum's rise?* Retrieved from https://www.quantamagazine.org/does-nevens-law-describe-quantum-computings-rise-20190618/ Quanta magazine.

Health, N. (2018). Moore's law is dead: Three predictions about the computers of tomorrow. *TechRepublic*. Retrieved from https://www.techrepublic.com/article/moores-law-is-dead-three-predictions-about-the-computers-of-tomorrow/

Herman, A. (2019). The quantum revolution is coming, ready or not. *Forbes*. Retrieved from https://www.forbes.com/sites/arthurherman/2019/03/12/the-quantum-revolution-is-coming-ready-or-not/#3680ef55265a

Istrail, S., & Marcus, S. (2013). Alan Turing and John von Neumann - their brains and their computers. In E. Csuhaj-Varjú, M. Gheorghe, G. Rozenberg, A. Salomaa, & G. Vaszil (Eds.), Lecture Notes in Computer Science: Vol. 7762. *Membrane Computing. CMC 2012*. doi:10.1007/978-3-642-36751-9_2

Jensen, R. W. (2014). Why do we still have software development problems? In *Improving Software Development Productivity: Effective Leadership and Quantitative Methods in Software Management*. Prentice-Hall.

Kagermann, H., Helbig, J., & Wahlster, W. (2013). *Recommendations for implementing the strategic initiative INDUSTRIE 4.0. Final report of the Industrie 4.0 Working Group*. Forschungsunion.

Karypis, G., & Kumar, V. (1998). A fast and high quality multilevel scheme for partitioning irregular graphs. *SIAM Journal on Scientific Computing*, *20*(1), 359–392. doi:10.1137/S1064827595287997

Kirke, A. J. (2019). Applying quantum hardware to non-scientific problems: Grover's algorithm and rule-based algorithmic music composition. *International Journal of Unconventional Computing*, *14*(3-4), 349–374.

Lardinois, F. (2019). *IBM unveils its first commercial quantum computer*. Retrieved from https://techcrunch.com/2019/01/08/ibm-unveils-its-first-commercial-quantum-computer/

Lemos, A. L., Daniel, F., & Benatallah, B. (2016). Web service composition: A survey of techniques and tools. *ACM Computing Surveys*, *48*(3), 1–41. doi:10.1145/2831270

Lodwich, A. (2016). *Understanding Error Correction and its Role as Part of the Communication Channel in Environments composed of Self Integrating Systems*. Retrieved from https://arxiv.org/abs/1612.07294

Lombardi, O., Holik, F., & Vanni, L. (2016a). What is Shannon information? *Synthese*, *193*(7), 1983–2012. doi:10.100711229-015-0824-z

Lombardi, O., Holik, F., & Vanni, L. (2016b). What is quantum information? *Studies in History and Philosophy of Modern Physics*, *56*, 17–26.

Manin, Y. I. (1999). *Classical computing, quantum computing and Shor's Factoring Algorithm.* arXiv:quant-ph/9903008v1

McClure, R. M. (2001). *The NATO Software Engineering Conferences.* Retrieved from http://homepages.cs.ncl.ac.uk/brian.randell/NATO/Introduction.html

McHugh, O., Conboy, K., & Lang, M. (2012). Agile practices: The impact on trust in software project teams. *IEEE Software, 29*(3), 71–76.

Messier, D. (2019). *China's quantum satellite establishes photon entanglement over 1,200 km.* Retrieved from http://www.parabolicarc.com/2019/06/19/china-quantum-satellite-establishes-photon-entanglement-1200-km/

Moore, G. E. (1965). Cramming more components onto integrated circuits. *Electronics (Basel), 38*(8), 114–116.

Mulder, H. (1994). *The Standish Group Report Chaos.* The Standish Group.

Musser, G. (2015). Spooky Action at a Distance: The Phenomenon That Reimagines Space and Time--and What It Means for Black Holes, the Big Bang, and Theories of Everything. *Scientific American.*

Naur, P., & Randell, B. (Eds.). (1968). Software Engineering: Report of a conference sponsored by the NATO Science Committee. Garmisch, Germany: NATO.

Neilsen, M. A., & Chuang, I. L. (2000). *Quantum Computation and Information.* Cambridge University Press.

Newell, A., & Simon, H. A. (1972). *Human Problem Solving.* Prentice-Hall.

Nguyen, A. T., Nguyen, H. A., Nguyen, T. T., & Nguyen, T. T. (2014). Statistical learning approach for mining API usage mappings for code migration. In *Proceedings of the 29th ACM/IEEE International Conference on Automated Software Engineering.* ACM. 10.1145/2642937.2643010

O'Connor, J. J., & Robertson, E. F. (2003). *John von Neumann,* Retrieved from http://www-history.mcs.st-andrews.ac.uk/Biographies/Von_Neumann.html

OMG. (2011). *Business Process Model and Notation (BPMN), Version 2.0.* Received from http://www.bpmn.org/

Ore, O. (1948). *Number Theory and its History.* Dover Publication.

Picard, R. W. (1995). *Affective Computing, M.I.T Media Laboratory Perceptual Computing Section Technical Report No. 321.* Retrieved from https://affect.media.mit.edu/pdfs/95.picard.pdf

Pieroni, A., Scarpato, N., & Scorza, M. (2018). Affective agile design: A proposal for a new software development model. *Journal of Theoretical and Applied Information Technology, 96*, 68–79.

Raattkaine, P. (2015). On the philosophical relevance of Godel's incompleteness theorems. *Revue Internationale de Philosophie, 234*, 513–534. Retrieved from https://www.cairn.info/revue-internationale-de-philosophie-2005-4-page-513.htm#

Randell, B. (2018). *Fifty years of software engineering or the view from Garmisch.* Paper presented at the meeting of the International Conference on Software Engineering (ICSE), Gothenburg, Sweden.

Richards, M. (2015). *The challenges of service-based architecture.* Retrieved from https://nofluffjuststuff.com/magazine/2015/10/the_challenges_of_service_based_architecture

Robinson, H., & Sharp, H. (2005). The social side of technical practices in extreme programing and agile processes in software engineering. Academic Press.

Rodriguez, N. D., Cuellar, M. P., Lilius, J., & Calvo-Flores, M. D. (2014). A Survey on Ontologies for Human Behavior Recognition. *ACM Computing Surveys, 46*(4), 1–33. doi:10.1145/2523819

Royce, W. (1970). Managing the development of large software systems. *Proceedings of IEEE WESCON, 8*, 328-338.

Russell, J. A. (2009). Emotion, core affect, and psychological construction. *Cognition and Emotion, 23*(7), 1259–1283. doi:10.1080/02699930902809375

Saxson, W. (1995). *Dr. George Stibitz, 90, inventor of first digital computer in '40.* Retrieved from https://www.nytimes.com/1995/02/02/obituaries/dr-george-stibitz-90-inventor-of-first-digital-computer-in-40.html

Shannon, C. E. (1948). A Mathematical Theory of Communication. *The Bell System Technical Journal, 27*(4), 623–656. doi:10.1002/j.1538-7305.1948.tb00917.x

Shannon, C. E., & Weaver, W. (1949). *The Mathematical Theory of Communication Urbana.* University of Illinois Press.

Siegel, E. (2019). *Could an Incompleteness in Quantum Mechanics Lead to Next Scientific Revolution?* Retrieved from https://www.forbes.com/sites/startswithabang/2019/04/17/could-an-incompleteness-in-quantum-mechanics-lead-to-our-next-scientific-revolution/#6dd6e27062ed. Forbes.

Stein, N. L., Trabasso, T., & Liwag, M. (1993). The representation and organization of emotional experience: Unfolding the emotion episode. In M. Lewis & J. M. Haviland (Eds.), Handbook of Emotions (pp. 279-300). Guilford Press.

Thackray, A., Brock, D. C., & Jones, R. (2015). *Moore's Law- The Life of Gordon Moore, Silicon Valley's Quiet Revolutionary*. Basic Books.

Timpson, C. G. (2004). Quantum Information Theory and The Foundations of Quantum Mechanics (PhD thesis). The Queen's College.

Turing, A. M. (1936). *On Computable Numbers with an Application to the Entscheidungs problem*. Retrieved from https://www.cs.virginia.edu/~robins/Turing_Paper_1936.pdf

Vincent, J. (2019). *IBM's new quantum computer is a symbol, not a breakthrough*. Retrieved from https://www.theverge.com/2019/1/8/18171732/ibm-quantum-computer-20-qubit-q-system-one-ces-2019

Wilde, M. M. (2019). *From Classical to Quantum Shannon Theory*. Cambridge University Press. Retrieved from http://www.markwilde.com/qit-notes.pdf

Xia, H., Chen, Y., Gao, H., Li, Z., & Chen, Y. (2010). Concept Lattice-Based Semantic Web Service Matchmaking. In *International Conference on Communication Software and Networks* (pp. 439-443). IEEE Explore.

Yu, X., & Petter, S. (2014). Understanding agile software development practices using shared mental models theory. *Information and Software Technology*, *56*(8), 911–921. doi:10.1016/j.infsof.2014.02.010

Zuse, H. (1991). *Software complexity measures and methods*. Berlin: Walter de Gruyter. doi:10.1515/9783110866087

Zuse, K. (1999). *Konrad Zuse*. Retrieved from https://www-history.mcs.st-andrews.ac.uk/Biographies/Zuse.html

KEY TERMS AND DEFINITIONS

Agile Methodology: It is an exciting and fascinating approach to software development. The agile process breaks a larger software project into several smaller parts that can be developed in increments and iterations. The purpose is to deliver a working software program quickly to the customer. The agile hierarchy in an agile team is based on competence, not authority. All members constantly explore ways to add more value to the customer. When compared with traditional methods, agile projects qualify that they are better in terms of overall business value, higher in quality, less costly, more productive, and show quicker time-to-market speeds. Lean, Kanban, Crystal, Extreme Programming (XP), Dynamic Systems Development Method and Feature-Driven Development are a few of the agile methodologies.

Emotional Labor: Emotion in software engineering has recently gained attention in both the research community and industry. Work performance and team collaboration that are the fundamental criteria of today's software development approaches depend on the positive emotional effects.

Hegelian Approach: This approach depends on dialectics. The dialectical method is a discourse between two or more people holding different points of view about a subject but wishing to establish the truth through reasoned arguments. Hegel (1771-1831) defined four concepts: (1) everything is finite and exists in the medium of time, (2) everything is composed of contradictions, (3) one force overcoming its leads to crisis, and (4) change is periodic without returning to the same point.

Incompleteness: Kurt Gödel wrote the incompleteness theorems in the 1930s. They are still valid as the subject of several of today's discussions and will continue to be effective in the future. These theorems show that any logical system consists of either contradiction or statements that cannot be proven. Therefore, they help to understand that the formal systems used are not complete. On the other hand, the trend of mathematicians in the 1900s was the unification of all theories for the solution of the most difficult problems in all disciplines. Before Gödel defined any system as consistent without any contradictions, and as incomplete with all or some disproved statements, Hilbert formulated all mathematics in an axiomatic form with Set Theory. Gödel's theorem showed the limitations that exist within all logical systems and laid the foundation of modern computer science. These theorems caused several results about the limits of computational procedures. A famous example is the inability to solve the halting problem. A halting problem finds out whether a program with a given input will halt at some time or continue to run into an infinite loop. This decision problem demonstrates the limitations of programming. In a modern sense, this means that it is impossible to build an excellent compiler or a perfect antivirus.

Information Theory: This term, originated in Shannon's work, which started the digital age. There is not a single definition accepted in the literature and over time different definitions have been made in different studies. Generally, information theory lies at the core of understanding computing, communication, knowledge representation, and action. Like in many other fields of science, the basic concepts of information theory play an important role in cognitive science and neuroscience.

Ontology: In computer science, ontology is a formal representation of the knowledge by a set of concepts within a domain and the relationships between those concepts. The domain is the type of objects, and/or concepts that exist and their properties and relations. The creation of domain ontologies is the fundamental of the definition of any enterprise framework. Every information system has its own ontology. Software agents can communicate with each other via messages that contain expressions formulated in terms of an ontology. It is important to use an ontology for the connection with the user interface component. The user browses the ontology to better understand the vocabulary and to formulate queries at the desired level. Application programs containing a lot of domain knowledge may not explicitly store information in the database for various reasons. In this case, it is possible to constitute a knowledge base by an ontology.

Software Conceptualization: During the elicitation of software requirements analysis, the customer's requirements are defined by visual diagrams or formal specifications (e.g., by the logic of first-order propositions, at the high level). An abstract solution closer to the customer side is realized. The design phase of the software visualization and the functional analysis of the previous development step are carried out in detail. Conceptualization at the design phase is closer to the implementation of the product.

Section 2
Some Cases on Object–Oriented Design and Architecture

Chapter 2
Lowering Coupling in Distributed Applications With Compliance and Conformance

José Carlos Martins Delgado

(iD) https://orcid.org/0000-0002-2536-4906

Instituto Superior Técnico, Universidade de Lisboa, Portugal

ABSTRACT

The interaction of applications in distributed system raises an integration problem that application-developing methods need to solve, even if the initial specifications change, which is actually the normal case. Current integration technologies, such as Web Services and RESTful APIs, solve the interoperability problem but usually entail more coupling than required by the interacting applications, since they share data schemas between applications, even if they do not actually exercise all the features of those schemas. The fundamental problem of application integration is therefore how to provide at most the minimum coupling possible while ensuring at least the minimum interoperability requirements. This chapter proposes compliance and conformance as the concepts to achieve this goal by sharing only the subset of the features of the data schema that applications actually use, with the goal of supporting a new architectural style, structural services, which seeks to combine the advantages of both SOA and REST.

DOI: 10.4018/978-1-7998-2142-7.ch002

INTRODUCTION

A complex software system typically involves many interacting modules, with many decisions to take and many tradeoffs to consider, not only in each module but also in the ways in which the various modules interact. Object-oriented software design tries to minimize the semantic gap (Sikos, 2017) between a problem specification and the architecture of the software application that deals with that problem, by providing a close correspondence between the problem entities and the corresponding software modules (classes).

Ideally, classes should not have dependencies on others, avoiding constraints on one another and exhibiting completely independent lifecycles. This would allow separate development of each class and elimination of software design and programming inefficiencies due to interaction between the specifications of classes, which usually cause iterations in requirements for other classes and consequent changes.

However, classes do need to interact and to cooperate, to fulfill collectively the goals of the system. Therefore, a fundamental tenet in software design is to reduce class coupling as much as possible (Bidve, & Sarasu, 2016) without hindering the interaction capabilities necessary to support the required class interoperability.

Decoupling also translates into higher changeability (a change in a class is less likely to have a significant impact in other classes), higher adaptability (less constraints require less effort to adapt to changes in other classes), higher reusability (a class with less requirements and constraints has an increased applicability range) and higher reliability in a distributed context (a smaller set of requirements simplify the task of finding an alternative in case of failure).

Although decoupling constitutes a fairly obvious goal, as a means to reduce dependencies and constraints, tuning it to the right degree in practice is not an easy task. In general, the fundamental problem of application design, in terms of interaction, is how to provide (at most) the minimum coupling possible while ensuring (at least) the minimum interoperability requirements. This means that the main goal is to ensure that each interacting class knows just enough about the others to be able to interoperate with them but no more than that, to avoid unnecessary dependencies and constraints. This is an instance of the principle of least knowledge (Hendricksen, 2014).

Historically, interoperability has been the main goal in Web-based distributed systems, whereas decoupling has been one of the top concerns in software engineering, when developing an application, along with other metrics such as cohesion.

Software development methods emphasize decoupling, changeability and agility, which means structuring classes of an application so that a change somewhere affects the remaining classes as little as possible and an application developer can deal with it easily and in a short time. Interoperability between classes of a local application is the easy part, since there is usually a single programming language with a shared class inheritance hierarchy.

The interaction between distributed applications is completely different. Interoperability is hard, since these applications are developed, compiled, and linked independently. Most likely, this means different type names, inheritance hierarchies, programming languages, execution platforms, and data formats. Inheritance-based polymorphism, one of the main workhorses of object-oriented software design to increase decoupling, is no longer usable. Current technologies base interoperability on strict data format matching (sharing of data schema). Although decoupling is of paramount importance, application developers have treated it as a side issue in distributed contexts, a best-effort endeavor after achieving the primary goal, interoperability (Delgado, 2019a).

The two most used application integration approaches, Service-Oriented Architecture (SOA) (Erl, Merson, & Stoffers, 2017) and Representational State Transfer (REST) (Fielding, Taylor, Erenkrantz, Gorlick, Whitehead, Khare, & Oreizy, 2017) hardly comply with the principle of least knowledge. They achieve interoperability but do not solve the coupling problem, since they require that the schemas used by the interacting applications are the same. The use of polymorphism is restricted and has no formal underlying model.

SOA is good at modeling distributed systems based on the service paradigm (an extension the class-based paradigm for distributed applications) but involves rather complex and static software specifications and entails sharing schemas between client and server, which is a heavy form of coupling. Changing the interaction between Web Services is not a trivial task. REST is much simpler, justifying its increasing popularity, but is rather low level and not the best match for general-purpose, behavior-oriented distributed applications. It also entails a high level of coupling, since it requires that both interacting applications share the same media type specification.

In addition, the SOA and REST architectural styles use different modeling paradigms, since behavior (services) is the guiding concept of SOA, whereas state (resources) is the fundamental concept in REST. SOA defines which application types are used and establishes the set of operations provided by each, whereas REST starts with a state diagram, without relevant concern about distinguishing which state belongs to which application.

This chapter revisits the integration problem with an open mind, without considering *a priori* the restrictions of specific technologies, such as Web Services for SOA and RESTful APIs for REST. The only assumption is that there are applications that need to interact, by using messages. The main goal is to propose and describe a new architectural style, Structural Services, which combines the best characteristics of the SOA and REST styles. On the one hand, services have a user-defined interface that enable to publish, to discover, and to use them. On the other hand, resources have structure (composed of other resources) and implement services. Operations are first class resources and messages are themselves resources, able to include references to other resources. As a result, developers can design applications in pure SOA or REST styles, or as a tunable mix of the two, according to the needs of the problem at hand.

Structural Services is an extension of the object-oriented paradigm to distributed application contexts, reintroducing the polymorphism capability (the ability to deal in the same way with different, distributed applications) without requiring the declaration of a shared specification, based either on an inheritance relation or on an interface.

This is achieved by basing the interoperability mechanism on the concepts of compliance (Czepa, Tran, Zdun, Kim, Weiss, & Ruhsam, 2017) and conformance (Carmona, van Dongen, Solti, & Weidlich, 2018), which allow partial interoperability, rather than on sharing data schemas. This makes all the difference. Unlike Web Services, there are no declared schemas that a client is forced to use. Unlike RESTful applications, the client and server do not have to agree on a specific data type. Each resource (dataset, message or distributed application) has its own schema, stemming from its service (interface) definition. Checking for interoperability between two resources (for example, between a message and the parameter required by an operation) is structural, component-by-component, in a recursive way until reaching primitive resources.

The structure of the rest of the chapter is as follows. It starts by describing the integration problem and deriving a coupling model. Then it describes and illustrates the concepts of compliance and conformance. Next, the chapter proposes a model that encompasses resources, services and processes, to serve as the foundation for the Structural Services architectural style, conceived to bridge the advantages of both SOA and REST while minimizing the disadvantages, namely coupling. Finally, the chapter lays down the lines of future research and draws some conclusions.

BACKGROUND

Connectedness in the computer-based world is nowadays higher than ever, in a huge distributed context generically known as the Internet. The world has entered a digital era (Chamoux, 2018), in which digital-based technologies such as cloud computing (Varghese, & Buyya, 2018), mobile computing (Page, & Thorsteinsson, 2018), and the Internet of Things (Paul, & Saraswathi, 2017) started to become ubiquitous and disruptive, and people and organizations in general became more acquainted and at ease with digital services.

Many applications, designed and managed in a distributed way, need to interact and collaborate with an increasing scale, since systems are becoming more complex and diversified. An example is the recent 4.0 trend (Dornberger, 2018), in which collaboration means generating and exchanging more and more data, either at business, personal, or sensor levels. The fourth industrial revolution, commonly known as Industry 4.0 (Liao, Deschamps, Loures, & Ramos, 2017), in which agile reconfigurability of the production supply chain is a fundamental objective, is just an example. The current trend of reducing the granularity of applications, from monoliths to small microservices (Yuan, 2019), also increases the scale of the integration requirements.

All this raises the application integration problem to a completely new level, in which conventional integration technologies expose their limitations and require new solutions (Delgado, 2019b).

Panetto and Whitman (2016) broadly define *integration* as the act of instantiating a given method to design or adapt two or more systems, so that they cooperate and accomplish one or more common goals. To interact, applications must be interoperable, i.e., able to meaningfully operate together.

Integration can be seen at all levels of abstraction and complexity, from low-level cyber-physical systems (Zanero, 2017) to high-level enterprise value chains (Kanade, 2019), targeting capabilities such as those required by Industry 4.0 (Xu, Xu, & Li, 2018).

Interoperability (Agostinho, Ducq, Zacharewicz, Sarraipa, Lampathaki, Poler, & Jardim-Goncalves, 2016) is a characteristic that relates systems with this ability and that the ISO/IEC/IEEE 24765 standard (ISO, 2010) defines as "the ability of two or more systems or components to exchange information and to use the information that has been exchanged". This means that merely exchanging information is not enough. Interacting applications must also be able to understand it and to react according to each other's expectations.

Another problem is *coupling* (Bidve, & Sarasu, 2016), which provides an indication of how much applications depend on each other. Some degree of coupling is unavoidable, since some form of mutual knowledge is necessary to make interoperability possible. Interoperability and a coupling as low as possible need to be combined to achieve an effective cooperation in the integration of distributed applications.

The two most used integration approaches are the Software-Oriented Architecture (SOA) (Erl, Merson, & Stoffers, 2017) and Representational State Transfer (REST) (Fielding, Taylor, Erenkrantz, Gorlick, Whitehead, Khare, & Oreizy, 2017), with the corresponding technological solutions for distributed interoperability, Web Services (Zimmermann, Tomlinson, & Peuser, 2012) and RESTful APIs (Pautasso, 2014), respectively.

The literature comparing the SOA and REST architectural styles is vast (Bora, & Bezboruah, 2015; Soni, & Ranga, 2019), usually with arguments more on technology issues than on conceptual or modeling arguments. There are also several proposals to integrate SOA and RESTful services (Dahiya, & Parmar, 2014; Sungkur, & Daiboo, 2016; Thakar, Tiwari, & Varma, 2016).

Web Services and RESTful APIs use data description languages such as XML (Fawcett, Ayers, & Quin, 2012) and JSON (Bassett, 2015). Although they have achieved the basic objective of interconnecting independent and heterogeneous systems, supporting distributed application interoperability, they are not effective solutions from the point of view of coupling, since they require that the data schemas of the messages exchanged by the interacting applications are the same.

Several metrics have been proposed to assess the maintainability of service-based distributed applications, based essentially on structural features, namely for service coupling, cohesion and complexity (Babu, & Darsi, 2013). Other approaches focus on dynamic, rather than static, metrics for assessing coupling during program execution (Geetika, & Singh, 2014). There are also approaches trying to combine structural coupling with other levels of coupling, such as semantics (Alenezi, & Magel, 2014).

Compliance (Czepa, Tran, Zdun, Kim, Weiss, & Ruhsam, 2017) is a concept that serves as a foundation mechanism to ensure partial interoperability and thus minimize coupling. It has been studied in specific contexts, such as choreography (Capel & Mendoza, 2014), modeling (Brandt & Hermann, 2013), programming (Preidel & Borrmann, 2016), and standards (Graydon, Habli, Hawkins, Kelly, & Knight, 2012). Conformance (Carmona, van Dongen, Solti, & Weidlich, 2018) is another concept underlying partial interoperability, enabling an application to replace another if it conforms to it (supports all its features).

THE PROBLEM OF APPLICATION COUPLING

Distributed Application Interaction

Applications that interact in a distributed environment require some network to send each other messages. In each message transaction (sending a request and processing a response), both sender and receiver need to understand and react appropriately upon receiving request and response messages. A given application, in the role of server, publishes the set of request messages to which it is able to respond, which defines the interface of the functionality offered by that application (its Application Programming Interface – API). In the role of client, another application may send one of the acceptable request messages to the server and invoke the corresponding functionality. Applications can also express their APIs in terms of exposed features, such as operations. Each operation can accept its own set of request messages.

Figure 1 illustrates a typical interaction, initiated by the client, which sends a request message to the server through the interconnecting network. This usually causes the server to answer with a response message, upon executing the request.

The server needs to be able to understand the client's request and to react and respond according to what the client expects. Otherwise, the interaction will not produce the intended effects.

In a distributed environment, interacting applications evolve independently from each other and cannot rely on names of local data types or inheritance hierarchies. However, the messages exchanged must be correct and meaningful in both the contexts of the interacting applications. The goal of achieving a simple interaction such as the one depicted in Figure 1 is decomposable into the following objectives:

- There must be an addressable interconnecting network and a message-based protocol, supporting a request-response message exchange pattern.
- The server needs to validate the request message, ensuring that it is compatible with one of those acceptable by the server's API.
- The reaction of the server and the corresponding effects, as a consequence of executing the request message, must fulfil the expectations of the client regarding that reaction. The server needs to do what the client expects.
- The client needs to validate the eventual response message, ensuring that it is one of those acceptable by the client as a response.
- The client must react to the response appropriately, fulfilling the purpose of the server in sending that response, as well as completing the purpose of the client in initiating the interaction.

This means that both request and response messages need to be validated and understood (correctly interpreted and reacted upon) by the application that receives it. In addition, many other factors can influence application interoperability, such

Figure 1. Message-based interaction between two distributed applications

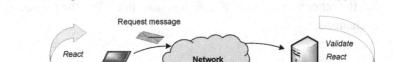

as performance, scalability, reliability, and security, although this chapter focus on the coupling aspects.

Coupling expresses the mutual dependencies between applications. The goal is to reduce it as much as possible, to avoid unnecessary constraints to the evolution and variability of applications, while trying to achieve a balance between two contradictory goals:

- On the one hand, two uncoupled applications (with no interactions between them) can evolve freely and independently, which favors adaptability, changeability and even reliability (if one fails, there is no impact on the other).
- On the other hand, applications need to interact to cooperate towards common or complementary goals, which means that some degree of previously agreed mutual knowledge must exist. The more they share with the other, the easier interoperability gets, but the greater coupling becomes.

The fundamental problem of application integration is how to provide *at most* the minimum coupling possible, while ensuring *at least* the minimum interoperability requirements. The main goal is to ensure that each interacting application knows just enough about the others to be able to interoperate with them but no more than that, avoiding unnecessary dependencies and constraints.

Existing data interoperability technologies, such as XML and JSON, assume that interacting applications share the same message schema, as depicted by Figure 2. This is *symmetric interoperability*, reminiscent of the first days of the Web and HTML documents, in which the client read the document produced by the server and both needed to use the same document specification. Today, data separate contents from their specification (schema), but both client and server still work on the same information. Application developing methods have not improved coupling.

The problem is that a server may need to serve several different clients and a client may need to send requests to several different servers. Sharing a schema couples both client and server for the whole set of messages that the schema can describe, even if the client only uses a subset of the admissible requests and the server only responds with a subset of the admissible responses.

The net effect of this symmetry is that, in many cases, coupling between client and server is higher than needed and changes in one application may very likely imply changing the other as well, even if a change does not affect the messages that are actually exchanged.

Figure 2. Schema sharing in symmetric message-based distributed application interaction

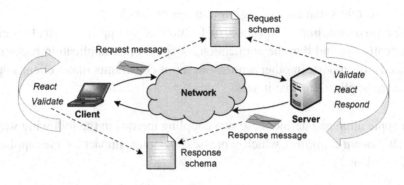

Coupling Metrics

Qualifying with *initial* an application that does not receive requests from any other and with terminal an application that does not send requests to any other, and considering the set of all the possible interactions between applications, any application that is not initial or terminal will usually take the roles of both client and server, as shown in Figure 3. Both the left and right parts of this figure entail the client-server relationship depicted in Figure 2.

Any interaction requires some form of dependency (coupling), stemming from the knowledge required to establish that interaction in a meaningful way. One way of assessing coupling is by evaluating the fraction of the features of one application (operations, messages, data types, semantic terms, and so on) that impose constraints on another application that interacts with it. There are two perspectives in which to express coupling, shown in Figure 3:

Figure 3. Backward and forward coupling

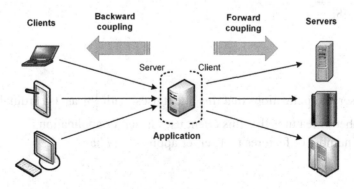

- **Backward coupling**: The subset of features of an application that it requires its clients to use according to that application's rules. In other words, the set of constraints that an application imposes on its clients.
- **Forward coupling**: The subset of features of an application that its clients actually use and that the application, or some other application replacing it, needs to support. In other words, the set of constraints that a client imposes on the applications that it uses.

An application can define these two coupling metrics in the following way:

C_B (*backward coupling*), which expresses how much impact a server application has on its clients:

$$C_B = \frac{\sum\limits_{i \in C} \dfrac{Uc_i}{Tc \cdot M}}{|C|} \tag{1}$$

where:

C - Set of clients that use this application as a server, with $|C|$ as its cardinality

Uc_i - Number of features of this application that client i uses

Tc - Total number of features that this application has

M - Number of known applications that are compatible with this application and can replace it, as a server

C_F (*forward coupling*), which expresses how much a client impacts its server applications:

$$C_F = \frac{\sum\limits_{i \in S} \dfrac{Us_i}{Ts_i \cdot N_i}}{|S|} \tag{2}$$

where:

S - Set of server applications that this client uses, with $|S|$ as its cardinality

Us_i - Number of features that this client uses in server application i

Ts_i - Total number of features that server application i has

N_i - Number of server applications with which this client is compatible, in all uses of features of server application i by this client

These coupling metrics yield values between 0, expressing completely unrelated and independent applications, and 1, in the case of completely dependent applications, constrained by all features. These metrics lead to the following interpretation:

- Equation (1) means that having clients use as few features as possible of a server application reduces the overall system dependency on it and the impact that it may have on its potential clients (its backward coupling C_B).
- Equation (2) indicates that the existence of alternative servers to a given client application reduces its forward coupling C_F, since having more server applications with which this client application is compatible dilutes the dependencies.

Reducing the fraction of features needed for compatibility to the bare minimum required by the interaction between applications helps in finding alternative server applications. The smaller the number of constraints, the greater the probability of finding applications that satisfy them.

Therefore, both factors on which coupling depends (the fraction of features used, as a client, and the number of replacement alternatives available, as a server) work in the same direction, with the first reinforcing the second. Reducing coupling means reducing the fraction of features used, or the knowledge of one application about another. Therefore, the integration of applications designed with these issues in mind will be easier.

Technologies such as Web Services (Zimmermann, Tomlinson, & Peuser, 2012) and RESTful APIs (Pautasso, 2014) constitute poor solutions in terms of coupling, since Web Services rely on sharing a schema (a WSDL document) and RESTful APIs are usually based on previously agreed upon media types. These technologies support the distributed interoperability problem, but do not solve the coupling problem.

In conventional systems, searching for an interoperable application is done by schema matching with similarity algorithms (Elshwimy, Algergawy, Sarhan, & Sallam, 2014) and ontology matching and mapping (Anam, Kim, Kang, & Liu, 2016). These algorithms may find similar server schemas, but do not ensure interoperability. Manual adaptations are usually unavoidable.

The goal in this chapter is to be able to integrate applications with exact interoperability, rather than just approximate, even if the client and server schemas are not identical, as long as certain requirements hold. This does not mean being able to integrate any set of existing applications, but rather being able to change an application, due to a normal evolution in specifications, without impairing an existing interoperability. Less coupling means greater flexibility for accommodating changes.

COMPLIANCE AND CONFORMANCE: TOOLS TO MINIMIZE COUPLING

The Concepts of Compliance and Conformance

In symmetric interoperability (Figure 2), interacting applications must share the schemas of the messages that they exchange. This leads to a higher level of coupling than actually needed, since applications are constrained by all the features of those schemas, even if not all are used.

This chapter proposes to use *asymmetric interoperability*, in which the schema of a message, as generated by the sender, needs only partially match the schema of the messages expected by the receiver. Only the actually used features need to have a match. The receiver ignores features present in the message that it does not require. Optional receiver features not present in the message are assigned default values prior to processing the message at the receiver. In addition, structured features are checked structurally and recursively, component by component.

This means that a client can use (send request messages to) various servers, as long as these messages match the relevant parts of those servers' request schemas, even if they were not designed to work together.

It also means that a server can replace another one, with a different schema, as long as it can deal with all the requests that the replaced one could. This can occur due to evolution of the server (replaced by a new version) or by resorting to a new server altogether.

Allowing a server to be able to interpret request messages from different clients, and a server to be able to send response messages to different receivers, is precisely what equations (1) and (2) show that is required to decrease coupling.

These *use* and *replace* relationships lead to two important schema relations, which are central to asymmetric interoperability and are illustrated by Figure 4:

- **Client-server**: *Compliance* (Czepa, Tran, Zdun, Kim, Weiss, & Ruhsam, 2017). The client must satisfy (*comply with*) the requirements established by the server to accept requests sent to it, without which these cannot be validated and executed. It is important to note that any client that complies with a given server can use it, independently of having been designed for interaction with it or not. The client and server need not share the same schema. The client's schema needs only to be compliant with the server's schema in the features that it actually uses. Since distributed applications have independent lifecycles, they cannot freely share names, and the server must check schema compliance (between messages sent by the client and the interface offered by the server) in a structural way, feature by feature. Note that in a response the roles of schema compliance are reversed (the server is the sender and the client is the receiver).

- **Server-server**: *Conformance* (Carmona, van Dongen, Solti, & Weidlich, 2018). The issue is to ascertain whether a server S_2 can replace another server S_1 in serving a client, such that the client-server relationship enjoyed by the client is not impaired, or whether server S_2 is replacement compatible with server S_1. Conformance expresses the replacement compatibility between two servers. Server S_2 must possess at least all the characteristics of server S_1, therefore being able to take the form of (*conform to*) server S_1 and fulfill the expectations of the client regarding what it expects the server to be. In particular, the schema of server S_2 cannot include any additional mandatory component, regarding the schema of server S_1, otherwise it would impose more requirements on the client and the interoperability could break. The reasons for replacing a server with another may be varied, such as switching to an alternative in case of failure or lack of capacity, evolution (in which case server S_2 would be the new version of server S_1), or simply a management decision.

In asymmetric interoperability, the server does not know the schema used by the client to generate messages. In this context, two kinds of schema are considered:

Figure 4. Compliance and conformance

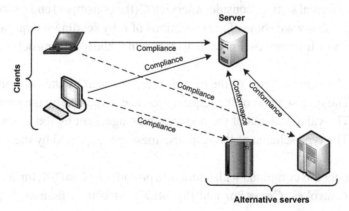

- **Type schema**: A description of the features of a set of messages, including the definition of each possible feature and whether it is optional or mandatory. This is what typically schema description languages such as XML-Schema provide.
- **Value schema**: The concrete definition of a specific message, with just the features that it actually has. Each message has its own value schema. This is simply a self-description and, unlike type schemas, includes no variability (range of structured values). A value schema satisfies an infinite number of type schemas (by considering an infinite number of optional features).

In symmetric interoperability, both the client and server share type schemas. The server must be able to deal with all the messages with value schemas that satisfy its type schema, since that is also the type schema that the client uses and therefore can send a message with any of those value schemas.

In asymmetric interoperability, there is no such restriction and, as long as the value schemas of the messages actually sent satisfy the type schema of the server, interoperability is possible, with a lower coupling.

In semantic terms, compliance means that the set of possible message values sent by a client is a subset of the set of values that satisfy the type schema of the server. Conformance means that the set of values that satisfy the type schema of an alternative server (Figure 4) is a superset of the set of values that satisfy the type schema of the original receiver.

As long as compliance and conformance hold, the server can accept messages from different clients. In addition, a client can start using an alternative server without noticing the difference with respect to the original server.

It is also useful to view client and server not merely as applications by as distributed services (with internal state that expose operations), in the role of consumer and provider, considering that a request message invokes one of the provider's operations and that a response message is sent back to the consumer.

In a more formal setting, consider a service C (the consumer) and a service P (the provider). C can invoke some of the operations of P by sending it request messages that trigger those invocations. For each operation in P, the following definitions hold:

- *Crq*: The value schema of the request message, sent by the consumer.
- *Prq*: The type schema of the request message, expected by the provider.
- *Prp*: The value schema of the response message, sent by the provider.
- *Crp*: The type schema of the response message, expected by the consumer.

A consumer C is compliant with (can *use*) a provider P ($C \blacktriangleleft P$) if, for all operations i of P that C invokes, $Crq_i \blacktriangleleft Prq_i$ and $Prp_i \blacktriangleleft Crp_i$. Structural assignment is used to assign the value components of a message received (either request or response) to the variable components of the type schema of the receiver (either provider or consumer, respectively).

In a similar way, a provider S is conformant to (can *replace*) a provider P ($S{\blacktriangleright}P$) if, for all operations i of P, $Srq_i{\blacktriangleright}Prq_i$ and $Prp_i{\blacktriangleright}Srp_i$.

Illustrating Compliance

Figure 5 illustrates a typical compliance-based (Czepa, Tran, Zdun, Kim, Weiss, & Ruhsam, 2017) client-server interaction, in which client and server need not share the same schema. The client must only satisfy (*comply with*) the requirements established by the server to accept requests sent to it. This means that the client's schema needs only to be compliant with the server's schema in the features that it actually uses, thereby reducing the coupling between the client and the server.

The compliance-based interoperability mechanism of Figure 5 includes the following aspects, for the request message (similar for the response message, with client and server roles reversed):

- The server publishes a request type schema, which describes the type of request message values that the server can accept.
- A value schema (specific of this message) describes the actual request message, sent by the client.
- When the request message arrives, the server validates the message's value schema by checking it for satisfaction of, or compliance with, the type schema

Figure 5. Illustrating compliance (showing only the request message validation, for simplicity)

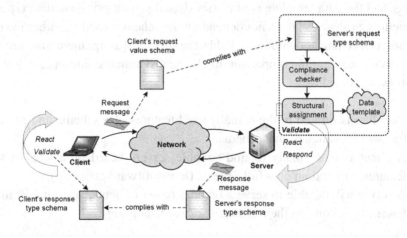

of the server, in the *compliance checker*. If compliance holds, the request message is one of those that satisfy the server's request type schema and is accepted.

- The request message's value is *structurally* assigned to the *data template*, which is a data structure that satisfies the server's type schema and includes default values for the components in the type schema that are *optional* (minimum number of occurrences specified as zero). Compliance will fail if the request message does not include at least the minimum number of occurrences specified for each component of data template.

- Structural assignment involves mapping the request message to the server's request type schema, by assigning the message to the data template, component by component, according to the following basic rules:
  - Structural assignment skips components in the message that do not comply with any component in the data template.
  - Components in the data template that are also present in the message have their values set to the corresponding message's component values.
  - Optional components in the data template missing from the message have their values set to the corresponding default values (specified in the data template).
  - Structural assignment deals with structured components by recursive application of these rules.

After this, the data template is completely populated and the server can access it. Each request message populates a new instance of the data template. Note that this mechanism is different from the usual data binding of existing technologies, since the server deals only with its own request message type schema. It does not know the value schema of the request message and there is no need for a data-binding stub to deal with it. The important issue is that the mapping between the request message and the data template is universal (based just on primitive data types and on structuring rules) and does not depend on the schemas used by either the client or the server. As long as compliance holds, the structural assignment rules are valid. This reduces coupling in comparison to classical symmetric interoperability, with the following advantages:

- Coupling is limited to the actually used features of a schema and not to the full set of features of that schema.
- A client is more likely to find suitable servers based on a smaller set of features, rather than on a full schema (lower forward coupling).
- A server will be able to serve a broader base of clients, since it will impose fewer restrictions on them (lower backward coupling).

Illustrating Conformance

Forward coupling limits the ability of one server application replacing another without impairing interoperability with existing clients. Replacing a server application can be useful in several cases, such as:

- An application evolves (the new version replaces the old one).
- An application migrates to another cloud or environment, eventually with differences in its interface.
- Usage of an alternative application, due to a failure or lack of capacity of the original application.
- To balance the load of requests, spreading them across several (not necessarily identical) server applications.
- Some management decisions imply using another application.

Figure 6 illustrates conformance (Carmona, van Dongen, Solti, & Weidlich, 2018) between the two servers, by depicting a situation in which a server S_1, serving a client, is replaced by another server S_2, while maintaining the client-server relationship in such a way that the client will not notice it.

Server S_2 has all the characteristics of server S_1 (and probably more) and is therefore able to take the form of (conform to) server S_1 and fulfill the expectations of the client regarding what it expects the server to be. If the schema of server S_2 has additional features, with respect to server S_1, these must be optional, otherwise it would impose more requirements on the client and the interoperability could be impaired.

By the definition of conformance, a client that complies with a server also complies with another server that conforms to the original server, as shown in Figure 4.

ARCHITECTURAL STYLES FOR APPLICATION INTEGRATION

Comparing the SOA and REST Architectural Styles

An *architectural style* is a collection of design patterns, guidelines and best practices (Sharma, Kumar, & Agarwal, 2015), in a bottom-up approach, or a set of constraints on the concepts and on their relationships (Erl, Carlyle, Pautasso, & Balasubramanian, 2012), in a top-down approach. Each architectural style has an underlying modeling paradigm, which serves as a guiding tenet.

SOA (Erl, Merson, & Stoffers, 2017) and REST (Fielding, Taylor, Erenkrantz, Gorlick, Whitehead, Khare, & Oreizy, 2017) are the most popular today in distributed

Figure 6. Illustrating conformance. A server application can replace another, as long as it supports the features that the clients of the original server application require

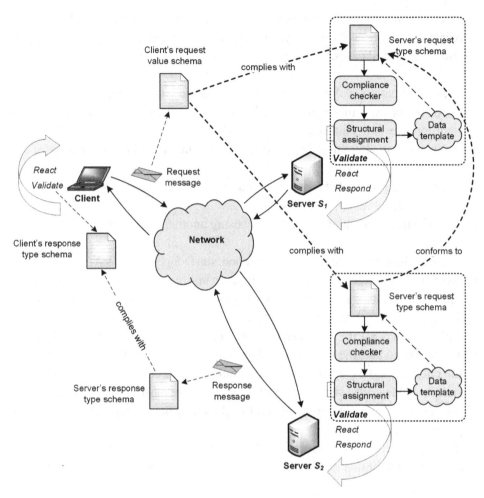

application integration and therefore those that this chapter analyzes and compares, although comparing architectural styles in abstract terms is not the same thing as comparing their practical instantiations.

SOA is easy to grasp, since it constitutes a natural evolution of the object-oriented style, with which analysts and application developers are already familiar. However, Web Services, with WSDL, XML Schema and SOAP, are complex to use, especially without adequate tools that usually automate or hide most of the development process.

REST can be comparatively counterintuitive at first, in particular for people with an object-oriented mindset, who tend to slide to the probably more familiar RPC (Remote Procedure Call) style (Kukreja & Garg, 2014), with operation parameters instead of dynamic resource references (Fielding, Taylor, Erenkrantz, Gorlick, Whitehead, Khare, & Oreizy, 2017). On the other hand, its instantiation over HTTP is relatively straightforward to use, even without elaborate tools, since what is involved is essentially plain HTTP messaging.

This chapter is more interested in the architectural styles themselves than on their instantiations, since these are heavily dependent on syntactic and protocol issues of existing interoperability tools and technologies. The goal is to compare styles, not their instantiations, since there are several ways to implement a style.

Both SOA and REST have advantages and limitations. This chapter proposes an architectural style that emphasizes the advantages of both and reduces their limitations, in particular with respect to the coupling problem.

SOA appeared in the context of enterprise integration, with the main goal of achieving interoperability between existing enterprise applications with the then emerging XML-based technologies, more universal than those used in previous attempts, such as CORBA (Common Object Request Broker Architecture) (Henning, 2008) and RPC (Kukreja & Garg, 2014). It was a natural evolution of the object-oriented style, now in a distributed environment and with large-grained resources to integrate. Therefore, developers modeled applications as black boxes, exposing their external functionality with an interface composed of a set of operations, application dependent. These models avoided exposing internal structure, as a measure to reduce coupling by applying the information hiding principle.

REST appeared in the context of Web applications, as a systematization of the underlying model of the Web and with scalability as the most relevant goal, since interoperability had already been solved by HTML (and, later, XML) and HTTP. REST is based on several architectural constraints, the most relevant of which are stateless interactions (only the client maintains the interaction state) and uniform interface (all resources have a service with the same set of operations, with variability on structure and with links to resources, rather than on service interface). These constraints had decoupling as their main motivation, to support scalability. When potentially thousands of clients connect to a server, server applications need to be able to scale and to evolve as needed and as independently as possible from the clients.

Coupling was therefore a main concern for both architectural styles, although many arguments contributed to fuel a lively debate between SOA and REST proponents. In particular, REST has been heralded as much simpler and providing a better decoupling between interacting systems (Pautasso, Zimmermann, & Leymann, 2008). A simple example, however, indicates that these two architectural styles are not that different, in essence.

Figure 7 describes a typical online product purchase scenario, using the process paradigm and Business Process Modeling Notation (BPMN) (Chinosi & Trombetta,

2012) to illustrate the interactions between a customer, a seller, and a logistics company to deliver the product.

A developer needs to conceive, design, and implement, as much independently as possible, each of the three roles in this process choreography, since applications with different goals and characteristics can perform the roles. The overall goal is to minimize coupling.

This example also compares the approaches based on SOA and REST. Figure 8 depicts just the Customer process, for simplicity, using UML. Figure 8a represents the SOA approach, with a resource structure mimicking the three actors and the corresponding sequence diagram, reflecting their interactions. The REST approach goes directly to modeling interaction states, which Figure 8b reflects by a state diagram.

Apart from details, it is noticeable that the flow of activities of the customer in SOA is dual of the flow of states in REST. Figure 8a (SOA) uses activity-based flow graph, with activities performed in the nodes and state changed in the edges, whereas Figure 8b (REST) places state at the nodes and implements activities at the edges.

Behavior guides SOA and (representation of) state guides REST. In UML terminology, SOA uses a static class diagram and a sequence diagram (Figure 8a) as a first approach, to specify which resource types are used, to establish the set of operations provided by each, and their interactions, whereas REST starts with a state diagram (Figure 8b), without relevant concern about distinguishing which state belongs to which resource. In the end, they perform the same activities and go through the same states, although with different perspectives that stem from the approaches used to solve the same problem.

It is also clear that both SOA and REST tackle the fundamental problem of integration, to achieve interoperability while trying to minimize coupling and to

Figure 7. An example of business-level distributed interactions

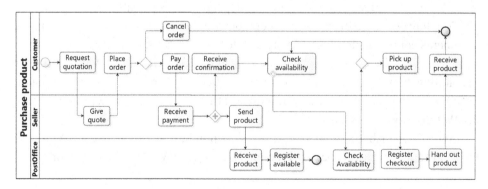

Figure 8. Modeling the customer process in (a) SOA and (b) REST styles

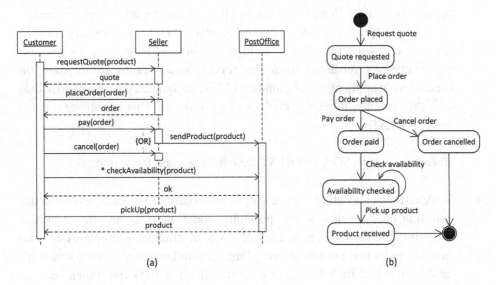

(a)　　　　　　　　　　(b)

comply with the information hiding principle by hiding the implementation of individual resources. However:

- SOA's approach is to hide resource structure (considering it part of the implementation), whereas REST's approach is to hide resource behavior (its service) by converting it into resource structure (each operation is a resource).
- SOA models resources as close as possible to real world entities, to reduce the semantic gap (Sikos, 2017). Since these are different from each other, offering a specific set of functionalities, the result is a set of resources with different interfaces (different set of operations). The client must know the specific interface of the server. This entails coupling and may only be acceptable if the number of clients for a given server is usually reasonably small and the system evolves slowly (to limit the maintenance effort).
- REST tries to avoid the interface coupling by decomposing complex resources into smaller ones (with links to other resources) until they are so primitive that they can all be treated in the same way, with a common interface. REST transfers interface diversity to the richness of the structure of the links between resources. This uniform interface for all resources, with a common set of operations is the most distinguishing feature of REST. This corresponds to separating the mechanism of traversing a graph (the links between resources) from the treatment of each node (resource). The goal is that a universal link follow-up mechanism, coupled with a universal resource interface, leads to decoupling between server and clients, allowing servers to change what they

send to the clients because these will adapt automatically, by just navigating the structure and following the links to progress in the interaction process.

- SOA has no dynamic visibility control mechanism for operations. In contrast, REST limits what the client can do to the links contained in the resource representations retrieved from the server, which helps to increase the robustness of applications. Amundsen (2014) designated the idea of providing only the currently allowable choices as *affordances*. This is a strong point in favor of REST.

Unfortunately, both SOA and REST have fallacies and limitations:

- SOA assumes that all resources (applications) are at the same level and that exposing their services is just providing some interface and the respective endpoint. The fallacy is to assert that resource structure is unimportant. This may be true when integrating very large-grained resources, but not in many applications that include lists of resources that need to expose their services individually. The limitation is in changeability. Changing the interface of the server will most likely require changes in the clients as well.
- REST imposes a uniform interface, which allows treating all the resources in the same way. The fallacy is to consider only a syntactic interface, or even semantic (Verborgh, Harth, Maleshkova, Stadtmüller, Steiner, Taheriyan, & Van de Walle, 2014), but forgetting behavior. Application integration also needs to consider the reaction of resources to requests, which means that resources cannot follow a link blindly. The client needs to know which kind of reaction the server is going to have. In the same way, traversing a structured resource implies knowing the type of that resource, otherwise which link should be followed next may not be known. This only means one thing: since there is no declaration of resource types, applications need to know in advance all types of resources that they use, either standardized or previously agreed upon (with custom media types). This is a relevant limitation of REST. What happens in practice is that developers are more than happy to agree on simple resource structures and on an aligned API to match. REST's advocates contend that an initial link (an URI – Universal Resource Identifier –, for example) is the only API's entry point and that the client must dynamically discover the entire functionality of the API simply by exploring links. However, this requires a set of fixed resource types (predefined or previously agreed upon). Resource structure can vary, which is a good advantage of REST, but only within the boundaries of resource types known in advance. This is nothing more than sharing schemas (Figure 2) or, in other words, coupling.

SOA is a better option for large-grained, slowly evolving complex resources, whereas REST is a better option for small-grained, structured resources that are relatively simple. In search for simplicity and maintainability, many service providers (including cloud-computing providers) have stopped using SOA APIs in favor of REST, by modeling operations as resources, using naturally occurring lists of resources as structured resources with links, and dynamically building URIs instead of resorting to operation parameters. Decoupling in REST, however, is not as good as its structure dynamicity seems to indicate. Applications need to know all the resource types (media types, in REST terminology) in advance and the client may break if the server uses a new media type unknown to the client. In addition, even when the client knows the type used, it cannot invent what to do and which link to choose when it receives a resource representation of a given type. Collaboration requires that both server and client implement behavior and deal with its effects, which means that they cannot be agnostic of each other. Rather, the design of applications needs to take into account that they must work together.

In Search of a Better Architectural Style

This SOA-REST dichotomy means that the application integration paradigm to adopt has to be chosen at the very beginning of an integration project and maintained throughout the whole project, since changing at some point practically means starting over with a completely different architecture.

However, integration projects are usually a mixture of different applications with different requirements, in which the respective APIs are sometimes more adequate to expose structured resources and sometimes better expressed by a set of services that expose functionality.

Naturally, SOA can access structured resources and REST can implement a service-based API. However, these are not the native uses for these architectural styles, and require tricks that translate into more development effort and a higher risk of failure to comply with the specifications.

In search of an architectural style that alleviates the disadvantages of SOA and REST and enhances their advantages, without forcing an application developer to choose between one and the other, it is noticeable that two of the main problems of SOA and REST are:

- The lack of flexibility of the underlying model. SOA has just services, without resource structure, and REST has just structured resources, with a fixed service at the syntactic level. REST does not provide a good support for the process paradigm, given the low level of resources and the stateless client-server interactions from the point of view of the server.

- The coupling stemming from the use of shared schemas, which in practice requires designing applications specifically to work together (e.g., building client stubs based on WSDL specifications of the servers, in SOA, or restricting messages to a standard or application-specific media type, in REST).

The ideal would be to use an architectural style that could:

- Deal natively with both state and behavior, exposing both structured resources and services. This requires a new model underlying the architectural style, encompassing both structured resources and services. The following section describes this.
- Avoid the requirement of sharing schemas, using compliance and conformance instead. Combining the new architectural model with the compliance and conformance relationships described above can be achieve this goal.

This means that this style could support better any application style or a mixture of applications with different styles, at the same time that would provide better integration, with lower application coupling.

This architectural style does not yet exist. Table 1 provides a summary of the main characteristics of the most relevant existing architectural styles, showing the evolution that leads to the requirements enunciated for the sought-after architectural style, proposed by this chapter with the *Structural Services* designation, precisely because it combines both structured state and behavior (services).

STRUCTURAL SERVICES: MOVING BEYOND SOA AND REST

Unifying Resources, Services and Processes in a Common Model

In a single application, the object-oriented architectural style is probably the best in the non-declarative programming world, with its low semantic gap (Sikos, 2017), information reuse (inheritance), polymorphism and ability to expose both behavior and structure. These characteristics are very similar to the goals of the new architectural style, Structural Services, introduced in the last row of Table 1.

Unfortunately, in a distributed environment pointers to objects can no longer be used and inheritance stops working, since the lifecycles of the objects are not synchronized (they can be modified, recompiled and linked independently).

Extending the object-oriented paradigm to the distributed realm requires viewing objects as resources in a message-based network, each implementing a service

Table 1. Main characteristics of various architectural styles

Style	Brief Description	Examples of Characteristics or Constraints
Object-Oriented	• Resources and services follow the Object-Oriented paradigm.	• Resources are classes. • Services are interfaces. • References are pointers. • Reactions discretized into operations. • Polymorphism based on inheritance.
Distributed	• Interacting resources have independent lifecycles.	• References cannot be pointers. • Type checking cannot be name-based. • Services and resources may use heterogeneous technologies.
SOA	• Style similar to Object-Oriented, but with distributed constraints.	• Resources have no structure. • The interface of services is customizable. • No polymorphism. • Integration based on common schemas and ontologies.
Process	• Behavior modeled as orchestrations and choreographies.	• Services are the units of behavior. • A process is an orchestration of services. • Processes must obey the rules of choreographies.
REST	• Resources have structure but a fixed service.	• Client and server roles distinction. • Resources have a common set of operations. • Stateless interactions.
Structural Services	• Structured resources, customizable services, minimum coupling.	• Resources have structure (like REST). • Services have a customizable interface (like SOA). • Interoperability based on structural compliance and conformance (new feature).

defined by its interface, and application interactions as service transactions that constitute a distributed process.

The relationship between resources, services and processes (core concepts of the REST, SOA, and Process architectural styles in Table 1) obeys the following considerations:

- A *service* is a set of logically related operations of a resource, or a facet of that resource that makes sense in modeling terms. A service is pure behavior, albeit the implementation of concrete operations may depend on state, which needs a resource as an implementation platform.
- A *resource* is a module that implements a service and that interacts with others by exchanging messages with them. A resource X that sends a message to a resource Y is in fact invoking the service of Y. This constitutes a service transaction between these two resources, in which the resources X and Y perform the role of service consumer (client) and service provider (server), respectively. A service transaction can entail other service transactions, as part of the chain reaction to the message on part of the service provider. The

definition of a service should be in terms of reactions to messages (external view) and not in terms of state transitions or activity flows (internal view).

- A *process* is a graph of all service transactions that can occur in a valid way, starting with a service transaction initiated at some resource X and ending with a final service transaction, which neither reacts back nor initiates new service transactions. The process corresponds to a use case of resource X and usually involves other resources as service transactions flow.

An abstract model can express the relationships between the entities described above, so that applications can deal with interoperability in a uniform way, as shown in Figure 9, using UML (Unified Modeling Language) notation. A resource provides implementation for a service, namely its operations. Services invoke each other through service transactions, forming a process. Interaction is message based, assuming that an adequate channel and message protocol are available. Resources can be composed of other resources (composition) and have references to other resources (aggregation). Distributed references are themselves resources and included as components (but not the resources they reference) in their containers.

Association classes describe relationships (such as Transaction and the message Protocol) or roles, such as Message, which describes the roles (specialized by Request and Response) performed by resources when they are sent as messages.

An interaction between resources corresponds to an interaction between services, since the service represents the active part (behavior) of a resource and exposes its operations. The mention of interaction between resources actual refers to the interaction between the services that they implement.

Resources entail structure, state and behavior. Services refer only to behavior, without imposing a specific implementation. Processes are a view on the behavior sequencing and flow along services, which resources implement. Services and processes are dual of each other, having resources as the structural entities. Where there is a service, there is a process and vice-versa. The question is which paradigm should be used first and foremost in modeling the architecture of a system, with the other derived from it. In a distributed application context, and in terms of modeling, adaptability and changeability, the service paradigm constitutes a better approach than the process paradigm (Baghdadi, 2014).

This model encompasses both behavior and structure, and is fundamental to apply the compliance and conformance in lowering coupling in a service-based, distributed application context.

Figure 9. A simple model of distributed application interaction

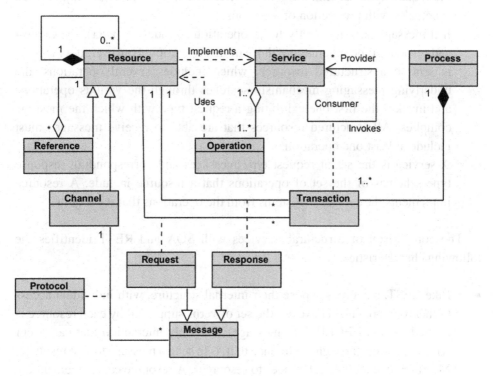

The Structural Services Architectural Style

This chapter contends that it can partially solve the problems identified in SOA and REST, limited only by the constraints of the specifications of the applications to integrate, not by the architectural style adopted, and proposes the Structural Services architectural style for that effect. The goal is to combine the best features of SOA and REST, by adopting Figure 9 as the underlying model in the following arrangement, the basis of the Structural Services architectural style:

- The basic unit of distribution is the resource, an entity accessible through distributed references (e.g., URIs – Uniform Resource Identifiers) and that can be atomic (not composed of other resources) or structured, recursively composed of other structured resources and operations.
- An operation is an atomic resource with a request type schema (see Figure 5), which expresses the type of messages it is able to receive (by compliance), and a response type schema, which expresses the kind of messages it is able to send back as a response. Reception of a message that complies with

the request type schema triggers the actions that the operation implements, eventually with production of a response.

- If a message is sent directly to an operation (through its URI), the request and response type schemas are those of that operation. However, if a message is sent to a structured resource, which includes several operations, the underlying messaging mechanism searches through the various operations and invokes the first one exhibiting a request type with which the message complies. All structured resources that are able to receive messages must include at least one operation.
- A service is the set of request type messages and corresponding response type schemas of the set of operations that a resource include. A resource implements the service that stems from the operations that it contains.

The comparison of Structural Services with SOA and REST identifies the following characteristics:

- Like REST, resources expose their internal structure, with individual access to their components. However, the set of verbs supported by each resource is limited to one: RECEIVE (a message). The only interaction that can occur with a resource, through a reference to it, is to send a message to that resource. Messages can include references to resources. A resource can implement the typical CRUD style (Create, Read, Update, and Delete) of REST's architectural model, as long as it supports the corresponding four operations. Therefore, the name of the operation is the last part of the resource reference's path and not a predefined operation of the message protocol. Resource interaction can use any communications protocol that is able to send a message and return a response.
- Unlike REST, the semantics of the reaction of that message is not to return a representation of the resource or to change its state, but rather to invoke the programmed actions and to return the corresponding response. The action may very well be to return a representation as a response, or to change the state with the request's content, but these are just two possibilities. All depends on the internal structure of the operations of that resource and the compliance mechanism to choose which operation to invoke.
- Like SOA, it is up to each resource to determine what the reaction and response will be regarding a given message received. Different resources can offer different functionality and different reactions to the same message.
- Unlike SOA, the basic unit of distribution is the resource, not the service. This means that the targets of messages are resources, not services, and therefore a distributed reference can identify a structure and not merely a one-level,

flat service. Different resources can actually implement the same service in different ways. This brings polymorphism back, now in a distributed context, thanks to compliance.

One of the advantages of the Structural Services style is the ability to lean more towards SOA or REST, according to modeling convenience, and mix several approaches and patterns in the same problem.

In particular, note that the object-oriented style bases the inheritance-based polymorphism on the assumption that objects belonging to classes inheriting from a common base class share a common set of features (variables and operations of the base class).

In Structural Services, resources do not belong to any class (or, better said, each resource is a singleton, with its own value schema) and there is no inheritance, but polymorphism still works on similar grounds, thanks to compliance and conformance. The server never deals with the request messages themselves, only with the data template (Figure 5). All the request messages that can be morphed into the data template (all for which compliance holds) will be seen as having a common set of features (those of the data template) and will be treated in the same way, exactly as in inheritance-based polymorphism, but now with the added advantage of supporting application distribution.

It is also important to acknowledge that the REST style requires a fixed set of operations, without stating which operations should be in that set. The HTTP implementations use some of the HTTP verbs, but this is just one possibility. The Structural Services style allows a further step in flexibility, by opening the possibility of using several fixed set of operations in the same problem. Now not only both extremes are possible (each resource with its specific set of operations, SOA style, or one common set of operations for all resources, REST style), but also any intermediate combination can be used, with different sets of operations for different sets of resources. This includes the distributed polymorphism mechanism based on compliance. Each server's type schema in Figure 5 specifies, in practice, a set of features common to all the resources that comply with that type schema.

Table 2 summarizes the main differences and advantages of the Structural Services architectural style regarding SOA and REST, in the light of the discussion above.

In the context of distributed application environments, the Structural Services architectural style, and in particular its partial interoperability features (compliance and conformance), can be useful in circumstances such as:

- Using compliance to support integration, even between applications not designed to interoperate, as long as one, in the role of client, complies with the requirements of the other, in the role of server (Figure 5). In addition, it is

63

Table 2. Comparing SOA, REST and Structural Services

	SOA	REST	Structural Services
Basic tenet	• Behavior.	• Hypermedia (structure + links).	• Tunable between pure behavior and pure hypermedia.
Distinguishing features	• Resource-specific interface. • Operations are entry points to a service. • Design-time service declaration.	• Uniform interface. • Operations are resources. • Clients react to structure received (do not invoke resource interfaces).	• Variable resource interface. • Resources are structured. • Operations are resources. • Applications need not know resource types at design time.
Structure exposed	• Behavior.	• State.	• State and behavior.
Best applicability	• Large-grained resources (application integration).	• Small-grained resources (CRUD-oriented APIs).	• Wide range (small to large, behavior to structured-oriented).
Interoperability based on	• Schema sharing.	• Predefined media types.	• Structural polymorphism (compliance and conformance).
Self-description	• Repository (e.g., WSDL document).	• Content type declaration in resource representations.	• Included in each message to match request type schemas.
Design time support	• High	• Low	• High
Main advantages	• Low semantic gap (resources model closely real world entities).	• Structured resources, with representations with links to other resources (hypermedia).	• Low semantic gap. • Structured resources. • Messages with links. • Polymorphism. • Self-description. • Tunable between SOA and REST styles.
Main fallacy	• Resource structure is unimportant.	• Hypermedia increases decoupling.	• None identified.
Main limitation	• No polymorphism (coupling higher than needed).	• Fixed interface (semantic gap higher than needed).	• None identified.

important to realize that compliance is a universal concept and can be applied not just to software applications but also in many more contexts, such cyber-physical systems or even people (in terms of characteristics or skills). This is important to complex distributed application scenarios, such as enterprise architectures.

• Using conformance for service discovery. A consumer application can send to potential providers the description of the service provider that it needs.

Those that conform can perform the role of service provider, as if they were exactly what the consumer seeks.
- Using compliance and conformance to enable the construction of enterprise value chains, by building a list of potential customers and suppliers (Figure 3).

A Simple Example

The notation to specify messages, type schemas, structured resources, operations, and so on, does not yet exist in a way that supports an actual implementation of the Structural Services style. This section illustrates the compliance and conformance concepts, and the Structural Services style, in a simulated way by resorting to existing technologies, namely Web Services to illustrate the service style and URIs to illustrate the REST style.

Consider the interoperability needed between the Customer and the Seller, in Figure 7. For a customer, this involves not only finding a suitable seller but also avoiding lock-in with it, by allowing the replacement of that seller by another with a compatible interface. Partial interoperability (compliance and conformance) allows reducing the coupling to the bare minimum necessary.

The Seller is a Web Service offering several operations, including one called getQuote that allows the Customer to implement its RequestQuotation activity in Figure 5.

Listing 1 contains a fragment of a seller's WSDL file, showing only the relevant parts. A WSDL file describes the interface of a Web Service, including the operations it supports and the respective parameters and results. To keep it simple, Listing 1 depicts just the operation getQuote. It receives the specification of a product (the model and the seller's department it belongs to) and the information returned includes a quote for each product of that model found, with an optional boolean that indicates whether that product is in stock. The Customer needs a client program to deal with this Web Service.

Now consider Listing 2, with the equivalent WSDL fragment of another seller's Web Service, compatible with this one but not identical to it. Its getQuote operation provides the same overall functionality and has the same name, so that a syntactical interface match is possible. For simplicity, this example does not tackle semantics. It also obtains a quote on the product, specified by a description and the product category it belongs to, and returns up to three pairs of product ID and respective price. The description may take one or two strings, so that brand and model, for example, can be separate, if required, and the category is optional but supports two strings to specify, for example the product's division and unit.

Listing 1. A fragment of the WSDL of one seller's Web Service

```
<types>
    <xs:schema xmlns:xs="http://www.w3.org/2001/XMLSchema"
            targetNamespace="http://example.com/schema/seller1"
            xmlns="http://example.com/schema/seller1"
            elementFormDefault="qualified">
        <xs:element name="product" type="Product"/>
        <xs:element name="prodInfo" type="ProdInfo"/>
        <xs:complexType name="Product">
            <xs:sequence>
                <xs:element name="model" type="xs:string"/>
                <xs:element name="department"
type="xs:string"/>
            </xs:sequence>
        </xs:complexType>
        <xs:complexType name="ProdInfo">
            <xs:sequence minOccurs="0" maxOccurs="unbounded">
                <xs:element name="ID" type="xs:string"/>
                <xs:element name="cost" type="xs:decimal"/>
                <xs:element name="inStock" type="xs:boolean"
                        minOccurs="0"/>
            </xs:sequence>
        </xs:complexType>
    </xs:schema>
</types>
<interface name="Seller_1">
    <operation name="getQuote"
                pattern="http://www.w3.org/ns/wsdl/in-out">
        <input messageLabel="In" element="seller1:product"/>
        <output messageLabel="Out" element="seller1:prodInfo"/>
    </operation>
</interface>
```

These two WSDL fragments correspond to two different schemas and the usual way to invoke the respective services would be to generate two different clients, one for each service. However, by looking at both the WSDL fragments, it is noticeable that:

Listing 2. A fragment of the WSDL of another seller's Web Service

```
<types>
    <xs:schema xmlns:xs="http://www.w3.org/2001/XMLSchema"
            targetNamespace="http://example.com/schema/seller1"
            xmlns="http://example.com/schema/seller2"
            elementFormDefault="qualified">
        <xs:element name="productSpec" type="ProductSpec"/>
        <xs:element name="productInfo" type="ProductInfo"/>
        <xs:complexType name="ProductSpec">
            <xs:sequence>
                <xs:element name="description" type="xs:string"
                        minOccurs="1" maxOccurs="2"/>
                <xs:element name="category" type="xs:string"
                        minOccurs="0" maxOccurs="2"/>
            </xs:sequence>
        </xs:complexType>
        <xs:complexType name="ProductInfo">
            <xs:sequence minOccurs="0" maxOccurs="3">
                <xs:element name="productID" type="xs:string"/>
                <xs:element name="price" type="xs:decimal"/>
            </xs:sequence>
        </xs:complexType>
    </xs:schema>
</types>
<interface name="Seller_2">
    <operation name="getQuote"
                pattern="http://www.w3.org/ns/wsdl/in-out">
        <input messageLabel="In"
element="seller2:productSpec"/>
        <output messageLabel="Out"
element="seller2:productInfo"/>
    </operation>
</interface>
```

- The In element of the getQuote operation in Listing 1, of type Product, *complies* with the In element of the operation in Listing 2, of type ProductSpec. In other words, supplying a model and department with one string each is within the requirements of the operation in Listing 2;

- The Out element of the operation in Listing 2, of type ProductInfo, *conforms* to the Out element of the operation in Listing 1, of type ProdInfo. This means that all the values returned by the operation in Listing 2 are just as valid as if the operation in Listing 1 returned them.

This means that, although the services are different, a client generated to invoke the service to which Listing 1 belongs can also invoke the service to which Listing 2 belongs, without changes, as long as the getQuote operation in Listing 2 conforms to that of Listing 1. This is equivalent to relaxing the constraint of using the same schema in both interacting parties (scenario of Figure 2) and becoming entitled to simply using compatible ones, through compliance and conformance (scenario of Figures 5 and 6). This increases the range of compatible services and translates into lower coupling.

If the implementation of the scenario of Figure 7 used the Structural Services architectural style with a service-based slant (SOA-style):

- The Seller would be a resource containing several operation resources, including getQuote.
- The Customer would send a message to a URI such as seller/getQuote, with a content compliant with the request type schema Product, expect a response message conformant to response type schema ProdInfo, both in Listing 1.
- Had Customer sent the same message to the Seller of Listing 2, it would have not noticed the difference (given that compliance and conformance hold), but the actual response would be the one produced by the alternative Seller.

If the implementation of the scenario of Figure 7 used the Structural Services architectural style with a resource-based slant (REST-style):

- Each product resource provided by the Seller would have to implement the operation getQuote, catering for the specifics of each product.
- The Seller would provide an operation called products (returning a list of URIs to the available products), which the Customer would invoke by sending an empty message to an URI such as seller/products.
- The Customer could then choose the URI of product X and then send a message to an URI such as seller/productX/quote, eventually with content specifying the quotation conditions required, which would then return the quotation result. Note that the names of these operations are in line with the REST-style.
- In a more purist REST-style, request messages should all be empty, i. e., only the URIs should indicate the resource to target as the message recipient.

Then the quote resource should not be an operation, but a structured resource with several operations, such as those with URIs seller/productX/quote/conditionA or seller/productX/quote/conditionB. It is a matter of API design.

FUTURE RESEARCH DIRECTIONS

For now, the Structural Services architectural style is just a proposal, as there is currently no implementation. This is a limitation inherent to the development of a new architectural style, not to its intrinsic capabilities. There are several possibilities on how to proceed to a practical implementation, namely:

- To extend WSDL files with another section (which could be designated Structure), in which component resources and links can be exposed, thereby allowing Web Services to have structure;
- To allow REST resources to have their own service description (e.g., an extended WADL file), thereby allowing the coexistence of the uniform and non-uniform interface approaches in REST.

An analysis of existing solutions to expose APIs for applications need to take into account the capabilities of the Structural Services architectural style, so that a feasible and effective proposal can be derived to describe resources and services according to the model described by Figure 9.

Compliance and conformance are basic concepts that are applicable to all domains and levels of abstraction and complexity. Although work exists on its formal treatment in specific areas, such as choreographies (Yang, Ma, Deng, Liao, Yan, & Zhang, 2013), an encompassing and systematic study needs to be conducted to formalize the definition of compliance and conformance.

The coupling problem is also relevant for the interoperability of non-functional aspects, namely in context-aware applications and in those involving the design and management of SLR (Service Level Requirements) with respect to enterprise-class applications and their supply chain interactions. Detailing how to apply compliance and conformance in these cases requires additional research.

CONCLUSION

Integrating applications is a fundamental problem in distributed information systems. Two of the most common integration technologies are Web Services (Zimmermann, Tomlinson, & Peuser, 2012) and RESTful APIs (Pautasso, 2014), but they focus more on the interoperability side of the issue than on coupling. In both cases, previous knowledge of the types of the resources involved in the interaction is required, which leads to more coupling than actually needed because interacting applications must share data schemas. Web Services usually require a link to the schema shared by the client and by the server, whereas RESTful applications usually agree beforehand on a given schema, or media type. If an application changes the schema it uses, the others interacting with it must adapt to these changes in order to maintain the interaction.

Both aspects, interoperability and coupling, need to be dealt with in a balanced way. The fundamental problem of application integration is how to achieve the minimum possible coupling while ensuring the minimum interoperability requirements, in order to keep dependencies between applications that hinder changeability at a minimum level and applications are able to interact in an effective way.

Structural compliance (Czepa, Tran, Zdun, Kim, Weiss, & Ruhsam, 2017) and conformance (Carmona, van Dongen, Solti, & Weidlich, 2018) relax the constraint of having to share message schemas and therefore constitute an improved solution over existing integration technologies. Any two applications can interoperate as long as that share at least the characteristics actually required by interoperability, independently of knowing the rest of the characteristics, thereby minimizing coupling and increasing the number of servers that are compatible with a client, and the number of clients that are compatible with a server.

Compliance and conformance are not universal solutions to find a server adequate for any given client, due to the huge variability in application interfaces, but can cater for client and/or server variants while supporting the substitution principle. This means that an application can be replaced by another (as a server) without breaking the service, or remain in service while a variant serves additional clients for a more balanced load distribution.

REFERENCES

Agostinho, C., Ducq, Y., Zacharewicz, G., Sarraipa, J., Lampathaki, F., Poler, R., & Jardim-Goncalves, R. (2016). Towards a sustainable interoperability in networked enterprise information systems: Trends of knowledge and model-driven technology. *Computers in Industry*, *79*, 64–76. doi:10.1016/j.compind.2015.07.001

Alenezi, M., & Magel, K. (2014). Empirical evaluation of a new coupling metric: Combining structural and semantic coupling. *International Journal of Computers and Applications*, *36*(1). doi:10.2316/Journal.202.2014.1.202-3902

Amundsen, M. (2014). APIs to Affordances: A New Paradigm for Services on the Web. In C. Pautasso, E. Wilde, & R. Alarcon (Eds.), *REST: Advanced Research Topics and Practical Applications* (pp. 91–106). New York, NY: Springer. doi:10.1007/978-1-4614-9299-3_6

Anam, S., Kim, Y., Kang, B., & Liu, Q. (2016). Adapting a knowledge-based schema matching system for ontology mapping. In *Proceedings of the Australasian Computer Science Week Multiconference* (p. 27). New York, NY: ACM Press. 10.1145/2843043.2843048

Babu, D., & Darsi, M. (2013). A Survey on Service Oriented Architecture and Metrics to Measure Coupling. *International Journal on Computer Science and Engineering*, 5(8), 726–733.

Baghdadi, Y. (2014). Modelling business process with services: Towards agile enterprises. *International Journal of Business Information Systems*, 15(4), 410–433. doi:10.1504/IJBIS.2014.060377

Bassett, L. (2015). *Introduction to JavaScript Object Notation: A to-the-point Guide to JSON*. Sebastopol, CA: O'Reilly Media, Inc.

Bidve, V. S., & Sarasu, P. (2016). Tool for measuring coupling in object-oriented java software. *IACSIT International Journal of Engineering and Technology*, 8(2), 812–820.

Bora, A., & Bezboruah, T. (2015). A Comparative Investigation on Implementation of RESTful versus SOAP based Web Services. *International Journal of Database Theory and Application*, 8(3), 297–312. doi:10.14257/ijdta.2015.8.3.26

Brandt, C., & Hermann, F. (2013). Conformance analysis of organizational models: A new enterprise modeling framework using algebraic graph transformation. *International Journal of Information System Modeling and Design*, 4(1), 42–78. doi:10.4018/jismd.2013010103

Capel, M., & Mendoza, L. (2014). Choreography Modeling Compliance for Timed Business Models. In *Proceedings of the Workshop on Enterprise and Organizational Modeling and Simulation* (pp. 202–218). Berlin, Germany: Springer. 10.1007/978-3-662-44860-1_12

Carmona, J., van Dongen, B., Solti, A., & Weidlich, M. (Eds.). (2018). *Conformance Checking: Relating Processes and Models*. Cham, Switzerland: Springer. doi:10.1007/978-3-319-99414-7

Chamoux, J. (Ed.). (2018). *The Digital Era 1: Big Data Stakes*. Hoboken, NJ: John Wiley & Sons. doi:10.1002/9781119102687

Chinosi, M., & Trombetta, A. (2012). BPMN: An introduction to the standard. *Computer Standards & Interfaces*, *34*(1), 124–134. doi:10.1016/j.csi.2011.06.002

Christudas, B. (2019). Introducing Microservices. In *Practical Microservices Architectural Patterns*. Berkeley, CA: Apress. doi:10.1007/978-1-4842-4501-9_14

Czepa, C., Tran, H., Zdun, U., Kim, T., Weiss, E., & Ruhsam, C. (2017). On the understandability of semantic constraints for behavioral software architecture compliance: A controlled experiment. In *Proceedings of the International Conference on Software Architecture* (pp. 155-164). Piscataway, NJ: IEEE Computer Society Press. 10.1109/ICSA.2017.10

Dahiya, N., & Parmar, N. (2014). SOA AND REST Synergistic Approach. *International Journal of Computer Science and Information Technologies*, *5*(6), 7045–7049.

Delgado, J. (2019a). Improving Application Integration by Combining Services and Resources. In A. Cruz & M. Cruz (Eds.), *New Perspectives on Information Systems Modeling and Design* (pp. 197–226). Hershey, PA: IGI Global. doi:10.4018/978-1-5225-7271-8.ch009

Delgado, J. (2019b). Enterprise Integration With the Structural Services Architectural Style. In L. Ferreira, N. Lopes, J. Silva, G. Putnik, M. Cruz-Cunha, & P. Ávila (Eds.), *Technological Developments in Industry 4.0 for Business Applications* (pp. 352–392). Hershey, PA: IGI Global. doi:10.4018/978-1-5225-4936-9.ch015

Dornberger, R. (Ed.). (2018). *Business Information Systems and Technology 4.0: New Trends in the Age of Digital Change* (Vol. 141). Cham, Switzerland: Springer. doi:10.1007/978-3-319-74322-6

Elshwimy, F., Algergawy, A., Sarhan, A., & Sallam, E. (2014). Aggregation of similarity measures in schema matching based on generalized mean. *Proceedings of the IEEE International Conference on Data Engineering Workshops* (pp. 74-79). Piscataway, NJ: IEEE Computer Society Press. 10.1109/ICDEW.2014.6818306

Erl, T., Carlyle, B., Pautasso, C., & Balasubramanian, R. (2012). *SOA with REST: Principles, Patterns & Constraints for Building Enterprise Solutions with REST*. Upper Saddle River, NJ: Prentice Hall Press.

Erl, T., Merson, P., & Stoffers, R. (2017). *Service-oriented Architecture: Analysis and Design for Services and Microservices*. Upper Saddle River, NJ: Prentice Hall PTR.

Fawcett, J., Ayers, D., & Quin, L. (2012). *Beginning XML.* Indianapolis, IN: John Wiley & Sons.

Fielding, R., Taylor, R., Erenkrantz, J., Gorlick, M., Whitehead, J., Khare, R., & Oreizy, P. (2017). Reflections on the REST architectural style and principled design of the modern web architecture. In *Proceedings of the 2017 11th Joint Meeting on Foundations of Software Engineering* (pp. 4-14). New York, NY: ACM Press. 10.1145/3106237.3121282

Geetika, R., & Singh, P. (2014). Dynamic coupling metrics for object oriented software systems: A survey. *Software Engineering Notes, 39*(2), 1–8. doi:10.1145/2579281.2579296

Graydon, P., Habli, I., Hawkins, R., Kelly, T., & Knight, J. (2012). Arguing Conformance. *IEEE Software, 29*(3), 50–57. doi:10.1109/MS.2012.26

Hendricksen, D. (2014). *12 More Essential Skills for Software Architects.* Upper Saddle River, NJ: Addison-Wesley Professional.

Henning, M. (2008). The rise and fall of CORBA. *Communications of the ACM, 51*(8), 52–57. doi:10.1145/1378704.1378718

ISO. (2010). *Systems and software engineering – Vocabulary. ISO/IEC/IEEE 24765:2010(E) International Standard* (p. 186). Geneva, Switzerland: International Organization for Standardization.

Kanade, S. (2019). Extending the Enterprise Using Enterprise Application Integration (EAI) Technologies for the Cloud. *International Journal of Applied Evolutionary Computation, 10*(2), 37–42. doi:10.4018/IJAEC.2019040105

Kukreja, R., & Garg, N. (2014). Remote Procedure Call: Limitations and Drawbacks. *International Journal of Research, 1*(10), 914–917.

Liao, Y., Deschamps, F., Loures, E., & Ramos, L. (2017). Past, present and future of Industry 4.0 - a systematic literature review and research agenda proposal. *International Journal of Production Research, 55*(12), 3609–3629. doi:10.1080/00207543.2017.1308576

Page, T., & Thorsteinsson, G. (2018). Emerging Technologies in Interaction with Mobile Computing Devices-A Technology Forecast. *Journal on Mobile Applications and Technologies, 5*(1), 1.

Panetto, H., & Whitman, L. (2016). Knowledge engineering for enterprise integration, interoperability and networking: Theory and applications. *Data & Knowledge Engineering, 105*, 1–4. doi:10.1016/j.datak.2016.05.001

Paul, P., & Saraswathi, R. (2017). The Internet of Things – A comprehensive survey. In *Proceedings of the International Conference on Computation of Power, Energy Information and Communication* (pp. 421-426). Piscataway, NJ: IEEE Computer Society Press. 10.1109/ICCPEIC.2017.8290405

Pautasso, C. (2014). RESTful web services: principles, patterns, emerging technologies. In A. Bouguettaya, Q. Sheng, & F. Daniel (Eds.), *Web Services Foundations* (pp. 31–51). New York, NY: Springer. doi:10.1007/978-1-4614-7518-7_2

Pautasso, C., Zimmermann, O., & Leymann, F. (2008). Restful web services vs. "big"' web services: making the right architectural decision. In *International conference on World Wide Web* (pp. 805-814). ACM Press. 10.1145/1367497.1367606

Preidel, C., & Borrmann, A. (2016). Towards code compliance checking on the basis of a visual programming language. *Journal of Information Technology in Construction*, *21*(25), 402–421.

Sharma, A., Kumar, M., & Agarwal, S. (2015). A Complete Survey on Software Architectural Styles and Patterns. *Procedia Computer Science*, *70*, 16–28. doi:10.1016/j.procs.2015.10.019

Sharma, R., & Panigrahi, P. (2015). Developing a roadmap for planning and implementation of interoperability capability in e-government. *Transforming Government: People, Process and Policy*, *9*(4), 426–447.

Sikos, L. (2017). The Semantic Gap. In *Description Logics in Multimedia Reasoning* (pp. 51–66). Cham, Switzerland: Springer. doi:10.1007/978-3-319-54066-5_3

Soni, A., & Ranga, V. (2019). API Features Individualizing of Web Services: REST and SOAP. *International Journal of Innovative Technology and Exploring Engineering*, *8*(9S), 664–671.

Sungkur, R., & Daiboo, S. (2016). Combining the Best Features of SOAP and REST for the Implementation of Web Services. *International Journal of Digital Information and Wireless Communications*, *6*(1), 21–33. doi:10.17781/P001923

Thakar, U., Tiwari, A., & Varma, S. (2016). On Composition of SOAP Based and RESTful Services. In *Proceedings of the 6th International Conference on Advanced Computing* (pp. 500-505). Piscataway, NJ: IEEE Computer Society Press. 10.1109/IACC.2016.99

Varghese, B., & Buyya, R. (2018). Next generation cloud computing: New trends and research directions. *Future Generation Computer Systems*, *79*, 849–861. doi:10.1016/j.future.2017.09.020

Verborgh, R., Harth, A., Maleshkova, M., Stadtmüller, S., Steiner, T., Taheriyan, M., & Van de Walle, R. (2014). Survey of semantic description of REST APIs. In C. Pautasso, E. Wilde, & R. Alarcon (Eds.), *REST: Advanced Research Topics and Practical Applications* (pp. 69–89). New York, NY: Springer. doi:10.1007/978-1-4614-9299-3_5

Xu, L., Xu, E., & Li, L. (2018). Industry 4.0: State of the art and future trends. *International Journal of Production Research*, *56*(8), 2941–2962. doi:10.1080/00 207543.2018.1444806

Yang, H., Ma, K., Deng, C., Liao, H., Yan, J., & Zhang, J. (2013). Towards conformance testing of choreography based on scenario. In *Proceedings of the International Symposium on Theoretical Aspects of Software Engineering* (pp. 59-62). Piscataway, NJ: IEEE Computer Society Press. 10.1109/TASE.2013.23

Yuan, E. (2019). Architecture interoperability and repeatability with microservices: an industry perspective. In *Proceedings of the 2nd International Workshop on Establishing a Community-Wide Infrastructure for Architecture-Based Software Engineering* (pp. 26-33). Piscataway, NJ: IEEE Computer Society Press. 10.1109/ECASE.2019.00013

Zanero, S. (2017). Cyber-physical systems. *IEEE Computer*, *50*(4), 14–16. doi:10.1109/MC.2017.105

Zimmermann, O., Tomlinson, M., & Peuser, S. (2012). *Perspectives on Web Services: Applying SOAP, WSDL and UDDI to Real-World Projects*. New York, NY: Springer Science & Business Media.

ADDITIONAL READING

He, W., & Da Xu, L. (2014). Integration of distributed enterprise applications: A survey. *IEEE Transactions on Industrial Informatics*, *10*(1), 35–42. doi:10.1109/TII.2012.2189221

Imache, R., Izza, S., & Ahmed-Nacer, M. (2012). An enterprise information system agility assessment model. *Computer Science and Information Systems*, *9*(1), 107–133. doi:10.2298/CSIS101110041I

Kostoska, M., Gusev, M., & Ristov, S. (2016). An overview of cloud interoperability. In *Federated Conference on Computer Science and Information Systems* (pp. 873-876). Piscataway, NJ: IEEE Computer Society Press. 10.15439/2016F463

Liska, R. (2018). Management Challenges in the Digital Era. In R. Brunet-Thornton & F. Martinez (Eds.), *Analyzing the Impacts of Industry 4.0 in Modern Business Environments* (pp. 82–99). Hershey, PA: IGI Global. doi:10.4018/978-1-5225-3468-6.ch005

McLay, A. (2014). Re-reengineering the dream: Agility as competitive adaptability. *International Journal of Agile Systems and Management*, 7(2), 101–115. doi:10.1504/IJASM.2014.061430

Mezgár, I., & Rauschecker, U. (2014). The challenge of networked enterprises for cloud computing interoperability. *Computers in Industry*, 65(4), 657–674. doi:10.1016/j.compind.2014.01.017

Moreira, F., Ferreira, M., & Seruca, I. (2018). Enterprise 4.0–the emerging digital transformed enterprise? *Procedia Computer Science*, 138, 525–532. doi:10.1016/j.procs.2018.10.072

Popplewell, K. (2014). Enterprise interoperability science base structure. In K. Mertins, F. Bénaben, R. Poler, & J. Bourrières (Eds.), *Enterprise Interoperability VI: Interoperability for Agility, Resilience and Plasticity of Collaborations* (pp. 417–427). Cham, Switzerland: Springer International Publishing. doi:10.1007/978-3-319-04948-9_35

Ritter, D., May, N., & Rinderle-Ma, S. (2017). Patterns for emerging application integration scenarios: A survey. *Information Systems*, 67, 36–57. doi:10.1016/j.is.2017.03.003

KEY TERMS AND DEFINITIONS

Client: A role performed by a resource C in an interaction with another S, which involves making a request to S and typically waiting for a response.

Compliance: Asymmetric property between a client C and a server S (C is compliant with S) that indicates that C satisfies all the requirements of S in terms of accepting requests.

Conformance: Asymmetric property between two servers, S_1 and S_2 (S_1 conforms to S_2) that indicates that S_1 fulfills all the expectations of all the clients of S_2 in terms of the effects caused by its requests, which means that S_2 can replace S_1.

Coupling: A measurement of how much an application is dependent on the interface of another application.

Interoperability: Asymmetric property between a client C and a server S that holds if C is compliant with the set of requests allowed by S and S is conformant with the set of responses expected by C.

Resource: The computer-based implementation of a service.

Server: A role performed by a resource S in an interaction with another C, which involves waiting for a request from C, honoring it and typically sending a response back to C.

Service: The set of operations supported by an application that together define its interface (the set of reactions to messages that the application is able to receive and process) and behavior.

Chapter 3
Synthesis of MOF, MDA, PIM, MVC, and BCE Notations and Patterns

Jaroslaw Zelinski
iD https://orcid.org/0000-0002-8032-4720
Independent Researcher, Poland

ABSTRACT

Publications, including academic handbooks, contain numerous inconsistencies in the descriptions of applications of architectural methods and patterns hidden under the abbreviations such as MOF, MDA, PIM, MVC, BCE. An efficient analysis and the following software design, particularly when we are speaking of projects realized in large teams, requires standardization of the production process and the applied patterns and frameworks. This study attempted to sort out the system of notations describing this process and used to describe architectural patterns. Analysis of key notations—MOF and MDA, patterns MVC and BCE—was carried out, and a consistent system combining them into a whole was created.

INTRODUCTION

The study objective was to verify the current state of design methods and development of a concise system of notations and design patterns in the field of software logic design as its abstract model. Numerous publications on the analysis and design in the field of software engineering use the names of MVC (Model View Controller) and BCE (Boundary Control Entity) design patterns and the PIM (Platform Independent Model) model (OMG MDA, 2016; OMG MOF, 2016). Considering the frequent

DOI: 10.4018/978-1-7998-2142-7.ch003

often not too minor discrepancies in the interpretation of these methods and patterns, the author made an attempt to order their mutual interactions. This thesis is based on foundations of mentioned notations only. Main audience of my paper are people using formalism described in OMG notations.

BACKGROUND

In this study, Object Management Group notation systems have been used. MOF (Meta Object Facility) specification describes three abstraction levels: M1, M2, M3 and level M0 that is real items (OMG MOF, 2016). M0 is a real system, M1 level is abstraction of the items of this system (its model). Level M2 comprises of relationships between classes of these objects (names of their sets) that is system metamodel. M3 level is a meta-metamodel describing the modeling method with the use of named elements with specified semantics and syntactic.

The analysis and design process is based on the MDA (Model Driven Architecture) specifications. This process has three phases understood as creation of subsequent models: CIM (Computation Independent Model), PIM (Platform Independent Model), PSM (Platform Specific Model) and code creation phase. The CIM model is documented with the use of BPMN (Business Process Model and Notation) (OMG BPMN, 2013) and SBVR notation (Semantic of Business Vocabulary and Rules) (OMG SBVR, 2017). These are, respectively: business process models and notation models and business rules. PIM and PSM models are documented with the use of UML notation (Unified Modeling Language) (OMG UML, 2017).

Between CIM and PIM models, determination of the list of application services (system reactions) occurs, whose realization mechanism is described by PIM model. The standard pattern used for modeling application architecture is MVC pattern. Component Model of this pattern is modeled with the use of the BCE architectural pattern.

Semiotics vs. UML

Semiotics, as a science dealing with symbols and their meanings, provides us with the tool enabling determination of relationships between an object (thing), its name (expression) and definition of notation represented by the name (or sign, meaning). These relationships are referred to as the semiotic triangle. Figure 1 represents this triangle on the left (OMG SBVR, 2017).

The UML notation (OMG UML, 2017) operates instance classifier and class notations. To the right, Figure 1 demonstrates an equivalent to semiotic triangle expressed with those terms.

The UML notation further operates the general structure notation, which is the content of each correct UML diagram. Structures may express a conceptual model (Namespace) or model (also metamodel) of system architecture (e.g. software) in the form of a chart (Architecture).

Conceptual models are structures based on taxonomies, visualizing conceptual relationships (relationships between names) between them. The notation of class represents name (expression) of a set of designations. The notation of classifier refers to definition (meaning) of the notation. In the UML, definition of a class of objects is the set of their common traits that is attributes and operations. The notation of object refers to designations (thing). In the UML notation, we add the classifier name defining the object (class to which it belongs) to the name of the object after the colon.

In the UML conceptual models, generalization relationships (taxonomies) and associations (semantic relationships between them) are used, whereas architecture models use composition relationships (whole-part relationship), use relationships (dependency relationship) and realization relationships (specification and implementation relationship). Architecture models express the structure and mechanism of action of modeled systems.

MOF Specification Abstraction Levels

MOF specification (Figure 2) describes four basic levels of abstraction and model creation. Level M0 is the so called real world that is the subject of modeling. Level M1 is model being abstraction of this world, typically from a specified perspective. Model, as abstraction, is not a simplification. Abstraction is an image of specified reality in the specified context that is with omission of insignificant details for the context. Level M1 comprises of abstractions of notation designations, and with those notations we name entities of the real world.

Figure 1. Semiotics vs. UML

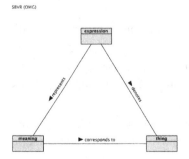
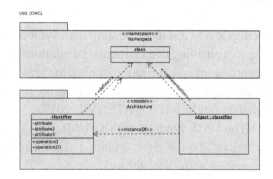

Level M2 operates classes (defined and named sets) of objects from the abstract layer of M1. This is a metamodel of M1 layer (metamodel: model comprising of classes of objects from M1 layer). Level M3 is a layer defining the M2 layer elements as one class of model elements (it is a meta-metamodel). This is the description of notation system.

Types of objects and classifier types can be created at levels M1 and M2. These layers are so called intermediate layers, and class and object types are labeled in UML with stereotypes. This tool-stereotyping-is used to create the so called profiles that is domain groups of object and class types (diagram types are thus formed, e.g. component diagram or communication diagram).

UML notation is M1 and M2 levels according to MOF.

MDA Specification and PIM Model

One of the basic traits of MDA is the separation of boundary contexts of the created models as given in Figure 3. Specification states MDA separates business and application logic from basic platform technology. MDA operates three context model types: CIM (Computation Independent Model), PIM (Platform Independent Model) and PSM (Platform Specific Model).

Figure 2. MOF Specification Abstraction Levels

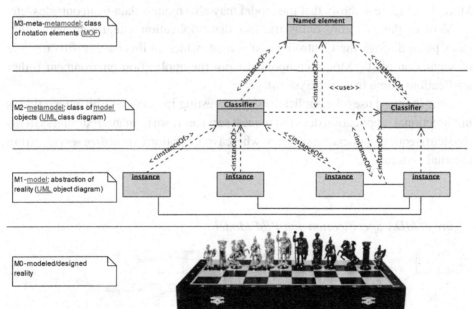

CIM is constructed in the context of actions of real world and its business rules (see MOF level M0). This model gathers descriptions of information structures (documents) and notation system used to classify information and actions (namespace). Based on CIM and the scope agreement (cases of use as requirement) a PIM is created. It is built in order to create a description of the mechanism of action of a software. This model disregards implementation. The Use Case Model, as a supplementary model (OMG UML, 2017), aims at determining the role of software (application services) in CIM business model.

PSM is description of software implementation. Relative to PIM model, it contains additional elements being a consequence of the so called non-functional requirements (usability, quality, security, etc.).

MVC Architectural Model

MVC architectural pattern (Fowler, 1997) assumes division of application architecture into three key components: Model realizes the whole of domain logic of the application that is management of information structures and implementation of their maintaining and processing. Controller realizes all technical aspects of application. View is responsible for handling the dialog between the application and the actor, which in this case is the user. Communication between MVC components has a potential two-way action: View relays requests to the Model component, but it can demonstrate its status to the user independently of these requests. View may request from the Controller (e.g. access to the services of external system application). Moreover, Figure 4 shows that the model may also request data from outsides, etc.

Most of the literature omits the fact that application integration with other takes place through the Controller component, which in this case fulfills the role of separation of the Model component from the application environment (other applications come from the System).

User (human) uses the application by requesting its services, this interaction is unidirectional (application does not request services from human). External systems (System) request application services, whereas application may utilize services from external systems.

Figure 3. MDA Specification and PIM Model

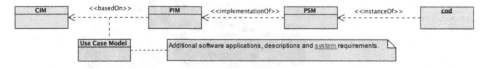

Figure 4. MVC Architectural Pattern

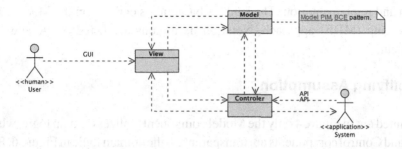

BCE Architectural Pattern

The BCE (Boundary Control Entity) as can be seen in Figure 5 is an architectural pattern known since 1990s. It assumes division of the code realizing application service (system usage case) into three separated components: boundary which is responsible for handling the dialog with the user, control responsible for realization of the business logic and entity responsible for information consolidation). This pattern is currently used also to design the so called micro services (singular application services).

Usage of this pattern facilitates analysis and design, as it forces separation and hermetization of these three responsibilities. It complies with the good practice of object architecture design, the OCP (Open Close Principia) stating that a good architecture is open for extensions and closed for changes.

This pattern, at the analysis and design stages, is adapted for design of Pattern model component MVC as described in the following section. In line with the object paradigm, all those components have operations (interfaces).

SOLUTIONS AND RECOMMENDATIONS

A concise notation system has been described based on definitions of MOF, MDA (PIM) specifications and on MVC and BCE architectural pattern models. A result has been obtained that enables unambiguous determination of the responsibility

Figure 5. BCE Architectural Pattern

of components of these patterns as well as to determine the boundaries between design and implementation. The study is based in its entirety on the Model-Driven Engineering (MDE) approach. Notation definitions are listed at the end of the document.

Simplifying Assumption

As pointed out in Figure 4 only the Model component realizes domain logic, whereas View and Control components are transparent for the domain logic in Figure 6. Figure 3 demonstrates that PIM contains the whole and only description of domain logic realization. Therefore, a safe simplifying inference can be assumed as visualized on the diagram Application abstraction at the stage of PIM creation for the purposes of analysis and design of use case (application services) realization may consist only of the Model component describing the mechanism of realization of application services (system domain model).

Integrated Model of Application Design Process Structure

Visualization of the described models in one flow chart requires the use of <<trace>> relationships to demonstrate tracing of elements of subsequent models as given in Figure 7.

CIM is a business model describing the analyzed domain. It is a model of business processes (BPMN notation) realized within modeled area of human activity.

The processes (activities creating specified value or products referred to as business) and business rules describe the mechanism of action of e.g. an organization. If, an organization, as a thus described system of people cooperating toward a determined target, is to contain an element being a software (application), then the requirements for this application are modeled as use cases, at this stage the Application is the so called black box. Such model is expressed as cases of use in UML notation. Here, a common business dictionary represented as Namespace is a significant element. All classes, attributes, operations etc. are names originating from this notation space (and defined within it).

Figure 6. Simplifying Assumption

The subsequent stage of work on the design of software is creation of model of the so called white box that is the mechanism of action of this application service, describing the manner in which reaction (effect) is formed in response to stimuli. This mechanism is modeled as PIM (architecture expressed as a diagram of classes of components in UML notation). This is solely a model of mechanism realizing the so called domain logic. At this stage we disregard the elements who do not realize domain logic. PIM architecture is here built upon the BCM architectural pattern described above. This model constitutes the Model component of the MVC pattern.

The PSM is an implementation plan with the use of specific technology, visualizing the remaining MVC pattern elements that is the View component realizing details of communication with user and the Controller component of the pattern.

Object models (object paradigm) do not refer directly to data as such, but to their named structures (they correspond to elements Data in the CIM model above). In other words, the entity object stores specific information, but we do not refer it to object attributes. The value of one object attribute may be e.g. even a very rich XML structure containing many so called data fields (representing Data on the business processes model BPMN). From the viewpoint of object operation this is

Figure 7. Integrated Model of Application Design Process Structure

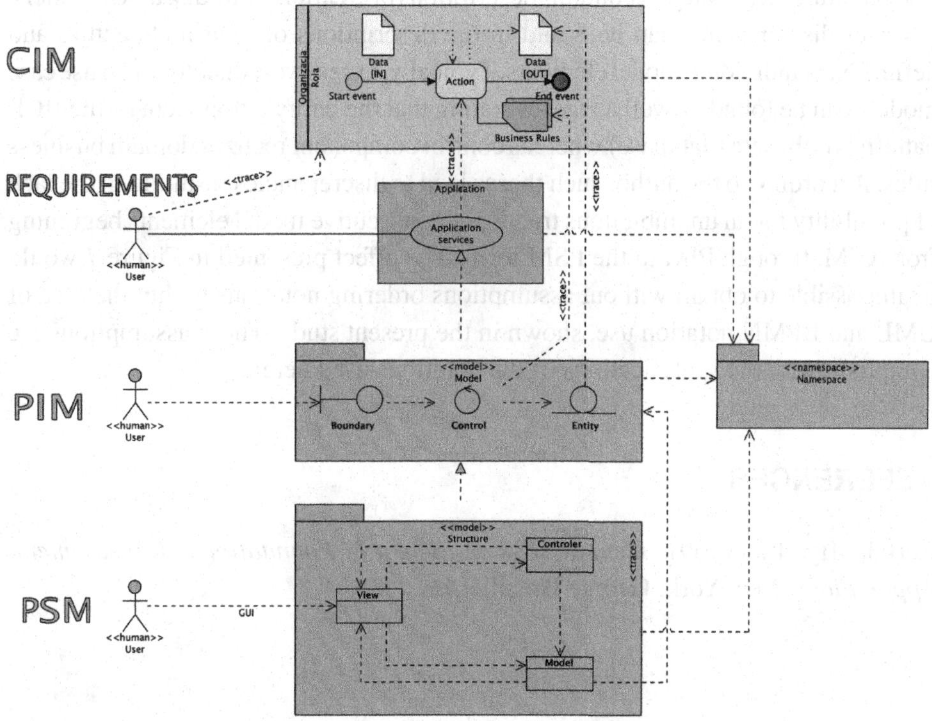

also insignificant, as a request as a calling for class operation may concern the entire data set and not one 'field' (it is a common bad practice to implement database fields as object attributes and creation of access interface to them in the form of set/get operation set for each such attribute).

The system of notations and architecture components described herein, constitutes, as a whole, a concise structure of models enabling the tracing of subsequent model elements from their more general precursors.

FUTURE RESEARCH DIRECTION

The author develops the described object model integration system in a direction enabling creation of a method of creation of domain metamodels as UML profiles in the M2 layer. The objective is to develop methodology for software design in an iterative-incremental approach based on metamodeling, enabling testing of the application feasibility before its implementation.

CONCLUSION

The literature on the subject contains descriptions of creation of the discussed models, however discrepancies can be found in the descriptions of their architecture and definition of individual model elements. Typically, excessively disintegrated use case models can be found as well as theses stating that the entity component of the BCE pattern is only data (database) whereas control component realizes domain business rules. According to the author such theses lead to discrepancies resulting in the lack of possibility for an unambiguous tracing of consecutive model elements beginning from CIM, through PIM to the PSM form. The effect presented in Figure 7 would be impossible to obtain without assumptions ordering notations within the area of UML and BPMN notation use, shown in the present study. These assumptions are compliant with the specifications of the notations used herein.

REFERENCES

Bertalanffy, L. (1969). *General System Theory: Foundations, Development, Applications*. New York: George Braziller Inc.

Breu, R., Grosu, R., Huber, F., Rumpe, B., & Schwerin, W. (1998). Systems, Views and Models of UML. In M. Schader & A. Korthaus (Eds.), *The Unified Modeling Language, Technical Aspects and Applications*. Heidelberg, Germany: Physica Verlag. doi:10.1007/978-3-642-48673-9_7

Cempel, C. (2008). Teoria i Inżynieria Systemówç. Radom: Wydawnictwo Instytutu Technologii Eksploatacji - PIB.

Dennis, A., Wixom, B. H., & Tegarden, D. (2005). *Systems Analysis and Design with UML Version 2.0 An Object Oriented Version*. John Wiley and Sons, Inc.

Díaz, V. G., Lovelle, J. M. C., García-Bustelo, B. C. P., & Martinez, O. S. (2014). *Advances and Applications in Model-Driven Engineering*. Academic Press.

Fowler, M. (1997). *Analysis Patterns. Reusable Object Models, Martin Fowler*. Addison-Wesley.

Karagiannis, D., Mayr, H. C., & Mylopoulos, J. (Eds.). (2016). *Domain-Specific Conceptual Modeling Concepts, Methods and Tools*. Springer. doi:10.1007/978-3-319-39417-6

Minati, G., Pessa, E., & Licata, I. (Eds.). (2018). *General System Theory: Perspectives in Philosophy and Approaches in Complex Systems*. MDPI.

OMG BPMN. (2013). *Business Process Model and Notation (BPMN) Version 2.0.2*. Object Management Group. Retrieved from http://www.omg.org/spec/BPMN

OMG MDA. (2019). *Object Management Group spec*. Model Driven Architecture. Retrieved from https://www.omg.org/mda/

OMG MOF. (2016). *Object Management Group Meta Object Facility (MOF) Core Specification Version 2.5.1*. Retrieved from https://www.omg.org/spec/MOF

OMG SBVR. (2017). *Object Management Group Semantics of Business Vocabulary and Business Rules Version 1.4*. Retrieved from https://www.omg.org/spec/SBVR/

OMG SysML. (2017). *Object Management Group Systems Modeling Language Version 1.5*. Retrieved from https://sysml.org/.res/docs/specs/OMGSysML-v1.5-17-05-01.pdf

OMG UML. (2017). *Object Management Group Unified Modeling Language Version 2.5.1*. Retrieved from https://www.omg.org/spec/UML/

Rosenberg, D., Collins-Cope, M., & Stephens, M. (2005). *Agile Development with ICONIX Process, People, Process, and Pragmatism*. APRESS.

Searle, J. R. (1990). Is the Brain a Digital Computer? *Proceedings and Addresses of the American Philosophical Association, 64*(3), 21–37. doi:10.2307/3130074

Zullighoven, H. (2005). *Object-Oriented Construction Handbook: Developing Application-Oriented Software with the Tools & Materials Approach.* Elsevier Inc.

KEY TERMS AND DEFINITIONS

Abstraction: Description from a certain perspective or in a certain context, consisting in omitting details that are irrelevant in this context, allowing an approach from a particular point of view and at a higher degree of generality.

Boundary, Control, Entity: Assumes modeling of structure of any application with the use of three construction blocks: Boundary (system boundary, interface), Control (the only place of system logic realization), Entity (place of information, data storage, memory); UML includes stereotypes of classes or objects, all should possess operations, abstract models may not have attributes; the pattern can be applied also for object organization modeling.

Business Model: A description of a company's activity that ensures its profit. This comes down to defining the role of the organization in the market value chain in which it operates and describing the mechanism of creating this value within the organization. Such models are expressed in the form of business models and structures as well as their dynamics. Typical elements of a business model: superior market value chain, internal value chain model, market five forces model, as well as SWOT context analysis.

Business Process Model and Notation: A notation system and graphic notation enabling modeling and documentation of business processes and procedures in a graphic form; it further enables modeling and documenting cooperation between organizations.

Component: A constituent forming a constructively closed element of a system, capable of being a separate subject of supply or realization, characterized by specified behavior (interface), own life cycle, can be replaced with another of the same external traits, without impact on the remaining system elements and system as a whole.

Computation Independent Model: Model (perspective) which is independent of the calculation system, understood as a model disregarding technology.

Fact: What occurred or occurs in reality, in SBVR notation an element combining notions in one context.

Information: Message about something or communication of something; data processed by computer.

Metamodel: Model generalization, in other words if a model is an abstraction of a specific reality, then metamodel is generalization of specific class (set) of such models (abstractions). Any metamodel represents all systems compliant with this metamodel. Moreover, metamodel as a class of models defines semantics and syntactic of the specified model class.

Model: Abstract representation of a product or system, enabling verification of its traits before commencement of its production, constitutes a set of assumptions, notions and relationships between them enabling description (modeling) a determined aspect of reality in a given context; model is not simplification, it is an abstraction; it can be expressed with mathematic formulas or a flow chart (nominal, abstract model) or as a simplified real construction (real model).

Model-Driven Architecture: An architecture based on open standards of Object Management Group, enabling separation in the analysis and design of business logic, application logic and its implementation.

Model-Driven Engineering: An analysis and design methodology orientated at the creation of models of the given domain, including notation models and others, built from various distinct perspectives in order to describe a problem and its specifics; it is based on the use of abstraction and models of mechanisms governing the given domain instead of individual calculations and algorithms.

Platform-Specific Model: Model describing application implementation architecture in the context of technology used for implementation.

Semantics of Business Vocabulary and Rules: Defining the method of creation of business rules and creation of business terms dictionary, the specification further includes a description of notation for the creation of the so called fact diagrams, which are graphic representation of business term dictionary and a method of modeling and control of cohesion of domain notation system (namespace).

System: Any notion or physical entity, comprising of mutually interlinked and interacting parts; a set of elements and relationships between them capable of realizing specified objectives; set of elements with specified structure and enabling logically ordered whole, arranged set of statements, views.

Use Case: Represents a behavior or set of system behaviors specified, initiated by the actor (user), whose objective is the predetermined result useful for the actor, it may include possible variants of its basic behavior, including special behavior such as error handling, means a specific (aiming at obtaining a concrete effect) System use; key notions associated with Use Cases are Actor and System creating a certain theory, log, a comprehensive and ordered set of tasks connected with the relations of logical result.

Chapter 4

Software Architecture Patterns in Big Data:
Transition From Monolithic Architecture to Microservices

Serkan Ayvaz
Bahçeşehir University, Turkey

Yucel Batu Salman
Bahçeşehir University, Turkey

ABSTRACT

Traditional monolithic systems are composed of software components that are tightly coupled and composed into one unit. Monolithic systems have scalability issues as all components of the entire system need to be compiled and deployed even for simple modifications. In this chapter, the evolution of the software systems used in big data from monolithic systems to service-oriented architectures was explored. More specifically, the challenges and strengths of implementing service-oriented architectures of microservices and serverless computing were investigated in detail. Moreover, the advantages of migrating to service-oriented architectures and the patterns of migration were discussed.

INTRODUCTION

With the widespread use of the Internet, and rapid technological advancements in big data, the amount of data in all parts of modern life such as finance, trade, health, and science has been increasing exponentially (Khan et al., 2014). Nowadays, the

DOI: 10.4018/978-1-7998-2142-7.ch004

amount of data created in a single day is estimated to be around 2.5 quintillion bytes (Petrov, 2019). The data created in the last two years alone exceeds 90% of entire data available in the world today. According to the DOMO report ("Data never sleeps," 2018), "By 2020, it's estimated that 1.7MB of data will be created every second for every person on earth."

Technological advancements have transformed how individuals access to information in recent decades. Now, data are being collected from variety of resources. Mobile phones, wearable technologies, and other smart devices have become essential part of daily life (Çiçek, 2015). Data are plentiful and made easily accessible. More than 80 percent of data are gathered from unstructured data from the web such as posts on social media sites, digital images, videos, news feeds, journals, blogs ("The most plentiful," 2016).

As a result, the software systems have been evolving over the decades to adapt the technological changes. Large scale software solutions require more complex system architectures nowadays. Monolithic systems and von Neuman architecture have served their purposes for a long time. Currently, the complex nature of enterprise software solutions demands scalable data abstraction for distributed systems (Gorton & Klein, 2014) and necessitates moving beyond von Neuman architecture.

From early days of Remote Procedure Calls (RPC) (Birrell & Nelson, 1984) in 1980s to Simple Object Access Protocol (SOAP) (Box et al., 2000) and Representational State Transfer (REST)(Fielding, 2000) over HTTP in early 2000s, the distributed technologies have evolved rapidly ("Beyond buzzwords," 2018). These technological advances heavily influenced the development of software systems that communicate over network in a distributed environment and led to wider industry adoption. Moving forward a few years, the progress in Cloud computing, virtualization and containerization technologies has provided infrastructure support for large scale distributed software systems. Concurrently, emergence of big data technologies such as Hadoop (Borthakur, 2007; White, 2012) and Spark (Zaharia, Chowdhury, Franklin, Shenker, & Stoica, 2010) enabled processing massive amount of data over distributed hardware over the cloud. These technologies facilitated breaking large software systems into smaller software components that serve for a single functionality over distributed hardware.

In the traditional monolithic systems, all components of software application are tightly-coupled, self-contained and composed into one unit. A major drawback of monolithic architecture is that all components of entire system must be compiled and deployed even when a simple update occurs in application logic (Fazio et al., 2016). Since entire code base must be regression tested, it hinders the stability of the system. Additionally, the costs of testing and deployment are high (Singleton, 2016). Thus, the code releases usually occur less frequently. The time from development to production is often very long. Monolithic architectures can satisfy the needs of the small to medium-sized systems. However, this pattern is not a well-suited solution for large scale software systems as they require frequent code releases for bug fixes, modifications, new features. Even successful small scale applications tend to grow rapidly over time. In such cases, small scale monolith applications can quickly become overwhelmingly large in size. Thus, management and maintenance can be extremely difficult as monolithic systems get more and more complex (Chen, Li, & Li, 2017). Consequently, the risks of monolithic system deployment may lead to delays in continued development of new features and fixing bugs.

The need for integration of fine-grained services and digitization of new products and services necessitates static enterprise software systems to adopt more dynamic and flexible software architectures (Zimmermann et al., 2016). Using new technologies doesn't automatically solve the scalability and performance issues in big data systems. The software architecture design deeply affects the performance of system development and productivity. The software development community has faced major setbacks when transitioning from monolithic development to a fine-grained service-oriented approach such as microservices and serverless architectures. Some of the extrinsic challenges including culture, organizational structure, and market pressures also play crucial role in adaption of architecture design pattern.

To efficiently develop and maintain such complex software systems, modular software architecture is needed. As the components can be tested separately and thus there are fewer parameters to test in each unit, it is easier to test and debug the issues in modular systems. Thus, software systems with modular architecture are more reliable and can be released more frequently. Serverless and microservice architecture approaches offer a versatile, modular and cost effective way to develop large scale software systems for information generation and big data processing (Herrera-Quintero, Vega-Alfonso, Banse, & Zambrano, 2018).

In this chapter, we explored various aspects of service-oriented software architecture patterns used in big data systems. From a data-driven software system perspective, the challenges and strengths of the patterns were further elaborated.

SERVICE-ORIENTED SOFTWARE ARCHITECTURE PATTERNS IN BIG DATA

Microservice Architecture

Microservice architecture is a modular solution to efficiently developing and maintaining complex software systems. The software systems comprise a collection of fine-grained and independent services (Soldani, Tamburri, & Van Den Heuvel, 2018). Each of the services is designed to serve a specific functionality. The communication between individual services is performed through exposed APIs. Due to its modular structure, its architecture is highly scalable and can support diverse collection of devices and systems including web, mobile and Internet of Things (IoT) devices.

In microservice architecture, the components of the system are services based on business functionalities and loosely coupled as small units as illustrated in Figure 1. Each of the services can be separately tested and deployed. Therefore, the costs of overall testing, deployment and maintenance become much lower since multiple services can be deployed simultaneously by different teams of developers.

Another benefit of microservice architecture is that it can contain different platforms and operating systems as the services communicate through APIs calls or messages. Furthermore, the microservice architecture is very suitable for cloud computing. The microservices can be scaled and deployed to a distributed computing in the cloud environment. The cloud itself can be thought as a very large microservices system that can be accessed through APIs over the internet. The location of the services and underlying platform become transparent to the client in cloud. Moreover, the service hardware and software updates are managed by a third party cloud service.

With cloud systems, the entire datacenter becomes the computer. Thus, the developers rather than worrying about system-level details such as race conditions, lock contention, reliability, fault tolerance, they can focus on the software system itself and build complex software systems efficiently.

Furthermore, another advantage of the microservices architecture is that it enables the collective use of various tools and technologies. IT teams can choose the best combination of tools and platforms for the users of services. Thus, it helps increase agility of the software systems by providing flexibility in the tool selection and facilitating experimentation. Consequently, the flexibility of tool selection may help improve fault tolerance and resilience of the system. The failures on a microservice should not prevent the other microservices from functioning properly unless the microservices have dependencies.

Microservice Architecture for Internet of Things

Microservices architecture can provide an efficient platform for data intensive applications in Internet of Things environments. IoT applications can be built as a collection of microservices in the cloud, in which the microservices are packaged and distributed over physical hardware (Fazio et al., 2016). Since IoT devices are designed to execute a specific functionality, they usually have limited resources (Fazio & Puliafito, 2015). Thus, they don't normally perform storage and data processing tasks. The integration of IoT devices to cloud computing enables implementation of new service architectures, in which IoT devices can manage limited storage and data processing tasks through microservices (Celesti, Mulfari, Fazio, Villari, & Puliafito, 2016). A major benefit of microservices based IoT approach is that some of the microservices can be independently designed to serve edge computing on nodes near IoT sensors. This way, some of the data processing tasks can be handled more efficiently near the data generation nodes before moving data to central repositories (Li, Seco, & Sánchez Rodríguez, 2019). This architecture prevents unnecessary data move. It also helps reduce the dependency between data processing from backend resource management.

As an emerging field, new IoT device protocols and technologies are still being developed. Since there is currently no universal standard protocol of IoT sensors, the IoT architectures often contain heterogeneous sensor technologies and protocols for communication (Viani et al., 2013). By using microservice architecture in IoT environments, the integration of various sensor technologies can be facilitated. The data generation and processing tasks from heterogeneous IoT devices can be bundled up to microservices. As a result, microservices hide the technological diversity of IoT devices. The communication between devices in the architecture can then be handled using standard microservices APIs exposed from IoT device interfaces (Vresk & Čavrak, 2016).

Figure 1. Overview of monolithic architecture and microservice architecture

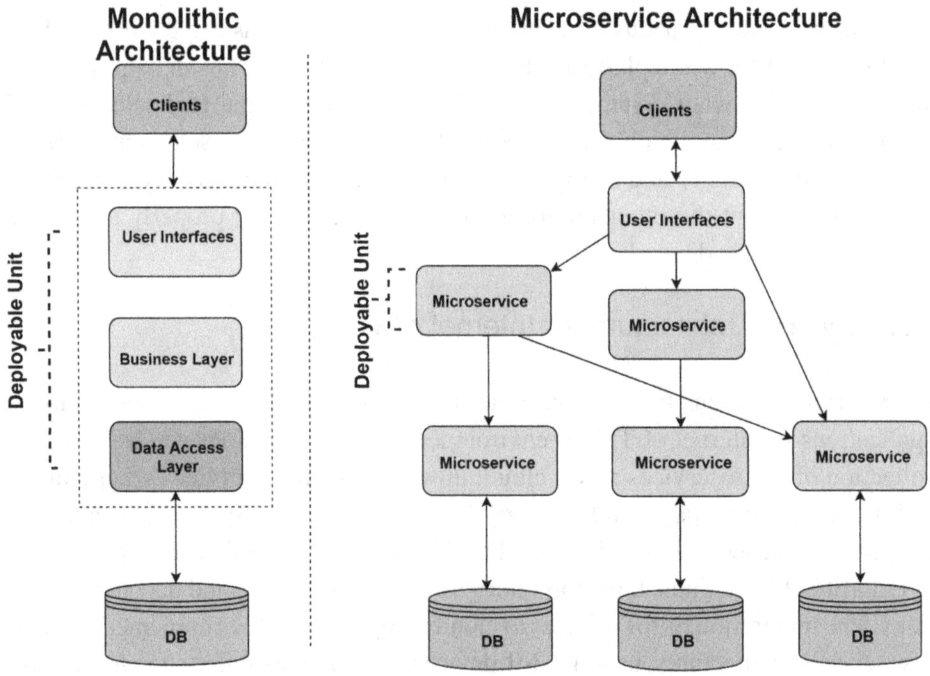

Cyber-Physical Microservices for IoT

With continuing development of big data technologies, cyber-physical microservices architecture, which is an IoT based infrastructure, has attracted a lot of attention from research community recently (Lu & Ju, 2017; Monostori et al., 2016; Kleanthis Thramboulidis, 2015). There have been many studies investigating applications of cyber-physical microservices in particularly manufacturing systems (Ciavotta, Alge, Menato, Rovere, & Pedrazzoli, 2017; Lu & Ju, 2017) and smart city infrastructures (Khanda, Salikhov, Gusmanov, Mazzara, & Mavridis, 2017; Krylovskiy, Jahn, & Patti, 2015) in the context of Industry 4.0. Thanks to its agility, scalability, and modularity, cyber-physical microservices architecture offers crucial benefits to large systems in fulfilling the changing requirements in those domains (Alshuqayran, Ali, & Evans, 2016; Innerbichler, Gonul, Damjanovic-Behrendt, Mandler, & Strohmeier, 2017). Some research studies demonstrated real-world examples of practical applications of microservices and big data in the industry and service sectors (Kleanthis Thramboulidis & Christoulakis, 2016).

While many frameworks using cyber-physical architecture for manufacturing systems utilizes service-oriented architecture on top of web technologies (Lu & Ju, 2017), Model-driven engineering approach (Schmidt, 2006) can be utilized to automate the development, integration and administration of the microservice and IoT based software systems (Lu & Ju, 2017; Kleanthis Thramboulidis, Vachtsevanou, & Solanos, 2018). As one of the applications of model-oriented engineering architecture, cyber-physical microservices architecture is likely to be utilized more commonly in various domains in the future (K Thramboulidis, Bochalis, & Bouloumpasis, 2017).

The Challenges of Microservices Architecture

Although the complexity of each single component in microservice architecture is lower than a monolithic application, the system's overall complexity does not decrease at all (Zimmermann et al., 2016). In microservices architecture, the communication between services are done through API calls and messages rather than simple function calls as in the case of monolithic systems. Breaking a large monolithic application into more micro-granular services moves the majority of software complexity from the inner component to the communication layer. Additional layer of communication components must be incorporated such as service catalogs for discovering available services, routing to suitable service instances and queuing the calls. Microservice architecture comes with a cost of communication overhead. Implementing APIs for service communications requires an extra code. Consequently, microservices demand additional computational resources.

One of the main advantages of using microservices is the fact that it enables technology independency and heterogeneity. Each component can be designed to use the most suitable technology. It also helps improving application resilience by reducing dependencies on outdated technologies and their potential limitations. That being said, having too many heterogeneous technologies in microservices may also cause potential maintenance issues for enterprise systems as it can quickly get out of control (Zimmermann et al., 2016). Furthermore, a strong DevOps team with the corresponding skills is needed to manage frequent deployments and maintain a variety of distributions based on diverse technologies and programming languages in microservices (Bass, Weber, & Zhu, 2015). The standardization of technology infrastructure and promoting the usage of a manageable set of technologies, and programming languages for microservices may help prevent the potential maintenance issues while allowing technological diversity.

Moreover, monitoring the performance of services and detection of errors require paying special attention. The optimum architectural setup saves resources in terms of time and money. Thus, the configurations should be available and systematically maintained.

Serverless Computing

Serverless architecture is considered as an extension of microservices. Serverless computing comprises a collection of components based on functionalities similar to microservices. In serverless architecture, the application code is executed as granular functions in isolated and stateless compute service. Main benefits of serverless architecture include cost effective scalability, rapid code development and releases, less burden on development and system administration.

Serverless computing has become popular paradigm for deployment of software and services on cloud recently. Cloud programming models and adoption of cloud technologies has played crucial role in the progress of serverless computing (Baldini et al., 2017). Amazon's AWS Lambda service, launched in 2015 boasted the popularity of serverless computing (Jonas et al., 2019). A major advantage of using serverless architecture is the ability to collect data from different data sources and manipulate the data for services using cost-effective cloud platforms (Cañon-Lozano, Melo-Castillo, Banse, & Herrera-Quintero, 2012; Herrera-Quintero et al., 2018).

In serverless computing, the computations still take place in servers but the allocation of servers and related administration tasks are handled by the cloud provider. Central to serverless computing are the concepts of the general purpose cloud functions, also known as Function as a Service (FaaS) and the middleware connecting applications to cloud services via APIs, also known as Backend as a service (BaaS).

Thanks to the simplified programming model of serverless computing, the developers simply focuses on writing the code for business logic rather than concerns on low level infrastructure management tasks such as provisioning of servers, scaling, modifying server configurations (Yan, Castro, Cheng, & Ishakian, 2016). More specifically, a developer can write a cloud function in a high-level language and determine the event triggering the function. The rest of the low-level server side tasks including provisioning of instances, fault tolerance, scaling, deployment, monitoring, logging, security patches are managed by the serverless platform automatically. Figure 2 demonstrates an architectural overview of typical serverless cloud platform.

The major differences between serverless and the traditional server oriented architectures are the separation of computation and storage, execution of code without the need for server administration, and estimation of billing based on resource usage rather than resource allocation (Jonas et al., 2019). Serverless platforms offer storage as a separate cloud service. The storage is provisioned and billed separately. The cloud provider supplies all necessary computational resources for the execution of user code. The computation takes place in stateless environment and its scales separately from the storage resources. Consequently, the users are charged based on actual usage of the computation and storage resources rather than resource allocation such as number of VM instances allocated or their sizes. In simple terms, a cloud service is defined serverless computing if it scales automatically without explicit

Figure 2. An overview of serverless cloud architecture
Source: Adapted from (Jonas et al., 2019).

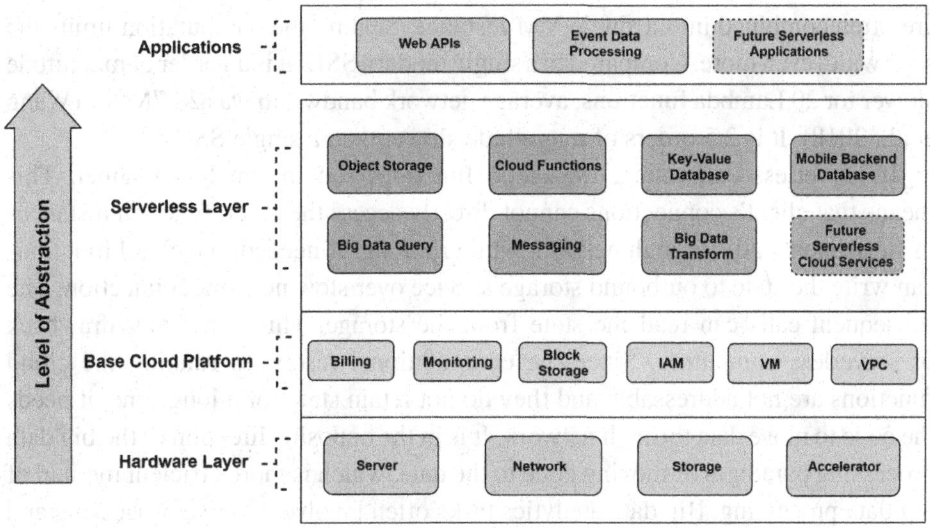

server provisioning and its users are charged based on resource utilization (Wang, Li, Zhang, Ristenpart, & Swift, 2018).

Serverless computing has gained significant popularity in industry and research communities recently. Thanks to its automatic server provisioning and ease of deployment, it helps senior developers to save time in development by concentrating on application code only and junior staff to deploy application code as cloud functions without concerning the server infrastructure. Moreover, another major benefit of serverless computing that makes it an attractive model is cost saving as the cloud functions get triggered only when events occur. The computation resources are allocated very efficiently. The users are billed on resource usage in a very fine-grained manner based on increments of 100 milliseconds at a time typically (Jonas et al., 2019).

The serverless cloud computing platforms provide big data applications an interface to the underlying cloud infrastructure. In data intensive big data ecosystems, a typical serverless layer consists cloud functions for computation and backend services including databases such as DynamoDB or BigTable, object storage i.e. AWS S3, and messaging i.e. Cloud Pub/Sub (Jonas et al., 2019). In the underlying infrastructure layer, these are complemented with integrated base services by the cloud platform such as virtual machines, private networks, authentication and access management, and billing and monitoring services.

The Issues of Serverless Computing

In serverless computing, storage is separated from computation and served as a cloud service over the network. Thus, code execution usually requires moving data between nodes and racks. Moreover, multiple cloud function calls from the same user are often combined into a single VM instance. Scaling the computation limits the bandwidth even more. Compared to a single modern SSD, it is an order of magnitude slower for 20 Lambda functions, average network bandwidth was 28.7Mbps (Wang et al., 2018). It is 2.5 orders of magnitude slower than a single SSD.

In serverless computing, the cloud functions run in stateless manner. This means that client's connections cannot directly access the cloud function instances in subsequent calls through network while running. If needed, the cloud functions can write the state to outbound storage service over slow network connection. The subsequent calls can read the state from the storage. This is a major drawback of serverless computing. Since the computational resources running the cloud functions are not addressable and they do not retain state for a long time, it needs the code to move data through network. It is in the opposite direction of the big data processing paradigm of moving code to the data, which is more efficient method of big data processing. Big data analytics tasks often involve iterative processing and data shuffling. Moving data between computation resources over network can be extremely slow and costly. While serverless computing has been built around the idea of event based distributed computation model with separated storage, event-driven processes often need state for coordination and iterative tasks, which is particularly common in big data use cases (Hellerstein et al., 2018).

Today's serverless computing cloud platforms provide generic all-purpose virtual machine instances with limited hardware resources. For example, the amount of memory that the largest Lambda instance offer is only 3GB RAM (Hellerstein et al., 2018). This hinders the usage of main-memory databases requiring large amount of memory for computation. Furthermore, these VMs are not customizable. The cloud function users have a limited control on hardware specifications. They do not have a way to configure specialized hardware resources for different computation needs. Typically, the memory amount and computation time limit can be determined by cloud function users only. However, computational tasks involving big data often demand special hardware resources as computation accelerators. Use of Graphical Processing Units (GPUs) and Tensor Processing Units (TPUs) is need for efficiently training deep learning models that can be order of magnitude performance improvement over CPUs.

One of the main limitations of current serverless computing platforms is the open source software restrictions. The vendors often restrict the cloud users to use their proprietary software (Hellerstein et al., 2018). The latest versions of commonly used libraries or software systems may not be supported by the serverless platforms. Moreover, the integration of new open source software may not be offered when using the infrastructure. Serverless platforms provide built-in services for management such as monitoring, logging, notifications, and authentication (Baldini et al., 2017). While these services ease the management tasks, the vendor lock-in prevents developers from using open-source or custom built tools on serverless platforms. The limitations of serverless computing on distributed data processing restrict the innovation of scalable open-source software.

SERVICE-ORIENTED DATA MODELLING IN BIG DATA ENVIRONMENTS

In big data environments, it is advantageous to use cloud services to move away from complex monolithic systems, and transition to the model of loosely coupled scalable microservices (Gan et al., 2019). Thanks to its benefits of agility and scalability, the cloud integration helps break the environmental monolith of applications (Li et al., 2019). Additionally, it can facilitate the collaboration on ideas and system modules with external organizations.

System integration is crucial for large enterprise software applications. System integration allows sharing data coming from different sources in various structures through data mediation subsystems. In big data environments, functionalities involving analytical data processing comprise a substantial part of large-scale software solutions. Analytical data modelling tasks using learning algorithms demand large data storage and compute intensive resources. Distributed data processing engines such as Hadoop and Spark facilitate parallel data processing in large-scale. The data analysis models are then scheduled as deployable artifacts in microservice architecture. The models can be deployed directly to an on-premise clusters or distributed computation services in the cloud. The analytical data processing components of software system can be published as microservices. Therefore, the data processing cluster becomes transparent to the client and managed by a third party service.

During data processing, data modelling algorithms often go through many iterations and intermediate stages. Moreover, finding the most optimal parameter values ends up running the same set of program packages iteratively, over and over again. This is a very time consuming and repetitive process, which also requires a powerful set of computational resources. The repetitive computation process must be configured and automated as well. Thus, the microservices system should also support horizontal scaling at runtime.

Big data storage is another important aspect of large-scale software system. Cloud providers such as Google, Amazon Simple Storage Service (S3)[1] offer data lakes for data storage in the cloud, in which the files can be compressed for efficient storage. When a service is requested to perform analysis on the stored data, the data are then retrieved from S3 or a similar storage service.

Software solutions often contain NoSQL databases in big data environments. They fit well with the microservice architecture. NoSQL databases such as MongoDB, HBase, CouchDB, DynamoDB Cassandra[2] are flexible, weakly consistent and scalable (Sadalage & Fowler, 2013). They have no constraint on schema. NoSQL databases can be exposed as database services. Data can be managed and queried through APIs by the programmer. The data are served to the worker nodes via database service. When a service requires data, it makes call to database service.

With continuing development of big data technologies, the number of available big data tools and frameworks has been rapidly increasing. Many competing technologies have emerged in recent years. The optimum architectural design and hardware specifications heavily depend on the decision of the selecting right set of technologies as they are designed to handle different big data tasks and functionalities (Mistrík, Bahsoon, Ali, Heisel, & Maxim, 2017). One fit for all infrastructure approach does not serve well for the purpose of all big data tasks.

The requirements concerning the hardware and architectural infrastructure are influenced by big data software architecture. For instance, MapReduce is a batch-oriented distributed programming model. Hadoop MapReduce is specifically designed to process big datasets sequentially. To make a good use of sequential data processing, the data in Hadoop file system are localized. This means that rather than moving data between nodes, the computation and I/O operations take place heavily in local data nodes. Thus, this decreases the need for network communication. However, MapReduce is not suitable for real-time processing and iterative machine learning tasks. NoSQL databases and computation engines such as Apache Spark, STORM provide interfaces for real-time data processing. As a data intensive framework, MapReduce gives higher precedence to IO operations on disk and access to memory over computation (Shamsi, Khojaye, & Qasmi, 2013). On the other hand, Machine Learning tasks require computation intensive resources. To perform Machine Learning tasks in big data efficiently, the frameworks demand computation intensive hardware resources such as GPUs and TPUs (Bonner, Kureshi, Brennan, & Theodoropoulos, 2017).

Scheduling and Container Orchestration

Microservices can be implemented as containers, or virtual machines that make abstraction of resources and hide low-level details. Containers are lightweight virtualization method similar to hypervisor virtualization that provides an environment for running applications in isolated way by packaging all dependencies. However, containers provide resource isolation for processes rather than simulating the hardware. Thus, they do not have the overhead of hypervisor virtualization that incurs from executing a kernel and virtually replicating the hardware ("What's a Linux container?," 2019). Containers simply do not save any state for running processes and are ideal solution for automating the deployment (Xavier et al., 2013). Figure 3 depicts the architectural difference between VMs and containers. It provides resource isolation that guarantees each process in deployed image to run in different platforms without having dependency issues. Multiple containers and virtual machines can run on physical servers.

Linux containers provided an efficient method to break complex monolithic systems into fine-grained composable parts that execute separately as isolated services. Each component making up the application can scale independently. The application simply becomes the collection of services running in containers. Based on Linux containers, Docker[3] later revolutionized the container technology by improving the accessibility, ease of use, and providing pre-built images of containers. Partially due to Docker's success, containers have become very popular since 2013. Efficiency and practical usage of containers also helped draw attention to microservices architecture.

Figure 3. Comparison of virtualization vs containerization

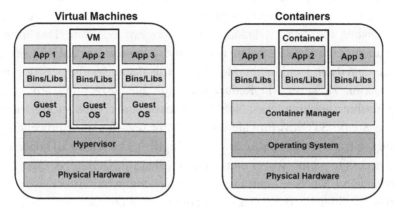

For scheduling and management of containers, cluster scheduling systems such as Apache Mesos[4], Kubernetes[5] are needed. Apache Mesos and Kubernetes are data center level scheduling and management systems that operate a collection of containers on virtual or physical servers. Mesos is deployed in master-slave relationship; masters are simply the nodes that are aware of the cluster's state and responsible to schedule any task attempts. Slave nodes simply obey the Mesos master node.

Every member of Mesos processes are deployed as Docker containers. Whenever service requires a new virtual machine labelled as worker (Mesos slave), a Mesos slave with proper configuration set including the master's address in the network can be automatically added to the cluster to expand computational resources.

Furthermore, the containers also include Spark binaries bundled with them. It is required when a Spark job scheduled for execution on any of them. Mesos masters and slaves discover themselves dynamically. Therefore, any new member of Mesos slave increases the total capacity of the cluster by the means of computational resources automatically. After service request is served on a slave node, corresponding virtual machine can be removed from the cluster to scale down.

Similar to Mesos, Kubernetes handles the management of computing environments. It simplifies the deployment and administration of containers for microservices. Different from serverless computing, Kubernetes provides a lot of flexibility in container configurations such as computation resources and network communication (Brewer, 2015). It allows deploying containers to both on-premise on local hardware and the cloud platforms. The operational administration tasks of containers are outsourced to Kubernetes but the developers still have a high degree of freedom to configure the containers. Kubernetes based containerized microservice architecture is in the middle of the architectural spectrum between monolithic architecture and serverless computing.

Migration to Service-Oriented Architecture

Microservices architectural design approach offers major benefits such as development simplicity, cost efficiency, scalability of application systems and smooth integration with the cloud. Having said that, moving from monolithic enterprise systems into microservices architecture involves many challenges. Firstly, the maintenance of legacy enterprise systems and the issues of migrating our previous monolithic enterprise systems must be considered. Laying a foundation on a set of agreed principles in terms of migration, orchestration, storage and deployment is the best first step in migration towards microservices architecture (Taibi, Lenarduzzi, & Pahl, 2018). It is worthwhile to begin microservices migration by modernizing monolithic legacy enterprise applications and enabling them to harness the benefits of cloud-computing environments can be beneficial rather than modifying the monolithic legacy applications code to use distributed database (Furda, Fidge, Zimmermann, Kelly, & Barros, 2017).

When migrating monolithic applications to microservices, a major challenge is the service decomposition process. Determination of right level of decomposition of components and features into services can be a daunting task. Many approaches to automatically break monolith to microservices have been proposed. Chen et al. proposed a dataflow-driven approach by decomposing into services by firstly developing decomposable dataflow diagram based on business logic from requirement analysis, and microservice candidates are automatically generated from the decomposable diagram, which is a directed graph (Chen et al., 2017).

Patterns of Migration Styles

Considering the patterns of applications migration style from monolithic to microservices, three different approaches appear to be followed commonly: API-Gateway pattern, service registry pattern, and hybrid pattern (Taibi et al., 2018).

In API-Gateway pattern, an API Gateway in the orchestration layer of the system is serving as the entry point that routes the requests from the clients to the microservices. The API Gateway hides the details of microservices and is responsible for communication between clients and microservices. It can also be implemented to handle various system administration tasks such as authentication, protocol transformation, load-balancing, and monitoring. While this approach provides easy extension and backward compatibility as custom APIs can be easily added, some potential issues must be considered such as potential gateway bottleneck and scalability issues with increasing number of microservices (Zimmermann et al., 2016).

In Service Registry pattern, the clients and microservices directly communicate to the microservices through exposed APIs. The virtualization platforms such as VMs or containers host the instances of microservices. A service registry is responsible for dynamic discovery of instances of microservices. Load balancers efficiently orchestrate the requests between clients and available microservices (Taibi et al., 2018).

The benefits of this approach include improved maintainability, easy and direct communication between services (O'Connor, Elger, & Clarke, 2016), increased resilience and auto-scaling, easier failure recovery as each microservice can be restarted without affecting others (Toffetti, Brunner, Blöchlinger, Dudouet, & Edmonds, 2015), ease of development since smaller isolated services can be developed separately, and ease of migration as legacy service can be easily replaced by updating the service registry with newly implemented microservices (Fowler & Lewis, 2014). However, the additional complexity of service registry requires paying special attention as it can reduce the performance of system (Potvin, Nabaee, Labeau, Nguyen, & Cheriet, 2016).

In the hybrid pattern, the service registry and API-Gateway are simultaneously used. Differently, the API-gateway is replaced with a message bus. Similar to Enterprise Service Bus concept in SOA architectures, the message bus facilitates the communication between services and clients (Taibi et al., 2018). The requests from clients and microservices are directed to appropriate microservices via the message bus. The advantages of this pattern include ease of migration for SOA application as microservices replacing the legacy services can utilize existing Enterprise Service Bus, and reduced learning curve for people with experience in SOA architectures (Kewley, Kester, & McDonnell, 2016; Taibi et al., 2018; Vresk & Čavrak, 2016). Similarity to SOA is also the main disadvantage of this pattern as it adds dependency to the message bus and restricts the state isolation, scalability and loose coupling of microservices (Taibi et al., 2018; Vianden, Lichter, & Steffens, 2014).

CONCLUSION

This chapter has explored the software architectures used in big data. Particularly, it covered the evolution of systems from monolithic systems to service-oriented architectures. Moreover, the issues and advantages of implementing service-oriented architectures of microservices and serverless computing were investigated. Microservices architecture is a modular software architecture, in which business functionalities are exposed as fine-grained services through APIs. The services are loosely coupled and thus can be tested and deployed separately. As each service is designed as a small unit, the complexity of testing and deployment is lower. However, microservice architecture carries the communication overhead from implementing APIs for communications between services. On the other hand, serverless computing provides a simplified model of computation in which, developers focus on application code without concerning the server infrastructure. The cloud platform handles the server provisioning and the management of infrastructure in a cost-effective way. Although services offered by the cloud providers ease the management tasks, the serverless cloud platforms currently are not flexible. The cloud providers restrict the cloud users to use their proprietary software. Additionally, the benefits of moving to service-oriented architecture and the patterns of migration were examined in detail. It appears that with the right architectural consideration and due diligence, microservices, serverless and cloud computing may present industry incumbents with an exit strategy to move from legacy infrastructure to adopt cloud based software deployment models. This has not observed in earlier legacy monolithic model with the serverless paradigm, in which the focus isn't on infrastructure but on delivering the required business functionalities that changes the economic model for IT service delivery.

REFERENCES

Alshuqayran, N., Ali, N., & Evans, R. (2016). A systematic mapping study in microservice architecture. *2016 IEEE 9th International Conference on Service-Oriented Computing and Applications (SOCA)*, 44–51.

Baldini, I., Castro, P., Chang, K., Cheng, P., Fink, S., & Ishakian, V. ... others. (2017). Serverless computing: Current trends and open problems. In Research Advances in Cloud Computing (pp. 1–20). Springer.

Bass, L., Weber, I., & Zhu, L. (2015). *DevOps: A software architect's perspective*. Addison-Wesley Professional.

Beyond buzzwords: A brief history of microservices patterns. (2018, October 10). Retrieved September 10, 2019, from IBM Developer website: https://developer.ibm.com/articles/cl-evolution-microservices-patterns/

Birrell, A. D., & Nelson, B. J. (1984). Implementing remote procedure calls. *ACM Transactions on Computer Systems*, *2*(1), 39–59. doi:10.1145/2080.357392

Bonner, S., Kureshi, I., Brennan, J., & Theodoropoulos, G. (2017). Exploring the Evolution of Big Data Technologies. In *Software Architecture for Big Data and the Cloud* (pp. 253–283). Elsevier. doi:10.1016/B978-0-12-805467-3.00014-4

Borthakur, D. (2007). The hadoop distributed file system: Architecture and design. *Hadoop Project Website*, *11*, 21.

Box, D., Ehnebuske, D., Kakivaya, G., Layman, A., Mendelsohn, N., Nielsen, H. F., … Winer, D. (2000). *Simple object access protocol (SOAP) 1.1*. Academic Press.

Brewer, E. A. (2015). Kubernetes and the path to cloud native. *Proceedings of the Sixth ACM Symposium on Cloud Computing*, 167–167. 10.1145/2806777.2809955

Cañon-Lozano, Y., Melo-Castillo, A., Banse, K., & Herrera-Quintero, L. F. (2012). Automatic Generation of O/D matrix for Mass Transportation Systems using an ITS approach. *2012 IEEE Colombian Intelligent Transportation Systems Symposium (CITSS)*, 1–6. 10.1109/CITSS.2012.6336681

Celesti, A., Mulfari, D., Fazio, M., Villari, M., & Puliafito, A. (2016). Exploring container virtualization in IoT clouds. *2016 IEEE International Conference on Smart Computing (SMARTCOMP)*, 1–6.

Chen, R., Li, S., & Li, Z. (2017). From monolith to microservices: a dataflow-driven approach. *2017 24th Asia-Pacific Software Engineering Conference (APSEC)*, 466–475.

Ciavotta, M., Alge, M., Menato, S., Rovere, D., & Pedrazzoli, P. (2017). A microservice-based middleware for the digital factory. *Procedia Manufacturing*, *11*, 931–938. doi:10.1016/j.promfg.2017.07.197

Çiçek, M. (2015). Wearable technologies and its future applications. *International Journal of Electrical. Electronics and Data Communication*, *3*(4), 45–50.

Data never sleeps. (2018). Retrieved May 31, 2019, from Domo website: https://www.domo.com/solution/data-never-sleeps-6

Fazio, M., Celesti, A., Ranjan, R., Liu, C., Chen, L., & Villari, M. (2016). Open issues in scheduling microservices in the cloud. *IEEE Cloud Computing*, *3*(5), 81–88. doi:10.1109/MCC.2016.112

Fazio, M., & Puliafito, A. (2015). Cloud4sens: A cloud-based architecture for sensor controlling and monitoring. *IEEE Communications Magazine*, *53*(3), 41–47. doi:10.1109/MCOM.2015.7060517

Fielding, R. (2000). Representational state transfer. *Architectural Styles and the Design of Netowork-Based Software Architecture*, 76–85.

Fowler, M., & Lewis, J. (2014). *Microservices a definition of this new architectural term*. Academic Press.

Furda, A., Fidge, C., Zimmermann, O., Kelly, W., & Barros, A. (2017). Migrating enterprise legacy source code to microservices: On multitenancy, statefulness, and data consistency. *IEEE Software*, *35*(3), 63–72. doi:10.1109/MS.2017.440134612

Gan, Y., Zhang, Y., Hu, K., Cheng, D., He, Y., Pancholi, M., & Delimitrou, C. (2019). Seer: Leveraging Big Data to Navigate the Complexity of Performance Debugging in Cloud Microservices. *Proceedings of the Twenty-Fourth International Conference on Architectural Support for Programming Languages and Operating Systems*, 19–33. 10.1145/3297858.3304004

Gorton, I., & Klein, J. (2014). Distribution, data, deployment: Software architecture convergence in big data systems. *IEEE Software*, *32*(3), 78–85. doi:10.1109/ MS.2014.51

Hellerstein, J. M., Faleiro, J., Gonzalez, J. E., Schleier-Smith, J., Sreekanti, V., Tumanov, A., & Wu, C. (2018). *Serverless computing: One step forward, two steps back*. arXiv Preprint arXiv:1812.03651

Herrera-Quintero, L. F., Vega-Alfonso, J. C., Banse, K. B. A., & Zambrano, E. C. (2018). Smart its sensor for the transportation planning based on iot approaches using serverless and microservices architecture. *IEEE Intelligent Transportation Systems Magazine*, *10*(2), 17–27. doi:10.1109/MITS.2018.2806620

Innerbichler, J., Gonul, S., Damjanovic-Behrendt, V., Mandler, B., & Strohmeier, F. (2017). Nimble collaborative platform: Microservice architectural approach to federated iot. 2017 Global Internet of Things Summit (GIoTS), 1–6.

Jonas, E., Schleier-Smith, J., Sreekanti, V., Tsai, C.-C., Khandelwal, A., & Pu, Q. (2019). *Cloud Programming Simplified: A Berkeley View on Serverless Computing*. arXiv Preprint arXiv:1902.03383

Kewley, R., Kester, N., & McDonnell, J. (2016). DEVS Distributed Modeling Framework-A parallel DEVS implementation via microservices. *2016 Symposium on Theory of Modeling and Simulation (TMS-DEVS)*, 1–8.

Khan, N., Yaqoob, I., Hashem, I. A. T., Inayat, Z., Ali, M., & Kamaleldin, W. (2014). … Gani, A. (2014). Big data: Survey, technologies, opportunities, and challenges. *The Scientific World Journal*, *2014*, 1–18. doi:10.1155/2014/712826

Khanda, K., Salikhov, D., Gusmanov, K., Mazzara, M., & Mavridis, N. (2017). Microservice-based iot for smart buildings. *2017 31st International Conference on Advanced Information Networking and Applications Workshops (WAINA)*, 302–308.

Krylovskiy, A., Jahn, M., & Patti, E. (2015). Designing a smart city internet of things platform with microservice architecture. *2015 3rd International Conference on Future Internet of Things and Cloud*, 25–30.

Li, Z., Seco, D., & Sánchez Rodríguez, A. E. (2019). Microservice-Oriented Platform for Internet of Big Data Analytics: A Proof of Concept. *Sensors (Basel), 19*(5), 1134. doi:10.339019051134 PMID:30845687

Lu, Y., & Ju, F. (2017). Smart manufacturing systems based on cyber-physical manufacturing services (CPMS). *IFAC-PapersOnLine, 50*(1), 15883–15889. doi:10.1016/j.ifacol.2017.08.2349

Mistrík, I., Bahsoon, R., Ali, N., Heisel, M., & Maxim, B. (2017). *Software Architecture for Big Data and the Cloud*. Morgan Kaufmann.

Monostori, L., Kádár, B., Bauernhansl, T., Kondoh, S., Kumara, S., Reinhart, G., ... Ueda, K. (2016). Cyber-physical systems in manufacturing. *CIRP Annals, 65*(2), 621–641. doi:10.1016/j.cirp.2016.06.005

O'Connor, R., Elger, P., & Clarke, P. M. (2016). Exploring the Impact of Situational Context—A Case Study of a Software Development Process for a Microservices Architecture. *2016 IEEE/ACM International Conference on Software and System Processes (ICSSP)*, 6–10.

Petrov, C. (2019, March 22). *Big Data Statistics 2019*. Retrieved May 31, 2019, from Tech Jury website: https://techjury.net/stats-about/big-data-statistics/

Potvin, P., Nabaee, M., Labeau, F., Nguyen, K.-K., & Cheriet, M. (2016). Micro service cloud computing pattern for next generation networks. In *Smart City 360* (pp. 263–274). Springer. doi:10.1007/978-3-319-33681-7_22

Sadalage, P. J., & Fowler, M. (2013). *NoSQL distilled: a brief guide to the emerging world of polyglot persistence*. Pearson Education.

Schmidt, D. C. (2006). Model-driven engineering. *Computer-IEEE Computer Society, 39*(2), 25–31. doi:10.1109/MC.2006.58

Shamsi, J., Khojaye, M. A., & Qasmi, M. A. (2013). Data-intensive cloud computing: Requirements, expectations, challenges, and solutions. *Journal of Grid Computing, 11*(2), 281–310. doi:10.100710723-013-9255-6

Singleton, A. (2016). The economics of microservices. *IEEE Cloud Computing, 3*(5), 16–20. doi:10.1109/MCC.2016.109

Soldani, J., Tamburri, D. A., & Van Den Heuvel, W.-J. (2018). The pains and gains of microservices: A Systematic grey literature review. *Journal of Systems and Software, 146,* 215–232. doi:10.1016/j.jss.2018.09.082

Taibi, D., Lenarduzzi, V., & Pahl, C. (2018). Architectural Patterns for Microservices: A Systematic Mapping Study. *CLOSER,* 221–232.

The most plentiful. (2016, October 7). Retrieved May 31, 2019, from IBM Business Analytics Blog website: https://www.ibm.com/blogs/business-analytics/data-is-everywhere/

Thramboulidis, K. (2015). A cyber–physical system-based approach for industrial automation systems. *Computers in Industry, 72,* 92–102. doi:10.1016/j.compind.2015.04.006

Thramboulidis, K., Vachtsevanou, D. C., & Solanos, A. (2018). Cyber-physical microservices: An IoT-based framework for manufacturing systems. *2018 IEEE Industrial Cyber-Physical Systems (ICPS),* 232–239.

Thramboulidis, K., Bochalis, P., & Bouloumpasis, J. (2017). A framework for MDE of IoT-based manufacturing cyber-physical systems. *Proceedings of the Seventh International Conference on the Internet of Things,* 11. 10.1145/3131542.3131554

Thramboulidis, K., & Christoulakis, F. (2016). UML4IoT—A UML-based approach to exploit IoT in cyber-physical manufacturing systems. *Computers in Industry, 82,* 259–272. doi:10.1016/j.compind.2016.05.010

Toffetti, G., Brunner, S., Blöchlinger, M., Dudouet, F., & Edmonds, A. (2015). An architecture for self-managing microservices. *Proceedings of the 1st International Workshop on Automated Incident Management in Cloud,* 19–24.

Vianden, M., Lichter, H., & Steffens, A. (2014). Experience on a microservice-based reference architecture for measurement systems. *2014 21st Asia-Pacific Software Engineering Conference, 1,* 183–190.

Viani, F., Robol, F., Polo, A., Rocca, P., Oliveri, G., & Massa, A. (2013). Wireless architectures for heterogeneous sensing in smart home applications: Concepts and real implementation. *Proceedings of the IEEE, 101*(11), 2381–2396. doi:10.1109/JPROC.2013.2266858

Vresk, T., & Čavrak, I. (2016). Architecture of an interoperable IoT platform based on microservices. *2016 39th International Convention on Information and Communication Technology, Electronics and Microelectronics (MIPRO),* 1196–1201.

Wang, L., Li, M., Zhang, Y., Ristenpart, T., & Swift, M. (2018). Peeking behind the curtains of serverless platforms. *Proceeding USENIX ATC '18 Proceedings of the 2018 USENIX Conference on Usenix Annual Technical Conference, 133*-145.

What's a Linux container? (2019). Retrieved June 7, 2019, from https://www.redhat.com/en/topics/containers/whats-a-linux-container

White, T. (2012). *Hadoop: The definitive guide*. O'Reilly Media, Inc.

Xavier, M. G., Neves, M. V., Rossi, F. D., Ferreto, T. C., Lange, T., & De Rose, C. A. (2013). Performance evaluation of container-based virtualization for high performance computing environments. *2013 21st Euromicro International Conference on Parallel, Distributed, and Network-Based Processing*, 233–240.

Yan, M., Castro, P., Cheng, P., & Ishakian, V. (2016). Building a chatbot with serverless computing. *Proceedings of the 1st International Workshop on Mashups of Things and APIs*, 5. 10.1145/3007203.3007217

Zaharia, M., Chowdhury, M., Franklin, M. J., Shenker, S., & Stoica, I. (2010). Spark: Cluster computing with working sets. *HotCloud, 10*(10), 95.

Zimmermann, A., Bogner, J., Schmidt, R., Jugel, D., Schweda, C., & Möhring, M. (2016). *Digital enterprise architecture with micro-granular systems and services*. Academic Press.

ENDNOTES

[1]   https://aws.amazon.com/blogs/big-data/introducing-the-data-lake-solution-on-aws/

[2]   http://cassandra.apache.org/

[3]   https://www.docker.com/

[4]   http://mesos.apache.org/

[5]   https://kubernetes.io/

Chapter 5
Big Data Processing:
Concepts, Architectures, Technologies, and Techniques

Can Eyupoglu

iD https://orcid.org/0000-0002-6133-8617

Turkish Air Force Academy, National Defense University, Turkey

ABSTRACT

Big data has attracted significant and increasing attention recently and has become a hot topic in the areas of IT industry, finance, business, academia, and scientific research. In the digital world, the amount of generated data has increased. According to the research of International Data Corporation (IDC), 33 zettabytes of data were created in 2018, and it is estimated that the amount of data will scale up more than five times from 2018 to 2025. In addition, the advertising sector, healthcare industry, biomedical companies, private firms, and governmental agencies have to make many investments in the collection, aggregation, and sharing of enormous amounts of data. To process this large-scale data, specific data processing techniques are used rather than conventional methodologies. This chapter deals with the concepts, architectures, technologies, and techniques that process big data.

INTRODUCTION

Today, data usage changes people's way of living, working and playing. Enterprises are utilizing generated data in order for enhancing customer experience, being more agile, developing new models and creating sources. The digital world nowadays constitutes the vast majority of people's daily lives which are based on reaching

DOI: 10.4018/978-1-7998-2142-7.ch005

goods and services, communicating with friends and having fun. The current world economy is substantially dependent on created and stored data. In times to come, this dependence will rise much more with the development and spread of technology. Companies collect large amounts of customer data for supplying more personalization and then consumers use social media, cloud, gaming and personalized services more. Because of this rising dependence on data, the size of the global datasphere will continuously increase. Furthermore, International Data Corporation (IDC) estimates that the global datasphere will reach to 175 zettabytes in 2025 as shown in Figure 1 (Reinsel, Gantz & Rydning, 2018).

In the big data age, the basic features of produced data having complicated structures are enormous volume and high velocity. These data are created via sensors, social networks, online and offline transactions. In the fields of government, business, management, medical and healthcare, smart, informational and related decision making can be performed thanks to efficient processing of big data (Wang, Xu & Pedrycz, 2017).

To cope with and process such a huge amount of data effectively, new techniques and technologies are emerging day by day (Eyupoglu, Aydin, Sertbas, Zaim & Ones, 2017; Eyupoglu, Aydin, Zaim & Sertbas, 2018). This chapter describes what is required to handle big data. Before discussing big data processing, it is needed to address big data life cycle. For this purpose, firstly, big data life cycle is expressed in this chapter. Then, big data analytics which is essential to design efficient systems in order for processing big data is explained. Afterwards, big data processing using Apache Hadoop including HDFS and MapReduce is clarified in detail. Moreover, the main aim and contribution of this chapter are to provide general information to the researchers who will work in this field.

The rest of this chapter is organized as follows. In the second section, big data life cycle is explained. The third section expresses big data analytics. Big data

Figure 1. Annual size of the global datasphere

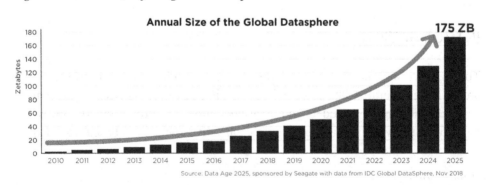

processing with Apache Hadoop is clarified in the fourth section. Finally, the fifth section concludes the chapter.

BIG DATA LIFE CYCLE

It is necessary to design effective and efficient systems for processing large-scale data coming from various sources and reaching astronomical speeds in order to overcome different aspects of big data with regard to volume, velocity and variety. Today, data are distributed. Therefore, researchers have focused on developing new techniques to process and store huge amount of data. Cloud computing based technologies like Hadoop MapReduce are investigated for this aim (Mehmood, Natgunanathan, Xiang, Hua & Guo, 2016). The life cycle of big data consists of three main stages shown in Figure 2. This section expresses these stages in detail.

Big Data Generation

Data are created from different distributed sources nowadays. Over the last few years, the amount of produced data has increased tremendously. To give an example, the web produces 2.5 quintillion bytes of data per day and 90% of the world's data has been generated in the last few years. Facebook alone produces 25TB of new data per day. Because of the fact that the created data generally associated with a particular field like Internet are big, varied and complicated, conventional technologies cannot cope with them (Mehmood et al., 2016). There are many technologies and areas in respect to big data generation such as universe observation, government sector, webpage, social network, business data, environment monitoring, large-scale scientific experiment, healthcare, UGC and e-commerce (Hu, Wen, Chua & Li, 2014).

Figure 2. Life cycle of big data

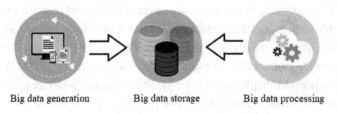

Big data generation   Big data storage   Big data processing

Big Data Storage

Big data storage stage is related to store and manage huge data sets. Data storage systems comprise of hardware infrastructure and data management parts (Hu et al., 2014). Hardware infrastructure is to utilize the resources of Information and Communication Technology (ICT) for a variety of tasks like distributed storage. On the other hand, data management is to manage, query and analyze large-scale data sets using software deployed on the hardware infrastructure. Furthermore, to interact with stored data, it should supply various interfaces (Mehmood et al., 2016). NoSQL, shared-nothing parallel databases, Google File System (GFS), MapReduce, HBase, MongoDB, SimpleDB, CouchDB, PNUTS, Dynamo, Dryad, Voldmort, BigTable, Redis, Casandra, All-Pairs and Pregel are the examples of technologies with regard to big data storage (Hu et al., 2014).

Big Data Processing

Big data processing stage consists of four steps which are data acquisition, data transmission, data preprocessing and data analysis (Figure 3). Data acquisition is necessary because of that data might come from different sources such as images, videos and text. In data acquisition step, data are collected from particular environment of data generation using special data acquisition techniques. In data transmission step, a high-speed communication method is needed to transmit data to a suitable repository for several analytical applications after raw data are collected from a particular data generation environment. In data preprocessing step, meaningless, unneeded and redundant parts of the data are removed for saving more data storage space. Finally, in data analysis step, to extract useful and meaningful information from data sets, excessive data and field-specific analytical mechanisms are used. Despite the fact that different areas of data analytics need to use particular data characteristics, a number of these areas might utilize similar techniques to derive value from data with the aim of examination, transformation and modelling (Hu et al., 2014; Mehmood et al., 2016). Big data analytics is with respect to data mining, text mining, web mining, statistical analysis, multivariate statistical analysis, multimedia analytics, network analytics, mobile analytics, social network analytics, recommendation, community detection and mobile community detection (Hu et al., 2014).

In big data processing stage, there are several fields and technologies related to data acquisition such as logfiles, sensor, web crawler, data integration, radio telescope, data cleansing, data compression, deduplication, Radio Frequency Identification (RFID), optic interconnect, Wavelength Division Multiplexing (WDM), Orthogonal Frequency Division Multiplexing (OFDM), 2-tier tree and 3-tier tree. Moreover, data transmission step can be classified into two phases as IP backbone transmission and

Figure 3. Big data processing steps

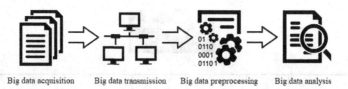

| Big data acquisition | Big data transmission | Big data preprocessing | Big data analysis |

data center transmission (Hu et al., 2014). Integration, cleansing and redundancy elimination are the techniques used for data preprocessing (Han, Pei & Kamber, 2011; Müller & Freytag, 2005; Noy, 2004). Besides, there are three types of approaches for data analysis, which are data visualization, data mining and statistical analysis (Anderson, 2003; Friedman, 2008; Wu et al., 2008).

BIG DATA ANALYTICS

The main goal of big data analytics is obtaining as much useful information as possible from large-scale data via experiment, measurement and observation. In addition, it is used to evaluate and predict the data, to decide how the data is used, to help decision-making, to give advice, to control whether the data is valid, to infer causes from fault and to estimate what will happen in the time to come (Hu et al., 2014).

With the increase in web usage recently, companies have started to invest more in analytical tools for extracting value from big data. Besides, understanding the necessities of big data analytics consisting of skills, processes, applications and technologies is required for companies (Wang & Hajli, 2017). Big data analytics can be used to transform organizational practices with ensuring traceability, decision support and predictive capabilities (Sivarajah, Irani, Gupta & Mahroof, 2019; Wang, Malthouse, Calder & Uzunoglu, 2019).

In terms of the depth of the analysis, data analytics is divided into three levels as descriptive, predictive and prescriptive analytics. Descriptive analytics utilizes historical data to explain what happened. Predictive analytics estimates future prospects and tendencies. Finally, prescriptive analytics examines effectivity and decision making (Blackett, 2013). Furthermore, there are six technical types of big data analytics, as shown in Figure 4.

Structured Data Analytics

Huge amounts of structured data are produced in the areas of business and scientific research nowadays. Relational Database Management System (RDBMS),

Figure 4. Types of big data analytics

Business Process Management (BPM), Online Analytical Processing (OLAP) and data warehousing are used to manage these structured data (Chaudhuri, Dayal & Narasayya, 2011). Data analytics is mostly based on statistical analysis and data mining which are researched in the last thirty years (Hinton, 2007). Deep learning, machine learning, statistical machine learning, temporal data mining, spatial data mining, privacy-preserving data mining and process mining are the examples of the research fields for structured data analytics (Chamikara, Bertok, Liu, Camtepe & Khalil, 2019; da Costa, Papa, Lisboa, Munoz & de Albuquerque, 2019; dos Santos Garcia et al., 2019; Gaber, Zaslavsky & Krishnaswamy, 2005; Jan et al., 2019; Qin & Chiang, 2019; Ucci, Aniello & Baldoni, 2019; Zhang, Yang, Chen & Li, 2018).

Text Analytics

Text analytics is to extract beneficial and meaningful information from unstructured text. It is thought that text analytics has more commercial impact than structured data mining because the majority of stored information consists of text which contains webpages, social media content, e-mails and business documents. Text analytics is also referred to as text mining that is an interdisciplinary area and related to machine learning, computational linguistics, statistics, information retrieval and especially data mining. Natural Language Processing (NLP) and text representation form the basis of most text mining systems (Hu et al., 2014). NLP is the field of computational modelling of natural languages and used to make computer systems discover and process languages (Eyupoglu, 2019a; Joshi, 1991). In the areas of information science, computer engineering, psychology and linguistics, several NLP techniques and applications have been developed. Natural language generation, speech recognition, expert systems, artificial intelligence, machine learning, machine translation, semantic search, sentiment analysis, summarization, question answering, information extraction, clustering, topic modeling, opinion mining and categorization are the examples of NLP applications (Balinsky, Balinsky & Simske, 2011; Blei,

2012; Chowdhury, 2003; Dreisbach, Koleck, Bourne & Bakken, 2019; Eyupoglu, 2019a; Ibrahim & Wang, 2019; Li, Hu, Lin & Yang, 2010; Liu & Zhang, 2012; Manning & Schütze, 1999; Nenkova & McKeown, 2012; Ritter, Clark & Etzioni, 2011).

Multimedia Analytics

Multimedia analytics is to extract desired information and find out the semantics in multimedia data such as audio, image and video. In most of the fields, multimedia data are various and have more knowledge than structured data and text data. Multimedia recommendation, multimedia annotation, multimedia summarization, multimedia event detection, multimedia indexing and retrieval are some of the examples of recent research areas in multimedia analytics (Ding et al., 2012; Hu, Xie, Li, Zeng & Maybank, 2011; Hu et al., 2014; Wang, Ni, Hua & Chua, 2012).

Multimedia data have become one of the widespread big data types by the reason of developments in mobile device technologies (Sadiq et al., 2015; Zhu, Cui, Wang & Hua, 2015). Studies on multimedia big data can improve big data handling issues such as analytics, utilization, sharing and storage. There are many challenges of multimedia big data that are common with big data. Some of these challenges are real time processing of multimedia big data, ensuring scalability, combining heterogeneous and unstructured multimedia big data, guaranteeing big data privacy and security, providing computing efficiency, discovering complexity of multimedia big data, guaranteeing quality of experience (QoE) and quality of service (QoS) (Kumari et al., 2018; Zhu et al., 2015). Furthermore, new challenges occur owing to Internet of Things (IoT) (Alvi, Afzal, Shah, Atzori & Mahmood, 2015; Atzori, Carboni & Iera, 2014; Eyupoglu, 2019b). Gathering sensor data located in different places is a challenging issue for multimedia big data because of the mobility of IoT devices (Kumari et al., 2018; Xu, Ngai & Liu, 2018).

Web Analytics

Web analytics is to automatically retrieve, extract and evaluate information from web services and documents in order for discovery of knowledge. The number of webpages has tremendously increased in the last decade, and because of that web analytics has become a hot topic. NLP, text mining, information retrieval and databases are the research fields of this topic. Moreover, there are three types of web analytics in terms of mining, which are web content mining, web usage mining and web structure mining (Pal, Talwar & Mitra, 2002). Web content mining is used to explore useful knowledge from content of websites such as text, metadata, hyperlinks, audio, image and video (Chakrabarti, 2000). Web usage mining is utilized in order to mine secondary data created by web actions and sessions. User profiles, user sessions, user queries, user transactions, registration data, cookies, bookmark data, mouse clicks, mouse scrolls, browser logs, web server access logs and proxy server logs are the sources of web usage data (Xu, Bu, Chen & Cai, 2012). Web structure mining is used to explore the model of link structures on the web. Link structure means the graph of links between websites or in a website. Furthermore, link structure model depends on the topology of hyperlinks, shows the relations between various websites and can be used to classify websites (Hu et al., 2014).

Mobile Analytics

Mobile analytics is to extract useful information from mobile terminals such as cell phones, mobile PCs, RFID and sensors. With the increase in smartphone usage in the last decade, mobile data traffic has increased extremely. According to the Ericsson Mobility Report (2018), total mobile data traffic is predicted to increase five times over the next six years, reaching 136 exabytes (EB)/month by the end of 2024 (Figure 5). This enormous increase in generated data leads to the emergence of mobile analytics.

With the advent of 4G and 5G technologies, mobile communication is highly improved and the conventional cellular network is evolved into a converged mobile network. Nowadays, the amount of data produced by mobile devices has increased enormously with the rise in the number of mobile applications developed by programmers (Jan et al., 2019). For instance, Yandex Maps is used by more than 20 million people all around the world.

Network Analytics

Network analytics is to obtain beneficial knowledge from network data and also known as social network analytics or social media analytics. Social media content including text, image, video, audio, comments and locations is created via social networking sites, social marketing sites, blogs, microblogs etc. Indeed, social media analytics is related to structured data analytics, text analytics and multimedia analytics. The techniques and applications used for data analytics, text analytics and multimedia analytics can also be utilized for social media analytics.

The concept of data streaming has become big data streaming with the widespread use of social networks. Billions of users generate and upload different types of data daily using various social media platforms including LinkedIn, Instagram, Twitter and Facebook. With the increasing popularity of these social media platforms, new challenges arise in managing large-scale data. Several studies have been done related to characteristic representations in low and high level abstraction. For example,

Figure 5. Growth of global mobile data traffic

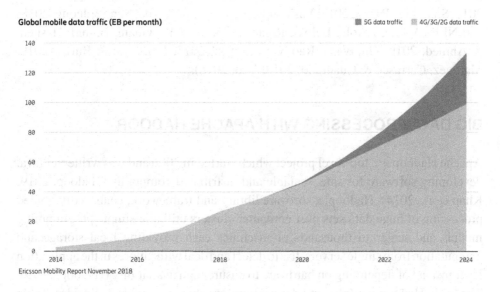

Global mobile data traffic (EB per month)   ■ 5G data traffic   ■ 4G/3G/2G data traffic

Ericsson Mobility Report November 2018

Facebook utilizes some machine learning methods in order for managing users' data and suggesting pages or friends that the user may be interested in (Jan et al., 2019).

In recent years, huge growth in social media usage causes an increase in the number of companies seeking knowledge from big data. Furthermore, companies can make well-timed and expressive business decisions thanks to using social media analytics which is an interdisciplinary research area. The aim of social media analytics is to associate, develop and adjust techniques for analysis of social media data. The process of social media analytics consists of four different steps which are data exploration, collection, preparation and analysis (Sivarajah et al., 2019; Stieglitz, Dang-Xuan, Bruns & Neuberger, 2014; Stieglitz, Mirbabaie, Ross & Neuberger, 2018).

Companies utilize social media big data analytical methods in order to make effective decisions instantly on the current situation. The data collected from social media platforms supply companies with exhaustive information on customer ideas and considerations related to the products. To analyze and exploit big data, companies should have proper abilities and means (Sivarajah et al., 2019; Wu, Zhu, Wu & Ding, 2014). In literature, many studies have been conducted based on various methods of social media big data analytics such as text mining (Cakir & Guldamlasioglu, 2016; Ibrahim & Wang, 2019; Ozbay & Alatas, 2019; Reddick, Chatfield & Ojo, 2017; Serna & Gasparovic, 2018; Shen, Chen & Wang, 2019), social network analysis (Bonchi, Castillo, Gionis & Jaimes, 2011; Can & Alatas, 2019; Jiang, Leung & Pazdor, 2016; Ren, Tang & Liao, 2019; Wang, Sun, Qian, Goh & Mishra, 2019), sentiment analysis (Kauffmann et al., 2019; Kumar, Srinivasan, Cheng & Zomaya,

2020; Ohbe, Ozono & Shintani, 2017; Sánchez-Rada & Iglesias, 2019; Shahare, 2017; Shanthi & Pappa, 2017; Vashishtha & Susan, 2019; Yoo, Song & Jeong, 2018) and NLP (Agerri, Artola, Beloki, Rigau & Soroa, 2015; Ghani, Hamid, Hashem & Ahmed, 2019; Gudivada, Rao & Raghavan, 2015; Liu, Shin & Burns, 2019; Marquez, Carrasco & Cuadrado, 2018; Yeo, 2018).

BIG DATA PROCESSING WITH APACHE HADOOP

Apache Hadoop is a top-level project which started in 2006 and was written in Java, developing software for safe, scalable and distributed computing (Hadoop, 2019; Khan et al., 2014). Hadoop, a software library and framework, enables distributed processing of huge data sets over computer clusters utilizing simple programming models and scales to thousands of machines each providing local storage and computation from single servers. It is to detect and deal with failures in the application layer instead of depending on hardware to ensure high availability (Hadoop, 2019). The basic Hadoop modules and descriptions are shown in Table 1. Besides, Table 2 demonstrates Hadoop based projects, definitions and functions.

In addition to these Hadoop based projects, Hadoop consists of several components such as Flume (2019), HCatalog (2019), Kafka (2019), Oozie (2019) and Sqoop (2019), demonstrated in Table 3.

HDFS and MapReduce

HDFS and MapReduce are the main components of Hadoop which are very relevant to each other. Each is deployed together to produce a single cluster (White, 2019). For this reason, storage and processing systems are physically interconnected. HDFS, a highly fault tolerant distributed file system, is developed to store huge-scale files for accessing streaming data and work on local file systems of cluster nodes.

Table 1. Basic Hadoop modules and descriptions

Module Name	Description
Hadoop Common	Supporting other Hadoop modules with common utilities
Hadoop Distributed File System (HDFS)	Supplying access to application data with high throughput
Hadoop YARN	Managing cluster resources and job scheduling
Hadoop MapReduce	Parallel processing of big data sets
Hadoop Ozone	Object storage
Hadoop Submarine	Machine learning engine

Table 2. Hadoop based projects, definitions and functions

Project Name	Definition	Function
Ambari	Web-based tool	Monitoring, organizing and managing Hadoop clusters
Avro	Data serialization system	Serializing data
Cassandra	Scalable multi-master database	Managing big data
Chukwa	Data collection system	Managing big distributed systems
HBase	Scalable and distributed database	Storing structured data for big tables
Hive	Data warehouse infrastructure	Ad hoc querying and data summarization
Mahout	Scalable library	Data mining and machine learning
Pig	Data flow language and execution framework	Parallel computation
Spark	Fast and comprehensive compute engine	Providing a simple and effective programming model for supporting a variety of applications such as Extract, Transform, and Load (ETL), stream processing and machine learning
Tez	Data flow programming framework	Ensuring a resilient engine for executing a complex Directed Acyclic Graph (DAG) of tasks to process data
ZooKeeper	High performance coordination service	High reliability coordination for distributed applications

It comprises of two kinds of nodes which are one namenode (master) and various datanodes (slaves). The task of the namenode is to manage the file system hierarchy and director namespace. File systems are introduced as a namenode which registers attributes including permission, modification, access time and disk space quotas. The file content is divided into big blocks. Every file block is independently replicated

Table 3. Other Hadoop components, definitions and functions

Component Name	Definition	Function
Flume	Distributed, reliable and available service	Collecting, aggregating and carrying huge-scale log data
HCatalog	Table and storage management layer	Sharing data across Hadoop tools such as Hive, MapReduce and Pig
Kafka	Scalable and fast messaging system	Durable, fault tolerant and high throughput messaging
Oozie	Workflow scheduler system	Managing Hadoop jobs
Sqoop	Transference tool	Bulk data transferring between Hadoop and structured datastores

between datanodes for the aim of backup and a report of all available blocks is sent to the namenode at certain intervals (Hashem et al., 2015). The system architecture of HDFS containing the relationship between the namenode, client and datanodes is shown in Figure 6 (Shvachko, Kuang, Radia & Chansler, 2010). Readers are referred to (Shvachko et al., 2010) for further details.

MapReduce, a simple programming model based on Google File System (GFS) (Ghemawat, Gobioff & Leung, 2003), is designed to process and generate big datasets containing real world tasks. In this programming model, programmers designate the computation as two functions that are map and reduce. A set of input key/value pairs is taken by the computation and a set of output key/value pairs is produced. The map function created by the programmer takes an input key/value pair and generates a set of intermediate key/value pairs. The reduce function takes an intermediate key and its values and then merges all intermediate values related to the same key. Finally, it generally produces zero or one output value for each reduce invocation (Dean & Ghemawat, 2008; Kalavri & Vlassov, 2013). Figure 7 demonstrates the programming model of MapReduce (Kalavri & Vlassov, 2013). Besides, the execution architecture of MapReduce is shown in Figure 8 (Dean & Ghemawat, 2008). Readers are referred to (Dean & Ghemawat, 2008) for further details.

CONCLUSION

In this chapter, the concepts, architectures, technologies and techniques associated with big data processing are explained and examined. For this aim, firstly, big data

Figure 6. System architecture of HDFS

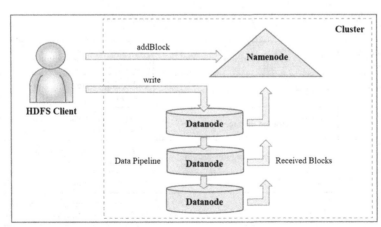

Figure 7. Programming model of MapReduce

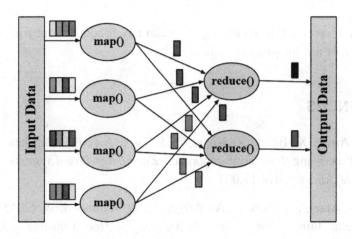

life cycle consisting of data generation, data storage and data processing stages is expressed in depth. Afterwards, big data analytics having six technical types which are structured data analytics, text analytics, multimedia analytics, web analytics, mobile analytics and network analytics is clarified. Finally, Apache Hadoop, a software library and framework used for big data processing, is explained with its main components which are HDFS and MapReduce. As a future work, big data processing methods to be proposed and new Hadoop based components may be discussed.

Figure 8. Execution architecture of MapReduce

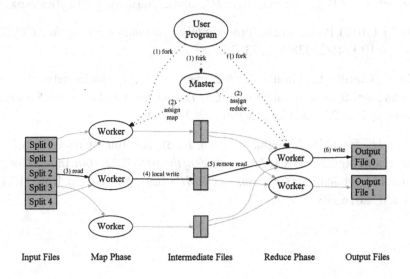

ACKNOWLEDGMENT

This research received no specific grant from any funding agency in the public, commercial, or not-for-profit sectors.

REFERENCES

Agerri, R., Artola, X., Beloki, Z., Rigau, G., & Soroa, A. (2015). Big data for Natural Language Processing: A streaming approach. *Knowledge-Based Systems*, *79*, 36–42. doi:10.1016/j.knosys.2014.11.007

Alvi, S. A., Afzal, B., Shah, G. A., Atzori, L., & Mahmood, W. (2015). Internet of multimedia things: Vision and challenges. *Ad Hoc Networks*, *33*, 87–111. doi:10.1016/j.adhoc.2015.04.006

Anderson, T. W. (2003). *An introduction to multivariate statistical analysis*. New York: Wiley.

Atzori, L., Carboni, D., & Iera, A. (2014). Smart things in the social loop: Paradigms, technologies, and potentials. *Ad Hoc Networks*, *18*, 121–132. doi:10.1016/j.adhoc.2013.03.012

Balinsky, H., Balinsky, A., & Simske, S. J. (2011, September). Automatic text summarization and small-world networks. In *Proceedings of the 11th ACM symposium on Document engineering* (pp. 175-184). ACM.

Blackett, G. (2013). *Analytics Network-O.R. Analytics*. Retrieved from http://www.theorsociety.com/ Pages/SpecialInterest/AnalyticsNetwork_anal%ytics.aspx

Blei, D. M. (2012). Probabilistic Topic Models. *Communications of the ACM*, *55*(4), 77–84. doi:10.1145/2133806.2133826

Bonchi, F., Castillo, C., Gionis, A., & Jaimes, A. (2011). Social network analysis and mining for business applications. *ACM Transactions on Intelligent Systems and Technology*, *2*(3), 22. doi:10.1145/1961189.1961194

Cakir, M. U., & Guldamlasioglu, S. (2016, June). Text mining analysis in Turkish language using big data tools. In *Proceedings of the 2016 IEEE 40th Annual Computer Software and Applications Conference (COMPSAC)* (pp. 614-618). IEEE. 10.1109/COMPSAC.2016.203

Can, U., & Alatas, B. (2019). A new direction in social network analysis: Online social network analysis problems and applications. *Physica A*, *535*, 122372. doi:10.1016/j.physa.2019.122372

Chakrabarti, S. (2000). Data mining for hypertext: A tutorial survey. *ACM SIGKDD Explorations Newsletter*, *1*(2), 1–11. doi:10.1145/846183.846187

Chamikara, M. A. P., Bertok, P., Liu, D., Camtepe, S., & Khalil, I. (2019). Efficient privacy preservation of big data for accurate data mining. *Information Sciences*. doi:10.1016/j.ins.2019.05.053

Chaudhuri, S., Dayal, U., & Narasayya, V. (2011). An overview of business intelligence technology. *Communications of the ACM*, *54*(8), 88–98. doi:10.1145/1978542.1978562

Chowdhury, G. G. (2003). Natural language processing. *Annual Review of Information Science & Technology*, *37*(1), 51–89. doi:10.1002/aris.1440370103

da Costa, K. A., Papa, J. P., Lisboa, C. O., Munoz, R., & de Albuquerque, V. H. C. (2019). Internet of Things: A survey on machine learning-based intrusion detection approaches. *Computer Networks*, *151*, 147–157. doi:10.1016/j.comnet.2019.01.023

Dean, J., & Ghemawat, S. (2008). MapReduce: Simplified data processing on large clusters. *Communications of the ACM*, *51*(1), 107–113. doi:10.1145/1327452.1327492

Ding, D., Metze, F., Rawat, S., Schulam, P. F., Burger, S., Younessian, E., ... Hauptmann, A. (2012, June). Beyond audio and video retrieval: towards multimedia summarization. In *Proceedings of the 2nd ACM International Conference on Multimedia Retrieval* (p. 2). ACM. 10.1145/2324796.2324799

dos Santos Garcia, C., Meincheim, A., Junior, E. R. F., Dallagassa, M. R., Sato, D. M. V., Carvalho, D. R., ... Scalabrin, E. E. (2019). Process Mining Techniques and Applications-A Systematic Mapping Study. *Expert Systems with Applications*, *133*, 260–295. doi:10.1016/j.eswa.2019.05.003

Dreisbach, C., Koleck, T. A., Bourne, P. E., & Bakken, S. (2019). A systematic review of natural language processing and text mining of symptoms from electronic patient-authored text data. *International Journal of Medical Informatics*, *125*, 37–46. doi:10.1016/j.ijmedinf.2019.02.008 PMID:30914179

Eyupoglu, C. (2019a). A two-level morphological description of Bashkir Turkish. *Computer Systems Science and Engineering*, *34*(3), 113–121.

Eyupoglu, C. (2019b). Big Data in Cloud Computing and Internet of Things. In *Proceedings of the 3rd International Symposium on Multidisciplinary Studies and Innovative Technologies*. IEEE.

Eyupoglu, C., Aydin, M. A., Sertbas, A., Zaim, A. H., & Ones, O. (2017). Büyük veride kişi mahremiyetinin korunması. *International Journal of Informatics Technologies*, *10*(2), 177–184.

Eyupoglu, C., Aydin, M. A., Zaim, A. H., & Sertbas, A. (2018). An efficient big data anonymization algorithm based on chaos and perturbation techniques. *Entropy, 20*(5), 373, 1-18.

Flume. (2019). *Apache Flume*. Retrieved from https://flume.apache.org/

Friedman, V. (2008). Data visualization and infographics. *Graphics. Monday Inspiration*, *14*, 2008.

Gaber, M. M., Zaslavsky, A., & Krishnaswamy, S. (2005). Mining data streams: A review. *SIGMOD Record*, *34*(2), 18–26. doi:10.1145/1083784.1083789

Ghani, N. A., Hamid, S., Hashem, I. A. T., & Ahmed, E. (2019). Social media big data analytics: A survey. *Computers in Human Behavior*, *101*, 417–428. doi:10.1016/j.chb.2018.08.039

Ghemawat, S., Gobioff, H., & Leung, S. T. (2003). The Google file system. In *Proceedings of the 19th ACM Symposium on Operating Systems Principles* (pp. 29-43). ACM.

Gudivada, V. N., Rao, D., & Raghavan, V. V. (2015). Big data driven natural language processing research and applications. In *Handbook of Statistics* (pp. 203–238). Elsevier.

Hadoop. (2019). *Apache Hadoop*. Retrieved from http://hadoop.apache.org/

Han, J., Pei, J., & Kamber, M. (2011). *Data mining: concepts and techniques*. Elsevier.

Hashem, I. A. T., Yaqoob, I., Anuar, N. B., Mokhtar, S., Gani, A., & Khan, S. U. (2015). The rise of "big data" on cloud computing: Review and open research issues. *Information Systems*, *47*, 98–115. doi:10.1016/j.is.2014.07.006

HCatalog. (2019). *Hive/HCatalog*. Retrieved from https://hortonworks.com/blog/hivehcatalog-data-geeks-big-data-glue/

Hinton, G. E. (2007). Learning multiple layers of representation. *Trends in Cognitive Sciences*, *11*(10), 428–434. doi:10.1016/j.tics.2007.09.004 PMID:17921042

Hu, H., Wen, Y., Chua, T. S., & Li, X. (2014). Toward scalable systems for big data analytics: A technology tutorial. *IEEE Access: Practical Innovations, Open Solutions*, *2*, 652–687. doi:10.1109/ACCESS.2014.2332453

Hu, W., Xie, N., Li, L., Zeng, X., & Maybank, S. (2011). A survey on visual content-based video indexing and retrieval. *IEEE Transactions on Systems, Man and Cybernetics. Part C, Applications and Reviews*, *41*(6), 797–819. doi:10.1109/TSMCC.2011.2109710

Ibrahim, N. F., & Wang, X. (2019). A text analytics approach for online retailing service improvement: Evidence from Twitter. *Decision Support Systems*, *121*, 37–50. doi:10.1016/j.dss.2019.03.002

Jan, B., Farman, H., Khan, M., Imran, M., Islam, I. U., Ahmad, A., ... Jeon, G. (2019). Deep learning in big data Analytics: A comparative study. *Computers & Electrical Engineering*, *75*, 275–287. doi:10.1016/j.compeleceng.2017.12.009

Jiang, F., Leung, C. K., & Pazdor, A. G. (2016, August). Big data mining of social networks for friend recommendation. In *Proceedings of the 2016 IEEE/ACM International Conference on Advances in Social Networks Analysis and Mining* (pp. 921-922). IEEE. 10.1109/ASONAM.2016.7752349

Joshi, A. K. (1991). Natural language processing. *Science*, *253*(5025), 1242–1249. doi:10.1126cience.253.5025.1242 PMID:17831443

Kafka. (2019). *Apache Kafka*. Retrieved from https://hortonworks.com/apache/kafka/

Kalavri, V., & Vlassov, V. (2013, July). Mapreduce: Limitations, optimizations and open issues. In *Proceedings of the 12th IEEE International Conference on Trust, Security and Privacy in Computing and Communications* (pp. 1031-1038). IEEE.

Kauffmann, E., Peral, J., Gil, D., Ferrández, A., Sellers, R., & Mora, H. (2019). A framework for big data analytics in commercial social networks: A case study on sentiment analysis and fake review detection for marketing decision-making. *Industrial Marketing Management*. doi:10.1016/j.indmarman.2019.08.003

Khan, N., Yaqoob, I., Hashem, I. A. T., Inayat, Z., Ali, W. K. M., Alam, M., ... Gani, A. (2014). Big data: Survey, technologies, opportunities, and challenges. *The Scientific World Journal*, *712826*, 1–18. PMID:25136682

Kumar, A., Srinivasan, K., Cheng, W. H., & Zomaya, A. Y. (2020). Hybrid context enriched deep learning model for fine-grained sentiment analysis in textual and visual semiotic modality social data. *Information Processing & Management*, *57*(1), 102141. doi:10.1016/j.ipm.2019.102141

Kumari, A., Tanwar, S., Tyagi, S., Kumar, N., Maasberg, M., & Choo, K. K. R. (2018). Multimedia big data computing and Internet of Things applications: A taxonomy and process model. *Journal of Network and Computer Applications*, *124*, 169–195. doi:10.1016/j.jnca.2018.09.014

Li, Y., Hu, X., Lin, H., & Yang, Z. (2010). A framework for semisupervised feature generation and its applications in biomedical literature mining. *IEEE/ACM Transactions on Computational Biology and Bioinformatics*, *8*(2), 294–307. PMID:20876938

Liu, B., & Zhang, L. (2012). A survey of opinion mining and sentiment analysis. In *Mining text data* (pp. 415–463). Boston, MA: Springer. doi:10.1007/978-1-4614-3223-4_13

Liu, X., Shin, H., & Burns, A. C. (2019). Examining the impact of luxury brand's social media marketing on customer engagement: Using big data analytics and natural language processing. *Journal of Business Research*. doi:10.1016/j.jbusres.2019.04.042

Manning, C. D., & Schütze, H. (1999). *Foundations of statistical natural language processing*. Cambridge, MA: MIT Press.

Marquez, J. L. J., Carrasco, I. G., & Cuadrado, J. L. L. (2018). Challenges and opportunities in analytic-predictive environments of big data and natural language processing for social network rating systems. *IEEE Latin America Transactions*, *16*(2), 592–597. doi:10.1109/TLA.2018.8327417

Mehmood, A., Natgunanathan, I., Xiang, Y., Hua, G., & Guo, S. (2016). Protection of big data privacy. *IEEE Access: Practical Innovations, Open Solutions*, *4*, 1821–1834. doi:10.1109/ACCESS.2016.2558446

Müller, H., & Freytag, J. C. (2005). *Problems, methods, and challenges in comprehensive data cleansing*. Professoren des Inst. Für Informatik.

Nenkova, A., & McKeown, K. (2012). A survey of text summarization techniques. In *Mining text data* (pp. 43–76). Boston, MA: Springer. doi:10.1007/978-1-4614-3223-4_3

Noy, N. F. (2004). Semantic integration: A survey of ontology-based approaches. *SIGMOD Record*, *33*(4), 65–70. doi:10.1145/1041410.1041421

Ohbe, T., Ozono, T., & Shintani, T. (2017, August). A sentiment polarity classifier for regional event reputation analysis. In *Proceedings of the International Conference on Web Intelligence* (pp. 1207-1213). ACM. 10.1145/3106426.3109416

Oozie. (2019). *Apache Oozie*. Retrieved from https://oozie.apache.org/

Ozbay, F. A., & Alatas, B. (2019). Fake news detection within online social media using supervised artificial intelligence algorithms. *Physica A*, 123174. doi:10.1016/j.physa.2019.123174

Pal, S. K., Talwar, V., & Mitra, P. (2002). Web mining in soft computing framework: Relevance, state of the art and future directions. *IEEE Transactions on Neural Networks*, *13*(5), 1163–1177. doi:10.1109/TNN.2002.1031947 PMID:18244512

Qin, S. J., & Chiang, L. H. (2019). Advances and opportunities in machine learning for process data analytics. *Computers & Chemical Engineering*, *126*, 465–473. doi:10.1016/j.compchemeng.2019.04.003

Reddick, C. G., Chatfield, A. T., & Ojo, A. (2017). A social media text analytics framework for double-loop learning for citizen-centric public services: A case study of a local government Facebook use. *Government Information Quarterly*, *34*(1), 110–125. doi:10.1016/j.giq.2016.11.001

Reinsel, D., Gantz, J., & Rydning, J. (2018). *The digitization of the world: from edge to core. IDC White Paper #US44413318*. Framingham: International Data Corporation. Retrieved from https://www.seagate.com/files/www-content/our-story/trends/files/idc-seagate-dataage-whitepaper.pdf

Ren, R., Tang, M., & Liao, H. (2019). Managing minority opinions in micro-grid planning by a social network analysis-based large scale group decision making method with hesitant fuzzy linguistic information. *Knowledge-Based Systems*, 105060. doi:10.1016/j.knosys.2019.105060

Report, E. M. (2018, November). *Mobile data traffic growth outlook*. Retrieved from https://www.ericsson.com/en/mobility-report/reports/november-2018/mobile-data-traffic-growth-outlook

Ritter, A., Clark, S., & Etzioni, O. (2011, July). Named entity recognition in tweets: an experimental study. In *Proceedings of the Conference on Empirical Methods in Natural Language Processing* (pp. 1524-1534). Association for Computational Linguistics.

Sadiq, B., Rehman, F. U., Ahmad, A., Rahman, M. A., Ghani, S., Murad, A., ... Lbath, A. (2015, November). A spatio-temporal multimedia big data framework for a large crowd. In *Proceedings of the 2015 IEEE International Conference on Big Data (Big Data)* (pp. 2742-2751). IEEE. 10.1109/BigData.2015.7364075

Sánchez-Rada, J. F., & Iglesias, C. A. (2019). Social context in sentiment analysis: Formal definition, overview of current trends and framework for comparison. *Information Fusion, 52,* 344–356. doi:10.1016/j.inffus.2019.05.003

Serna, A., & Gasparovic, S. (2018). Transport analysis approach based on big data and text mining analysis from social media. *Transportation Research Procedia, 33,* 291–298. doi:10.1016/j.trpro.2018.10.105

Shahare, F. F. (2017, June). Sentiment analysis for the news data based on the social media. In *Proceedings of the 2017 International Conference on Intelligent Computing and Control Systems (ICICCS)* (pp. 1365-1370). IEEE. 10.1109/ICCONS.2017.8250692

Shanthi, C., & Pappa, N. (2017). An artificial intelligence based improved classification of two-phase flow patterns with feature extracted from acquired images. *ISA Transactions, 68,* 425–432. doi:10.1016/j.isatra.2016.10.021 PMID:28209428

Shen, C. W., Chen, M., & Wang, C. C. (2019). Analyzing the trend of O2O commerce by bilingual text mining on social media. *Computers in Human Behavior, 101,* 474–483. doi:10.1016/j.chb.2018.09.031

Shvachko, K., Kuang, H., Radia, S., & Chansler, R. (2010). The hadoop distributed file system. In *Proceedings of the 26th Symposium on Mass Storage Systems and Technologies (MSST)* (pp. 1-10). IEEE.

Sivarajah, U., Irani, Z., Gupta, S., & Mahroof, K. (2019). Role of big data and social media analytics for business to business sustainability: A participatory web context. *Industrial Marketing Management.* doi:10.1016/j.indmarman.2019.04.005

Sqoop. (2019). *Apache Sqoop.* Retrieved from https://sqoop.apache.org/

Stieglitz, S., Dang-Xuan, L., Bruns, A., & Neuberger, C. (2014). Social media analytics-an interdisciplinary approach and its implications for information systems. *Business & Information Systems Engineering, 6*(2), 89–96. doi:10.100712599-014-0315-7

Stieglitz, S., Mirbabaie, M., Ross, B., & Neuberger, C. (2018). Social media analytics–Challenges in topic discovery, data collection, and data preparation. *International Journal of Information Management, 39,* 156–168. doi:10.1016/j.ijinfomgt.2017.12.002

Ucci, D., Aniello, L., & Baldoni, R. (2019). Survey of machine learning techniques for malware analysis. *Computers & Security, 81,* 123–147. doi:10.1016/j.cose.2018.11.001

Vashishtha, S., & Susan, S. (2019). Fuzzy rule based unsupervised sentiment analysis from social media posts. *Expert Systems with Applications, 138*, 112834. doi:10.1016/j.eswa.2019.112834

Wang, H., Xu, Z., & Pedrycz, W. (2017). An overview on the roles of fuzzy set techniques in big data processing: Trends, challenges and opportunities. *Knowledge-Based Systems, 118*, 15–30. doi:10.1016/j.knosys.2016.11.008

Wang, L., Sun, T., Qian, C., Goh, M., & Mishra, V. K. (2019). Applying social network analysis to genetic algorithm in optimizing project risk response decisions. *Information Sciences*.

Wang, M., Ni, B., Hua, X. S., & Chua, T. S. (2012). Assistive tagging: A survey of multimedia tagging with human-computer joint exploration. *ACM Computing Surveys, 44*(4), 25. doi:10.1145/2333112.2333120

Wang, W. L., Malthouse, E. C., Calder, B., & Uzunoglu, E. (2019). B2B content marketing for professional services: In-person versus digital contacts. *Industrial Marketing Management, 81*, 160–168. doi:10.1016/j.indmarman.2017.11.006

Wang, Y., & Hajli, N. (2017). Exploring the path to big data analytics success in healthcare. *Journal of Business Research, 70*, 287–299. doi:10.1016/j.jbusres.2016.08.002

White, T. (2009). *Hadoop: The Definitive Guide*. Sebastapol, CA: O'Reilly Media.

Wu, X., Kumar, V., Quinlan, J. R., Ghosh, J., Yang, Q., Motoda, H., ... Steinberg, D. (2008). Top 10 algorithms in data mining. *Knowledge and Information Systems, 14*(1), 1–37. doi:10.100710115-007-0114-2

Wu, X., Zhu, X., Wu, G. Q., & Ding, W. (2014). Data mining with big data. *IEEE Transactions on Knowledge and Data Engineering, 26*(1), 97–107. doi:10.1109/TKDE.2013.109

Xu, B., Bu, J., Chen, C., & Cai, D. (2012, April). An exploration of improving collaborative recommender systems via user-item subgroups. In *Proceedings of the 21st International Conference on World Wide Web* (pp. 21-30). ACM. 10.1145/2187836.2187840

Xu, G., Ngai, E. C. H., & Liu, J. (2018). Ubiquitous transmission of multimedia sensor data in Internet of Things. *IEEE Internet of Things Journal, 5*(1), 403–414. doi:10.1109/JIOT.2017.2762731

Yeo, H. (2018, December). A Machine Learning Based Natural Language Question and Answering System for Healthcare Data Search using Complex Queries. In *Proceedings of the 2018 IEEE International Conference on Big Data (Big Data)* (pp. 2467-2474). IEEE. 10.1109/BigData.2018.8622448

Yoo, S., Song, J., & Jeong, O. (2018). Social media contents based sentiment analysis and prediction system. *Expert Systems with Applications, 105*, 102–111. doi:10.1016/j.eswa.2018.03.055

Zhang, Q., Yang, L. T., Chen, Z., & Li, P. (2018). A survey on deep learning for big data. *Information Fusion, 42*, 146–157. doi:10.1016/j.inffus.2017.10.006

Zhu, W., Cui, P., Wang, Z., & Hua, G. (2015). Multimedia big data computing. *IEEE MultiMedia, 22*(3), 96–105. doi:10.1109/MMUL.2015.66

Chapter 6
A General Overview of RESTful Web Services

Eyuphan Ozdemir

(iD) https://orcid.org/0000-0002-4348-0783
Victoria University of Wellington, New Zealand

ABSTRACT

This chapter aims to present a general overview of today's dominant software architectural style for developing web services, namely REST, by comparing the core elements of this paradigm with the big web service model. The study evaluates the HTTP requests, responses, and thus, the SOAP/JSON payloads involved in consuming a big web service and a RESTful service that is developed in the ASP. NET Core Web API framework. After summarizing the REST constraints, the chapter elucidates how the example RESTful web service satisfies these constraints and lists some scenarios suited to each paradigm. The study notes the object-oriented elements that are inherent in RESTful services, specifically how polymorphism and abstraction principles can be applied to RESTful services.

INTRODUCTION

Web services are indispensable components of the programmable web. It is therefore of crucial importance that they are simple, efficient, scalable and maintainable. Although there are many ways to develop web services, they can be reduced to two major paradigms: The Big Web Services and RESTful services.

These paradigms are usually treated as rival methodologies for building web services. However, there is a considerable difference in the variety of solutions each paradigm offers. Unlike RESTful services, Big Web Services (hereafter, big

DOI: 10.4018/978-1-7998-2142-7.ch006

services) aim to work with different communication protocols and messaging exchange patterns. In this respect, comparing these paradigms is analogous to comparing a swiss army knife with a kitchen knife.

Apart from these general differences, they also differ in some more specific, fundamental regards, mostly related to the communication between the client and the web service. This chapter compares these paradigms not only in terms of their general characteristics and capabilities, but also in these specific regards. For such a comparison, the present study evaluates invocations of two example services, highlighting the most important differences between each paradigm in terms of difficulty in developing and consuming the web service, the way web methods are called and the payload submission and format. Another important aim of the study is to show in a concrete way how REST (Representational State Transfer) constraints are met by an ASP .Net Core RESTful service. The study also makes an overall comparison between paradigms, looking at the technical/technological capabilities and scenarios suited to each.

The resource-oriented nature of the RESTful paradigm makes it coherent with another dominant paradigm in software development: Object-Oriented software design. The current study aims to show in which senses RESTful services behave in an object-oriented way. The study also mentions some possibilities in which two important principles of Object-Oriented Programming (OOP) - Polymorphism and Abstraction - can be implemented by RESTful services.

The primary sections of this chapter are sequentially Big Services which focuses on three important disadvantages of big services, RESTful services which explains REST constraints and how to develop a web service with ASP.Net Core Web API framework in accordance with these constraints, and Overall Comparison between Big and RESTful Services Section.

BACKGROUND

A web service is defined by World Wide Web Consortium (W3C) as follows:

A Web service is a software system designed to support interoperable machine-to-machine interaction over a network. It has an interface described in a machine-processable format (specifically WSDL). Other systems interact with the Web service in a manner prescribed by its description using SOAP-messages, typically conveyed using HTTP with an XML serialization in conjunction with other Web-related standards. (Haas and Brown, 2004)

This definition appears outdated because of its central reference to SOAP (Simple Object Access Protocol) and XML (Extensible Markup Language). Nevertheless, it is useful to distinguish the first SOAP-based examples of web services from previous distributed object technologies. Among these technologies were DCOM (Distributed Component Object Model), CORBA (Common Object Request Broker Architecture) and Java RMI (Java Remote Method Invocation). However, these technologies failed to be efficient in terms of interoperability and security (Halili & Ramadani, 2018).

XML-RPC (XML-Remote Procedure Call) was designed as an alternative to these old technologies and can be seen as the prototype of today's modern web services in that it uses HTTP to transport the payload, supports request-response pattern, stores the payload in a text format and is interoperable. XML-RPC evolved to SOAP (Winer, 2002) which was almost the only game in the town before the emergence of RESTful services.[1] Today, RESTful and SOAP-based web services are the dominant web services, with the former being the most common (Gonzalo & Rakela, 2015; Santos, 2017).[2]

The W3C classifies web services into two categories: REST-compliant web services that manipulate representations of resources in a stateless manner and arbitrary web services that "may expose an arbitrary set of operations" (Booth et al., 2004). In a similar vein, Richardson and Ruby (2008) compare SOAP-based services with RESTful services in terms of how the web method and the data required by the method are indicated, rather than the messaging/envelope format the service uses. They consider SOAP and XML-RPC messages as describing RPC calls in that both contain arbitrary web method names and data the web method requires, whereas RESTful services determine the web method by the HTTP method of the request. This study also puts emphasis on the way the web method and the payload are indicated on the client-side and aims to show how SOAP-based and RESTful services differ from each other in this regard.

It is common to compare RESTFul services with SOAP Services. However, since SOAP is an envelope/messaging protocol and REST is an architectural style, this classification might be misleading, although the term is helpful in contrasting the typical SOAP-based services with RESTful services that do not depend on SOAP. Following Pautasso, Zimmermann, and Leymann (2008) and Richardson and Ruby (2008), any web service working with web service standards and specifications (such as SOAP, WSDL, WS-Notification, WS-Security and so on, which are collectively labeled as "WS-* stack") will be referred to as Big Web Services in the study.

As will be seen, Uniform Interface Constraint is the most distinctive REST constraint for a RESTful design. This general constraint involves four design principles: identification of resources, manipulation of resources through representations, self-descriptive messages, and hypermedia as the engine of the application state. Unsurprisingly, these four principles are given a special focus in the literature regarding REST. Thus, these principles, together with Statelessness, are listed as the five principles of a concrete ROA (Resource Oriented Architecture) in Richardson and Ruby (2008). Bouguettaya, Sheng, and Daniel (2014) list the same five principles as REST design constraints. These principles are treated as formulating REST in Fielding et al. (2017). Lastly, the Richardson Maturity Model also reflects this special focus on these principles. According to this model, three requirements for a web service to qualify as a RESTful service involve the addressability of resources, the use of various HTTP methods and connectedness (using hypermedia links) (Fowler, 2010). In parallel to these studies, this chapter also focuses on these principles and how they are implemented by the example ASP.NET Core RESTful service.

In the literature, it is common to compare Big Web Service with RESTful paradigms over four dimensions: the general features and capabilities, performance, relation to HTTP or web, and congruity with object-oriented software design.

Regarding general features and capabilities, RESTful services are simpler to develop, consume and maintain than big services. But, unlike big services, they support only HTTP and suffer from the lack of specific security and reliability models (Halili & Ramadani, 2018; Kumari, 2015; Wagh & Thool, 2012). Based on these reasons, RESTful services should be used for tactical, ad hoc integration over web whereas big services are more flexible and better for the enterprise application integration scenarios (Pautasso et al., 2008). These points are well recognized in the literature and will be echoed in the overall comparison of this study as well.

There is also a consensus on the better performance of RESTful services. The study briefly summarizes some recent studies that contrast the performance of RESTful services with that of big services (Kumari & Rath, 2015; Mumbaikar & Padiya, 2013; Tihomirovs & Grabis, 2016).

It is a well-recognized fact that RESTful services are much more compatible with HTTP, and thus the web logic (resource-based uniform interface and connectedness via hypermedia links), and that big services (mis)use HTTP only as a transport protocol, despite the fact that HTTP is an application layer protocol (Richardson & Ruby, 2008; Xiao-Hong, 2014). The study underlines the differences between the two paradigms in this dimension.

Another important difference between these paradigms is that the big service paradigm has a function-oriented nature (Gokhale et al., 2002), whereas the RESTful paradigm has an object-oriented nature ((Richardson & Ruby, 2008). This study provides some examples of how RESTful services behave in accordance with Polymorphism and Inheritance principles, and mentions some possibilities in which Polymorphism and Abstraction can be implemented by RESTful services.

BIG WEB SERVICES

This section will briefly explain both the relationship between big services and web service standards/specifications, plus how big services work. In so doing it will reveal three primary disadvantages of the big service paradigm.

Unlike RESTful services, big services work with standards and specifications that are collectively termed as WS-*. Among these specifications are three major components of a big service: UDDI, WSDL and SOAP. UDDI (Universal Description, Discovery, and Integration) is used to discover big web services. Clients can understand how to communicate with web services with the help of WSDL (Web Service Definition Language) files. The payload in this communication is enveloped in SOAP format. All these three components present their information in XML format.

The most important advantage of the big service paradigm is that it is independent of any network protocol and supports not only the request-response pattern, but also duplex and one-way messaging patterns. However big services have three major disadvantages. Firstly, the flexibility big services enjoy is provided at the cost of more complexity. Secondly, big services typically locate the payload in an extra envelope (SOAP envelope) within the request body. This makes the payload unnecessarily large and complex even for simple web methods. Lastly, big services cannot effectively benefit from HTTP features. The next three subsections will give concrete examples for these major downsides of the big service paradigm.

The Difficulty of Developing and Consuming the Service

Because big services are protocol-agnostic and contract-based services, and thus more extensible and complex, they are relatively difficult to develop even for basic functionality. The definition of different kinds of contracts/interfaces is usually required, as are configurations for both the server and the client-side. For example, WCF (Windows Communication Foundations) requires defining service contracts, operation contracts, data contracts, message contracts, data members, and so on. All these fine details are described in the service description file (WSDL file). Typically, the client application needs to access this WSDL file and create a service reference that includes the interfaces, classes and method signatures required for communicating with the service. Furthermore, since each further modification produces a new contract described in a new WSDL file, in most cases of modification to the web service the client must repeat this process.

A further difficulty is that the client-side must also put some information about how to call the service (such as the endpoints of the service) in the configuration file, while it is not unusual that the developer deals with some subtle details in the configuration files on both sides. The requirement to create service reference via WSDL file is not the only example of opacity and difficulty in consuming big services. This opacity can also be determined in the difficulty of calling a typical (non-AJAX enabled, non-RESTful) WCF service from JavaScript/AJAX code.

Big services have other disadvantages when it comes to handling data, mapping complex objects, and transferring files (Enríquez & Salazar, 2014). Enríquez & Salazar specify the difficulty in consuming a big service created in Java from a client developed in another language as follows:

In certain situations, even when consuming a web service created in Java from a .NET application, it ends up creating a service implemented in Java in the middle of both. This does not occur in RESTful web services, since in this case, the functionality is exposed through HTTP method invocations.

Complexity and Size Problem of the Payload

In order to see the other two problems with the Big Service paradigm - namely, complexity and largeness of the payload, and failure of the big service to use HTTP features - it would be helpful to evaluate the request, responses and SOAP messages when some sample methods in a simple big service (developed by WCF) are called by a client.

The sample service has two web methods: *GetEmployees* and *DeleteEmployee*. *GetEmployees* gets an integer argument called *departmentId* and will return an array of *Employee* objects. *Employee* class has *Id* and *name* properties. The sample method will return 5 employees in its response. The other method, *DeleteEmployee* needs an integer argument called *Id* to be passed and returns the deleted *Employee* object.

Big service frameworks send the payload in another envelope - the SOAP envelope - within the HTTP envelope. The data in the SOAP envelope is unnecessarily complex and large. This can be seen from the following request and response which were captured when the *GetEmployees* method of the service was called:

```
POST http://localhost:51663/EmployeeService.svc HTTP/1.1
Content-Type: text/xml;charset=UTF-8
Content-Length: 217
Host: localhost:51663
<soapenv:Envelope xmlns:soapenv="http://schemas.xmlsoap.org/
soap/envelope/" xmlns:tem="http://tempuri.org/">
   <soapenv:Header/>
   <soapenv:Body>
      <tem: GetEmployees >
         <tem: departmentId >1</tem: departmentId >
```

```
        </tem: GetEmployees>
     </soapenv:Body>
</soapenv:Envelope>
```

In this request, the first section before *soapenv* tag is the Header section. Among other details, this section provides some information about the HTTP method, URI of the service, request size, host and content type. Note that the HTTP method is POST and that the content type is XML. This is typical of the requests calling a big service.

The section below is the SOAP envelope located in the Body section of the request. This inner envelope also consists of a Header and a Body part. The large size of big services starts with this extra envelope. The proportion of the size of the data required by the web service (the length of *GetEmployees* plus the length of the value of *departmentId*) to the total size of the SOAP envelope is very small. This shows that the SOAP envelope uses more meta-data than the data itself in the case of simple web method calls.

The amount of the meta-data is even worse when it comes to the response. The response returned from the *GetEmployees* method is as follows:

```
HTTP/1.1 200 OK
Cache-Control: private
Content-Type: text/xml; charset=utf-8
Server: Microsoft-IIS/10.0
...
<s:Envelope xmlns:s="http://schemas.xmlsoap.org/soap/
envelope/">
  <s:Header>
  </s:Header>
  <s:Body>
    <GetEmployeesResponse xmlns="http://tempuri.org/">
      <GetEmployeesResult xmlns:a="http://schemas.datacontract.
org/2004/07/WCFSampleService" xmlns:i="http://www.w3.org/2001/
XMLSchema-instance">
        <a:Employee>
          <a:Id>1</a:Id>
          <a:Name>John</a:Name>
        </a:Employee>
        <a:Employee>
          <a:Id>2</a:Id>
          <a:Name>Suzan</a:Name>
```

```
          </a:Employee>
          <a:Employee>
            <a:Id>3</a:Id>
            <a:Name>Justin</a:Name>
          </a:Employee>
          <a:Employee>
            <a:Id>4</a:Id>
            <a:Name>Jonathan</a:Name>
          </a:Employee>
          <a:Employee>
            <a:Id>5</a:Id>
            <a:Name>Simon</a:Name>
          </a:Employee>
        </GetEmployeesResult>
      </GetEmployeesResponse>
    </s:Body>
</s:Envelope>
```

Field names (*Id* and *Name*) are repeated for each *Employee* object. Moreover, the values of these fields, which are the only substantial data, are in the 5. level in the XML hierarchy of the SOAP message following the *Envelope*, *Body*, *GetEmployeesResponse* and *GetEmployeesResult* elements, respectively.

Limited Use of HTTP Features

Since they are operation-oriented, typical big services use arbitrary method names when they indicate the web method, while different web method calls target the same service URI without mentioning resources. This is against the general resource-oriented logic of the web. In web logic, the client-side indicates the resource by URI and the method by the selected HTTP method. URIs are also often used to pass arguments to the web method. This logic provides web applications with a uniform interface and can provide the same uniformity to web services if the logic is followed in an orthodox way. The approach of big services is exactly the opposite of this canonical web model: It targets the same service URI that has no reference to the relevant resource, uses arbitrary web method names and tends to use the same HTTP method (POST).

This can be seen from the request above. The URI of the request, *http:// localhost:51663/EmployeeService.svc*, is the name of the service itself, showing that URIs of the big service calls remain the same no matter which method is called, since the web method (*<tem:GetEmployees/>*) and the arguments of the method (*<tem: departmentId >1</tem: departmentId>*) are indicated in the SOAP message.

The payload is typically sent to the server with POST method in big services. This tendency to use POST for any type of call is against the HTTP 1.1 specification according to which different HTTP methods should be used for different kinds of operations (Fielding et al., 2006). For instance, DELETE should be used to delete a resource, PUT should be used to update a resource.

Even for simple web methods, rather than passing data in URIs, big services also tend to use inflated XML-based SOAP data in the request body. For example, the SOAP message that is sent to the big service in order to delete an employee with the Id of 2 is as follows:

```
<soapenv:Envelope xmlns:soapenv="http://schemas.xmlsoap.org/
soap/envelope/" xmlns:tem="http://tempuri.org/">
   <soapenv:Header/>
   <soapenv:Body>
      <tem:DeleteEmployee>
         <tem:id>2</tem:id>
      </tem:DeleteEmployee>
   </soapenv:Body>
</soapenv:Envelope>
```

Note that the HTTP method (POST) and the URI (*http://localhost:51663/ EmployeeService.svc*) are the same as that of the previous request that calls *GetEmployees* method. However, the SOAP message of the request now refers to *DeleteEmployee* as the method information and *2* for the *Id* argument.

RESTFUL SERVICES

This section will define REST, articulate REST constraints, summarize the major components and processes in RESTful architecture, explain how to develop a simple web service with ASP .Net Core Web API framework in accordance with REST constraints, and give some examples of the object-oriented nature of RESTful services.

Although the term REST is used mostly for web services, REST is a coordinated set of architectural constraints for any kind of distributed information systems (Fielding, 2000). RESTful web services are applications of the REST philosophy to web services.

REST dates back to Roy Fielding's seminal dissertation. Fielding (2000) explains the close relationship between the general logic of web and REST, as well as what exactly "Representational State Transfer" means, as follows:

The name Representational State Transfer is intended to evoke an image of how a well-designed Web application behaves: a network of web pages (a virtual state-machine), where the user progresses through the application by selecting links (state transitions), resulting in the next page (representing the next state of the application) being transferred to the user and rendered for their use.

Fielding's dissertation presents five mandatory constraints for a fully RESTful compliant application and an optional constraint.

REST Constraints

The *Client-Server* constraint states that the client and the server should not depend on each other. In other words, the client-side and the server-side should be as loosely coupled as possible. Thus, RESTful services are more transparent than big services in that there is no need for WSDL or SOAP, and even an HTML file with some AJAX code can call a REST service. Due to this loose coupling between the client and the server in a RESTful web service, if you change something about the web method or its arguments, it might be enough for the client to change only the URI in order to adapt to this change.

The *Statelessness* constraint is described by Fielding (2000) as follows:

Each request from client to server must contain all of the information necessary to understand the request and cannot take advantage of any stored context on the server.

This is one of the most important REST principles not only for web services but also for web applications/web sites. HTTP, thus web, is stateless in nature. In other words, each web request is treated independently. However, most web applications and some web services hold information about the client or about the previous requests and need this information to perform the subsequent requests. Session variables are typical examples used for stateful applications. This constraint forbids all types of state. Fielding, for instance, considers cookies to be violating this constraint.

The *Cacheability* constraint states that the client-side should be able to understand from the response whether it can use the data in the response for later, identical requests. This reusable data is called cacheable data. The type of caching mentioned in this constraint is Response Caching (or HTTP Caching), in which web browsers can use the cached version of the resource according to the *Cache-Control* header of the response (Luo, Anderson, Smith, & Latham, 2019). Regarding cacheability, because the URIs of big service requests do not refer to a specific resource and thus the caching mechanism cannot know which resource to cache, REST architecture has a great advantage over big services. Moreover, as stated, big services typically make POST requests which browsers do not usually cache (MozDevNet, 2019).

The *Layered System* constraint specifies that A RESTful design allows the use of intermediaries between the client and the web service. These intermediaries are useful in modularizing the service and thus improving maintainability. Intermediaries should not break other REST constraints, such as statelessness and the separation of concerns between the client and the server. That is to say, the client should not need to know with which intermediaries it is communicating.

The *Uniform Interface* is the central constraint of the REST paradigm. A uniform interface simplifies and decouples the architecture of the whole system, thereby enabling each part of the system to evolve independently and increasing the visibility of interactions (Fielding, 2000).

This constraint requires implementing another four important constraints: *Identification of Resources, Manipulation of Resources through Representations, Self-Descriptive Messages,* and *Hypermedia as the Engine of Application State (HATEOAS)*.

Fielding (2000) defines resources as "any concept that might be the target of an author's hypertext reference" such as documents, images, entities, collections of resources and even a temporal service (e.g. "today's weather in Los Angeles"). The *Identification of Resources* constraint states that each resource should have a unique and consistent identifier. Any resource, such as, for example, a department in a company, should be accessible by the same URI. Different methods should address this fixed URI, as in the following web calls that access the information about the software department and delete it, respectively:

```
GET http://example.com/department/software
DELETE http://example.com/department/software
```

As can be noted, the expression of *department/software* functions as a persistent path that points to the same resource, namely the software department. In other words, the address of the software department is fixed and should be unique in the service ontology. The addressability of resources and representations is an important principle that RESTful services need to satisfy. This principle can be formulated as follows: a URI should represent one and only one resource, and every representation of a resource should have its own address/URI.

The *Manipulation of Resources through Representations* constraint states that communication between the components in REST architecture communicates through the representations of the resources (Fielding, 2000). A representation of a resource is a presentation of the resource in a specific format. This format might be the same format as the original format of the resource (e.g. a JPEG file) or a different one such as JSON or XML but in any case, this should not affect the communication between the client and the server.

Representations of resources can travel in two directions: from the server to the client and from the client to the server. In the first direction, the web service should be able to serialize and return the resource in the format that the client requested and can understand. This capability of the service is called *Content Negotiation* (Wasson, 2012). *Content Negotiation* is closely related to the addressability principle because it enables each different representation of the same resource to have its own address. To illustrate, we can imagine XML and JSON representations of the same software department that is addressed as, say, */department/software*. In this case, the client should be able to retrieve both types of representations by setting the *Accept* header of the request either to *application/XML* or *application/JSON*, or by calling an extended address that includes the address of the software department (*/department/software*) plus the extension of the representation format (*.XML* or *.JSON*). Thus, */department/software.XML* refers to the XML version of the software department, while */department/software.JSON* targets the JSON version. In the second direction, the server should also respect the media format of the payload that the client indicates in the *Content-Type* header of the request. In this way, the server can manipulate the resource through representations without binding itself to a single specific format.

According to the *Self-Descriptive Messages* constraint, for the request to be self-descriptive, standard HTTP methods and media types should be used, and the communication should be stateless. Moreover, the response should clearly indicate whether the desired resource is cacheable or not.

Standard methods mentioned here are HTTP methods such as GET, POST, DELETE, etc. each of which should be used for performing different operations. Table 1 lists the most commonly used HTTP methods, their conventional functions (Fielding et al., 2006) and some sample usages of them.

There are some important conventions about identifying the most appropriate HTTP method: GET and HEAD methods are safe methods in that they do not alter the resource in any way. GET, HEAD, PUT and DELETE methods are idempotent methods because, after the initial execution of these methods, re-execution of them does not further change the resource (Fielding et al., 2006). Only these idempotent methods should be used for idempotent operations. POST, for example, should not be used to perform any operation that is supposed to be idempotent.

Media types, also known as MIME (Multipurpose Internet Mail Extensions) types, such as *Application/XML* or *Text/CSV* are indicated by the *Accept* and *Content-Type*

Table 1. HTTP methods and usual functions

HTTP Method	Function	Example
GET	Reads the information about the resource.	To retrieve information about the software department: GET http://www.example.com/departments/software
POST	Creates a new subordinate resource and/or submits form data, posts articles, messages, etc.	To create a new department: POST http://www.example.com/departments
PUT	Updates a resource (or creates if the URI points to a resource that does not exist)	To update the software department: PUT http://www.example.com/departments/software
DELETE	Deletes a resource	To delete the software department DELETE http://www.example.com/departments/software

headers of the request and the *Content-Type* header of the response. *Cacheability* is provided through the *Cache-Control* header of the request and response. The values of these headers and the HTTP method collectively make the message self-descriptive.

Arguably, the most obvious and important differences between big services and RESTful services are in terms of this constraint and the constraint of Identification of Resource. As Figure 1 illustrates, typical big services tend to use the same HTTP method, (POST), and the same URI for different web method calls, while storing both web method description and parameters required for the web method in the SOAP envelope within the request body. They cannot benefit from HTTP Caching. On the other hand, RESTful services use the most appropriate HTTP method, pass simple parameters in the URI which clearly point to the relevant resource, and can use HTTP caching.

The *Hypermedia as the Engine of Application State (HATEOAS)* constraint, like other REST constraints, aims to make web services more similar to the web. Hypermedia links are the central components of the web sites/applications. They are located in the web pages that are sent back to the clients in response to their requests. With the help of hyperlinks, the user can navigate other resources on the web site. HATEOS simply refers to the same expectation from a web service: RESTful services should return hypermedia links in their responses. In this way, RESTful services can transfer the application states as hypermedia links to the client in their responses.

To illustrate, imagine that the client makes the following web service call:

Figure 1. Messaging in big and RESTful services

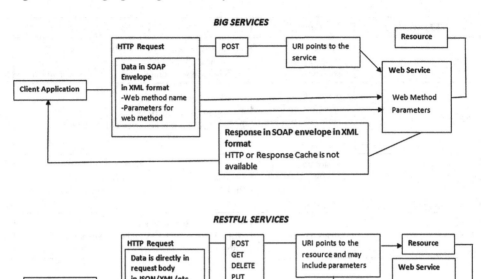

GET http://example.com/departments/software

The web service is supposed to return some information about the software department, but according to HATEOAS constraint it should also return some links pointing to possible states/resources into which the client can move. For example, in response to the request above, the payload of the response can include the following links:

GET http://example.com/departments/software/employees
DELETE http://example.com/departments/software

In this way, the client can navigate the employees of the software department by following the first link or can delete the software department by following the second link.

The web server typically returns non-executable data in specific formats such as JSON or XML, but according to the *Code-on-Demand* constraint, which is the only optional constraint in the REST architecture, the server can also send some executable code such as JavaScript code. This constraint is similar to HATEOS constraint in that it allows the web service to transfer additional functionality to the client.

In this section, REST constraints and some related concepts such as *Content Negotiation* were explained. Figure 2 illustrates how these constraints and concepts take place in the life cycle of HTTP requests and responses, thereby summarizing the working mechanism of a typical RESTful service.

As can be seen, a variety of clients running on different platforms can send HTTP requests which might first be welcomed by proxy servers. The request can be subjected to authentication and rate limit (the limit regarding the amount of data in the request or the number of request) controls. The caching filter checks if a cached response is already available. The request details can be logged. When the request reaches the RESTful service, the service determines the relevant web method, collects the parameters (required for the web method) from the request and creates the response. The response payload might be built with the help of microservices.[4] The service determines the payload format (content negotiation), can paginate the payload, add some links (HATEOAS), response status codes and other information (such as the values of cache-related headers) to the response. Finally, the client receives the response.

The next subsection briefly explains how some of these processes or concepts (such as content negotiation, request routing, collecting parameters from the request, caching and HATEOAS) can be implemented.

Developing and Observing a RESTful Service

In this subsection, a basic example of the development of a RESTFul service will be given, the communication between the client and the web service will be evaluated,

Figure 2. Main components and processes in RESTful service architecture [3]

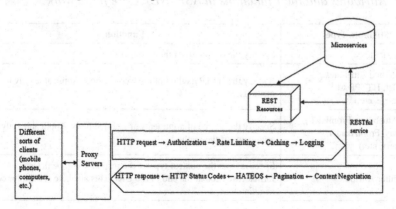

and how the example service implements REST constraints will be shown. The sample RESTful service will be developed in ASP.Net Core Web API framework, which is becoming increasingly popular in the development of RESTful services.

ASP.NET Core is a cross-platform and open-source framework for the development of web applications, web services and mobile applications (Anderson, Roth, & Luttin, 2019). The core element of the framework is the controller class that handles HTTP requests and directs them to a specific web method.

The framework uses conventions, automatic model binding and content negotiation mechanisms together with route/method/source/format attributes to build a RESTful service. Here are some important conventions:

- All of the public methods in a controller class are accepted as web methods.
- If the controller class name is *XController*, the service endpoint is set to X. If the class name is *EmployeesController*, for example, the service endpoint is set to http://example.com/employees
- Any method starting with an HTTP method name welcomes the request with that method. Thus, if the HTTP method of the request is DELETE, any method starting with "Delete", such as *DeleteEmployee,* is invoked.

With the help of these conventions, only a controller class that includes some public methods whose names start with an HTTP method can serve as a web service. The above-mentioned attributes can be used to further configure the service. These attributes can be applied to a specific web method if they are used just before the web method signature, or to all web methods if they are used just before the class definition. Table 2 shows the functions of these attributes:

Another way of implementing content negotiation is by using the *Accept* header of the request. Thus, the service returns the requested resource in XML format if

Table 2. Attributes and their functions in ASP .NET Core framework

Attribute Type	Function
Route Attributes	Specify the endpoints of the web methods
HTTP Method Attributes (HTTPGet, HTTPPost, HTTPDelete, etc.)	Specify the HTTP method of the web method. Applicable only to web methods.
Source Attributes (FromURL, FromBody, FromHeader, FromQuery, etc.)	Specify the source of arguments of web methods. Applicable only to arguments of the method.
FormatFilter Attribute	Specifies that the content type of the response will be determined by the format extension at the end of the URI. This attribute is used for content negotiation.

this header is set to *application/XML*, and it returns JSON representation if it is *application/JSON*. If this header is not present in the request, the framework assumes that the client desires the resource in JSON format.

It is also possible to welcome the payload of the request in different formats by looking at the *Content-Type* header of the request. Following the same logic as above, if the content-type of the request is *application/XML*, for example, the framework would understand that the payload is presented in XML format.

The ASP.NET Core Web API framework is also flexible when it comes to collecting the values of the arguments of web methods from the request. Collecting data from the request and converting this data from String to the corresponding .NET type is called Model Binding (Anderson, 2019). The model binding mechanism can collect the data from the request body, request headers, form values, path parameters and query string in the URI. The data source of the argument can be specified by decorating the argument with the source attributes. If there is no source attribute for an argument, the framework will do its best and look at all the sources available to find any value whose variable name matches the argument name.

Unlike the development of big services, the development of an ASP.NET RESTful service does not require the definition of service endpoints and contracts and does not need WSDL or any type of configuration. With the help of conventions, a class that extends the *ControllerBase* class and has some web methods is ready to serve.

The sample RESTful service exemplifies GET, POST, PUT and DELETE methods and works on the same Employee list (containing 5 employees) that was used in the sample big service. The *EmployeesController* service class is decorated with the route attribute of *[Route("API/employees")]* in order to indicate that the starting URI of the service is *api/employees*. The method signatures, with their attributes and brief explanations of them, are as follows:

- *public ActionResult<List<Employee>> Get([FromQuery]string search=""):* As indicated by its name (*Get*), this method will be invoked when the HTTP method is GET. It will return a list of employees. The method takes an optional argument called *search* to filter the results. Because of the source filter, *[FromQuery]*, the value of search will be collected from the query string. This method will be invoked by the default URI of the service (*api/employees*) because the method does not use any route attribute.
- [FormatFilter] [Route("{id}.{format?}")] *public ActionResult<EmployeeWithLinks> GetWithLinks(int id):* This method will be invoked when the HTTP method is GET and the URI is, for instance, */api/employees/1, /api/employees/1.json,* or */api/employees/1.xml,* in accordance with the route attribute stated before the method signature. It will return the specified employee along with some links.

- [HttpPut("{id}")] *public ActionResult<Employee> Put(int id, [FromBody] Employee emp):* It will run when the HTTP method is PUT and the URI is */api/employees/1,* for instance. The method will update the specified employee and return the updated employee. The model binding mechanism of the framework will automatically create an Employee object by collecting data from the request body.
- [HttpDelete("{id}")] *public ActionResult<Employee> Delete(int id):* This method will run when the HTTP method is DELETE and the URI is, say, */api/employees/1. It will* delete the specified employee and return the deleted employee.

Conventions, route/method/source/format attributes, automatic model binding and content-negotiation mechanisms make the development process for a RESTful service simpler than for big services. However, also important are the ease with which RESTful services can be consumed, and ease of communication between the client and the service. These will be addressed in the next two subsections.

The Simplicity of Consuming the Service

Consuming a RESTful service is easier than consuming big services because the client only needs to know the endpoint URI, required HTTP method type and web method signature. Moreover, RESTful services do not need to build and parse SOAP messages. Instead, the default message format for RESTful services is JSON which, mainly because it is this format that JavaScript uses to represent objects in a concise way, became the standard messaging format for communication between the components of a distributed system. Because of their greater transparency, and unlike typical big services, RESTful services can be consumed easily by any type of client that can make HTTP requests. As noted, even an HTML file that has some JavaScript (AJAX) code can consume a RESTful service.

Lastly, there is a loose coupling between the client and the RESTful service. Because the RESTful service determines the web method depending on the HTTP method, rather than the web method name, even if the name of the web method was altered, the client code would still run properly. In the case of consuming a big service, the client code would first need to update the WSDL reference and then change the method name on the client-side code, because the SOAP message would need to refer to the new web method name.

The Simplicity of Request and Payload in RESTful Services

Remember that when the sample big service call requested all the employees, the payload was enveloped in SOAP format and was unnecessarily complex and large. A sample request that calls a RESTful service for the same purpose would be as follows:

```
GET http://localhost:65386/api/employees/ HTTP/1.1
User-Agent: Fiddler
Host: localhost:65386
```

There is no extra envelope and the HTTP method is GET rather than POST. RESTful services work with simpler HTTP requests. Similarly, the response to this request does not use an extra envelope and presents the payload in JSON format as follows:

```
[{"id":1,"name":"John"},
 {"id":2,"name":"Suzan"},
 {"id":3,"name":"Justin"},
 {"id":4,"name":"Jonathan"},
 {"id":5,"name":"Simon"}]
```

Note that JSON representation is lightweight because it includes very limited meta-data. The same simplicity also holds for calling the service with other HTTP methods. For example, if the URI *http://localhost:65386/api/employees/1* was called with the PUT method, the request body would be

```
{"id":1,"name":"eyuphanModified"}
```

Alternatively, only using PUT method with the following URI that includes a query parameter would be enough.

```
http://localhost:65386/api/employees/1/name=eyuphanModified
```

Note again that the capability of using HTTP methods and URIs makes RESTful services more similar to the web applications/sites.

Identification of Resources and Self-Descriptive Messages

In the example RESTful service, every resource has its unique URI. This considerably increases the uniformity of interface and makes the web service calls self-descriptive.

As a result, after looking at some examples, it is easy to understand how to retrieve information about a specific resource and how to call other web methods. This is because each operation is performed on well-specified resource addresses, and the web methods are selected to run in accordance with the conventions regarding the HTTP methods. Table 3 shows this.

Note that the URI pattern *api/employees/{id}* serves as the starting point for dealing with an employee. As *api/employees/1/ContactInfo* exemplifies, any employee-related resource can be called after indicating this starting point. Note also that how to create, delete, update and retrieve resources can quite easily be surmised. For instance, it is obvious that the following web method call deletes a department with the id 3:

```
DELETE api/departments/3
```

Content Negotiation

RESTful services should determine the format of the response payload according to the *Accept* header of the HTTP request or the extension of the URI. The satisfaction of this requirement can be seen in the following example.

The request below tells the service that it demands the response in XML format.

Table 3. Self-descriptive messages with URIs and HTTP methods

Operation	URI	Required HTTP Method
Retrieve the collection of all employees	api/employees/	GET
Retrieve the collection of all employees whose names contain the search term	api/employees?search={searchTerm}	GET
Retrieve information about a specific employee	api/employees/{id}	GET
Create a new resource to the employee repository/collection	api/employees	POST
Update an employee	api/employees/{id}	PUT
Delete an employee	api/employees/{id}	DELETE
Retrieve the contact information of the specified employee	api/employees/{id}/contactInfo	GET

```
GET http://localhost:65386/api/employees/ HTTP/1.1
...
Accept: application/xml
```

The service complies and returns the following response:

```
HTTP/1.1 200 OK
Transfer-Encoding: chunked
Content-Type: application/xml; charset=utf-8
...
<ArrayOfEmployee xmlns:xsi="http://www.w3.org/2001/XMLSchema-
instance" xmlns:xsd="http://www.w3.org/2001/XMLSchema">
    <Employee>
        <Id>1</Id>
        <Name>John</Name>
    </Employee>
    <Employee>
        <Id>2</Id>
        <Name>Suzan</Name>
    </Employee>
    <Employee>
        <Id>3</Id>
        <Name>Justin</Name>
    </Employee>
    <Employee>
        <Id>4</Id>
        <Name>Jonathan</Name>
    </Employee>
    <Employee>
        <Id>5</Id>
        <Name>Simon</Name>
    </Employee>
</ArrayOfEmployee>
```

Note that the content type of the response is the same as the *Accept* header of the request, which is *application/XML*.

The other way of achieving content negotiation is by appending the extension of the desired format (such as *.XML* or *.JSON*) to the end of the URI. In this way, whether or not the content is returned in the specified format can be tested with web browsers.[5] For instance, calling *http://localhost:65386/api/employees/1.xml* would return the following employee with the *Id* 1 in XML format as follows:

```
<EmployeeWithLinks xmlns:xsi="http://www.w3.org/2001/XMLSchema-
instance" xmlns:xsd="http://www.w3.org/2001/XMLSchema">
    <employee>
        <Id>1</Id>
        <Name>John Brown</Name>
    </employee>
    <Links>
        <Link>
            <Href>/1/ContactInfo</Href>
            <Rel>ContactInfo of the employee</Rel>
            <Method>GET</Method>
        </Link>
        <Link>
            <Href>/1</Href>
            <Rel>DELETE the employee</Rel>
            <Method>DEL</Method>
        </Link>
        <Link>
            <Href>/1</Href>
            <Rel>Update the employee</Rel>
            <Method>PUT</Method>
        </Link>
    </Links>
</EmployeeWithLinks>
```

Because it enables different representations of the same resources to have specific addresses and makes the URI more self-descriptive and readable by explicitly stating the desired format, content negotiation increases the addressability and self-descriptiveness of the service.

HATEOAS

According to the HATEOAS constraint, web services should transfer some possible states/resources related to the requested resource. As can be noted, the response above includes not only employee information, but also some links related to the requested resource (the employee with the *Id* of 1 in this case).

The first link states that the URI of *http://localhost:65386/api/employees/1/ ContactInfo* can be called with the GET method to retrieve the contact information of the employee in question. Similarly, the second and third link state that the same resource can be deleted and updated with DELETE and PUT methods by using the respective URIs.

Cacheability

The sample controller class is decorated with the following attribute:

```
[ResponseCache(Duration = 30)]
```

This attribute simply adds a *Cache-Control* header to the response, as shown in the following example:

```
Cache-Control: public,max-age=30
Content-Type: application/JSON; charset=utf-8
...
```

This is a simple example of how to perform response caching (a.k.a HTTP Cache) in ASP.NET Core WEB API framework. The *ResponsseCache* attribute states that web browsers should use the cached version of any response that is returned from any web methods in the specified controller class for 30 seconds. In other words, the client should not really call the web service in the next 30 seconds. Instead, they should simply return the cached response. This attribute can also be used for web methods individually.

Object-Oriented Nature of RESTful Services

As noted, in the ontology of RESTful service, every resource is given an address, a unique URI, and the client targets the objects/resources via these URIs. For example, *api/employees/1* points to a particular object, in this case an employee. All operations concerning an employee can be done by calling this object/URI. Since, just as objects have fixed memory addresses and methods in OOP, resources have fixed addresses and (HTTP) methods, this makes the whole logic of the service object-orientated.

RESTful services call web methods in an object-oriented way (Richardson & Ruby, 2008). For example, The URI *api/employees/1* with *GET* method in a RESTful service resembles the statement *employee1.Get( )* in an OOP language. On the other hand, in the function-oriented spirit of big services, the SOAP message, which contains the method name and the arguments, is, as it were, passed to a common function that calls the web service. Thus, the web service request in big services is similar to the statement *CallWebService("GetEmployee",1)*.

RESTful services are also inherently polymorphic because the same HTTP method, say GET, behaves differently depending on the type of the object/resource. If the type of object is Employee, for instance, the *Get* method of Employee is invoked, whereas the *Get* method of Department is invoked if the type of the object is Department.

Two different representations returned from *api/employees/1.xml* and *api/employees/1.json*, for example, can be thought of as resources/objects of two different types, (Employee-as-XML and Employee-as-JSON), that inherit the same base type (Employee). This can be regarded as an example of the Inheritance principle of OOP. This can also be thought of as an example of Polymorphism because the same GET method behaves differently depending on the type (Employee-as-XML or Employee-as-JSON) that inherits the base type Employee.

Table 4 summarizes the points above.

OVERALL COMPARISON BETWEEN BIG AND RESTFUL SERVICES

This section will make an overall comparison between the big service and the RESTful paradigms in terms of the primary differences in general approaches, technical/technological differences and performance. Based on the details provided in the previous sections, the general characteristics of both paradigms can be summarized as follows in Table 5.

Table 6 lists technical differences including those that have not yet been covered, mostly with the help of Pautasso et al. (2008).

Table 4. OOP and RESTful services

	OOP	**RESTful Service**
Object	employee1	api/employees/1
Method call	employee1.Get()	api/employees/1 with GET method
Polymorphism	object.Get() method behaves differently when the object is an employee or a department	The same method, GET, behaves differently for api/employees/1 and api/departments/1
Inheritance and Polymorphism	EmployeeXML and EmployeeJSON classes inherit the Employee class. employee.Get() behaves differently when the type of employee is EmployeeXML or EmployeeJSON.	api/employees/1.XML and api/employees/1.JSON inherit api/employees/1. The same method GET behaves differently for api/employees/1.XML and api/employees/1.JSON.

Table 5. General differences between big services and RESTful services

Big Services	RESTful Services
Operation-oriented	Resource oriented
Full of standards (WSDL, SOAP, UDDI, etc.) establishing several specifications (such as WS-Addressing, WS-Discovery, WS-Federation, WS-Security)	No binding standard or specification.
Contract-oriented	Convention-oriented
Independent from HTTP	Powered by HTTP
Relatively strict coupling between the client and the server	Loose coupling
Complexity for enhanced extensibility	Simplicity for performance and scalability
RPC style web method invocation	Purely HTTP requests
Stateless or stateful depending on the transport protocol and the design	Stateless in principle

As can be noted from both tables, big services offer more extensible, secure, reliable and standardized solutions. However, this makes them more complex, slow and difficult to maintain and scale. Since Big Web Service paradigm is designed to support many protocols apart from HTTP, big services cannot benefit from HTTP features in a native and effective way.

On the contrary, RESTful services capitalize on HTTP methods, resource-oriented URL patterns, HTTP headers, and so on. Since they do not need any extra standard, configuration, or envelope, they are more scalable, faster, simpler and easier to develop and maintain. However, the most important disadvantages of RESTful services are also due to this practical dependency on HTTP, although REST constraints can in theory be implemented for other protocols. They offer endpoints only for HTTP and implement only the request-response exchange pattern.

Further, the simplicity of RESTful services comes with a downside: unlike big services, since they do not rely on any standard for security, reliability, service description and discovery, RESTful services are more susceptible to behave in arbitrary ways even if all REST constraints are satisfied.

When it comes to performance, there is a consensus on the better performance of RESTful services over big services. Mumbaikar and Padiya (2013) compare a SOAP-based service with a RESTful one by measuring the message sizes and response times of the representative services. They conclude that RESTful services have better performance mainly because of their smaller payloads. Kumari & Rath (2015) observe that RESTful services have better throughput and response times.

Table 6. Technical differences between big services and RESTful services

	Big Services	RESTful Services
Payload format	XML (SOAP)	Primarily JSON but supports any desired format such as XML
Supported transport protocols	Any protocol in principle: HTTP, TCP, SMTP, MSMQ, etc.	HTTP (but not limited to HTTP in principle)
Service identification	URI and WS-Addressing	URI
Service description	WSDL is used (but not necessary)	No binding definition but WADL or any other definition can be used.
Service discovery	UDDI	No standard
Security	HTTPS and WS-Reliability	HTTPS
Reliability	HTTPR, WS-Reliability, WS-Reliable Messaging, etc.	HTTPR (Reliable Hyper Text Transfer Protocol)
Message exchange patterns	Request-Response, One-way, duplex messaging	Only Request-Response
Using HTTP methods for identification of the web method	Not available because it is independent from HTTP. Also tends to overly use POST method.	Strongly relies on using different HTTP methods.
Using URL patterns	-	Extensively uses path parameters and query parameters
Resource relationship	-	HATEOAS
HTTP Cache	-	Natively supported
Approach to data	It makes data available as resource	It makes data available as services (Kumari, 2015)
Responsibility of invocation the web method, encoding the data and managing the connection	A layer of middleware between the client and the service is responsible	Client is responsible (Navarro & da Silva, 2016)

Lastly, it is found that RESTful services have faster execution speed, low memory consumption, and lower response times (Tihomirovs & Grabis, 2016).

Based on these differences, these paradigms fit better for the different scenarios listed below. The first scenario is the most obvious one: if one of the followings are required then big services should be chosen because RESTful services do not support them, at least for now:

- Endpoints for protocols other than HTTP
- One-way or duplex message patterns
- Strict standards for security, reliability, service description and discovery

But if the web service,

- Needs to be resource-oriented and/or needs HATEOS
- Will considerably benefit from model-binding, URI patterns and other HTTP features
- Will be developed based on conventions rather than contracts
- Will be relatively simple and accessible only from HTTP
- Needs to be fast and/or simple and/or considerably scalable
- Needs HTTP caching
- Will be called with different HTTP methods
- Needs content negotiation

then the RESTful paradigm would most probably be a better choice.

FUTURE RESEARCH DIRECTIONS

As noted, RESTful web services behave in an object-oriented way. However, the examples presented above can also be thought of as merely analogies rather than real applications of OOP principles. In any case, because it is resource-oriented, the RESTful paradigm seems natively suitable for the applications of OOP principles.

Indeed, Zhou et al. (2019) provide an application of Polymorphism principle to a RESTful service in which the RESTful service retrieves the resources from a resource registry depending on the mapping information in the request. They explain how the service implements Polymorphism as follows:

Because the process described above can handle REST requests from clients to access multiple, heterogeneous repositories, the REST server can be characterized as providing polymorphic REST services to those clients.

In a further possibility for such an application, when a web API uses some Abstract/Interface controllers to impose rules on controller classes, implementing these rules can be thought to implement the Abstraction principle. Web APIs can use these Interfaces as a protocol or contract that needs to be satisfied. Even runtime polymorphism can be achieved in this way. For instance, the service can behave differently for the same call (with the same HTTP method and the same resource) depending on a Header value that indicates which controller class will be used to implement the contract. We can also imagine that the methods of these Abstract/ Interface controllers can be addressed (as e.g. *api/IEmployees/1*) and called by clients, in which case they could, for example, return a blueprint that shows what the real data should look like.

There emerge many questions related to these ideas. REST differs from the object-oriented style in a very important sense: the former is stateless whereas the latter is stateful. So, how meaningful is it to talk about applying OOP principles to RESTful services? It is also important to consider whether the above examples, or similar applications, would break some REST constraints. Also of crucial importance is the question of the ways in which Web API frameworks can implement OOP principles in more useful, automated ways in accordance with web logic. All these questions deserve to be examined in further research and in greater detail.

CONCLUSION

A RESTFul service should comply with the five necessary REST constraints: Client-Server, Statelessness, Cacheability, Layered System and the Uniform Interface, with the last one being the most distinctive feature of RESTful services. ASP .Net Web API framework considerably smooths the way for developing RESTful services thanks to HTTP method, source and format attributes as well as content negotiation and model binding mechanisms.

RESTful services have important advantages over big services: They are easier to develop, maintain and consume, more scalable, less complex, and considerably benefit from HTTP features. Further, the payload in RESTful services, is more lightweight and not stored in an extra envelope.

However, unlike big services, RESTful services are limited to use of HTTP and request-response message exchange pattern. Further, big services capitalize on well-defined WS-* protocols and specifications which makes them more standardized, reliable and secure. The right design choice between these two paradigms depends on the requirements and technical constraints. However, it can be safely concluded that the RESTful paradigm would be a better choice for typical scenarios running on HTTP.

REFERENCES

Anderson, R. (2019). *Model binding in ASP.NET Core*. Retrieved from https://docs.microsoft.com/en-us/aspnet/core/mvc/models/model-binding?view=aspnetcore-3.0

Anderson, R., Roth, D., & Luttin, S. (2019). *Introduction to ASP.NET Core*. Retrieved from https://docs.microsoft.com/en-us/aspnet/core/?view=aspnetcore-3.0

Booth, D., Haas, H., McCabe, F., Newcomer, E., Champion, M., Ferris, C., & Orchard, D. (2004). *Web services architecture*. Retrieved from https://www.w3.org/TR/2004/NOTE-ws-arch-20040211/#relwwwrest

Bouguettaya, A., Sheng, Q. Z., & Daniel, F. (2014). *Web services foundations*. New York: Springer. doi:10.1007/978-1-4614-7518-7

Enríquez, R., & Salazar, A. (2014). *RESTful Java web services security*. Packt Publishing Ltd.

Fielding, R., Gettys, J., Mogul, J., Frystyk, H., Masinter, L., Leach, P., & Berners-Lee, T. (2006). Hypertext transfer protocol–HTTP/1.1, 1999. *RFC2616*.

Fielding, R. T. (2000). *REST: architectural styles and the design of network-based software architectures* (Unpublished doctoral dissertation). University of California, Irvine, CA.

Fielding, R. T., Taylor, R. N., Erenkrantz, J. R., Gorlick, M. M., Whitehead, J., Khare, R., & Oreizy, P. (2017). Reflections on the REST architectural style and principled design of the modern web architecture. *Proceedings of the 2017 11th Joint Meeting on Foundations of Software Engineering*. 10.1145/3106237.3121282

Fowler, M. (2010). *Richardson maturity model*. Retrieved from https://martinfowler.com/articles/richardsonMaturityModel.html

Gokhale, A., Kumar, B., & Sahuguet, A. (2002). Reinventing the wheel? CORBA vs. web services. *Proceedings of International World Wide Web conference*.

Gonzalo, N., & Rakela, B. (2015). *ICWE 2015 - REST web service description for graph-based service discovery*. Retrieved from https://www.slideshare.net/NikolasGonzaloBravoR/icwe-2015-rest-web-service-description-for-graphbased-service-discovery

GraphQL Working Group. (2019). *GraphQL is the better REST*. Retrieved from https://www.howtographql.com/basics/1-graphql-is-the-better-rest/

gRPC Working Group. (2019). *gRPC*. Retrieved from https://grpc.io/

Haas, H., & Brown, A. (2004). *Web services glossary*. Retrieved from https://www.w3.org/TR/2004/NOTE-ws-gloss-20040211/#webservice

Halili, F., & Ramadani, E. (2018). Web services: A comparison of soap and rest services. *Modern Applied Science, 12*(3), 175. doi:10.5539/mas.v12n3p175

Jamshidi, P., Pahl, C., Mendonça, N. C., Lewis, J., & Tilkov, S. (2018). Microservices: The journey so far and challenges ahead. *IEEE Software*, *35*(3), 24–35. doi:10.1109/MS.2018.2141039

JSON-RPC Working Group. (2013). *JSON-RPC 2.0 specification*. Retrieved from https://www.jsonrpc.org/specification

Kumari, S., & Rath, S. K. (2015). Performance comparison of soap and rest based web services for enterprise application integration. *2015 International Conference on Advances in Computing, Communications and Informatics (ICACCI)*. 10.1109/ICACCI.2015.7275851

Kumari, V. (2015). Web services protocol: SOAP vs REST. *International Journal of Advanced Research in Computer Engineering Technology*, *4*(5), 2467–2469.

Luo, J., Anderson, R., Smith, S., & Latham, L. (2019). *Response caching in ASP.NET Core*. Retrieved from https://docs.microsoft.com/en-us/aspnet/core/performance/caching/response?view=aspnetcore-3.0

Mehta, B. (2014). *RESTful Java patterns and best practices*. Packt Publishing Ltd.

MozDevNet. (2019). *HTTP caching*. Retrieved from https://developer.mozilla.org/en-US/docs/Web/HTTP/Caching

Mumbaikar, S., & Padiya, P. (2013). Web services based on soap and rest principles. *International Journal of Scientific and Research Publications*, *3*(5), 1–4.

Navarro, A., & da Silva, A. (2016). A metamodel-based definition of a conversion mechanism between SOAP and RESTful web services. *Computer Standards & Interfaces*, *48*, 49–70. doi:10.1016/j.csi.2016.03.004

Neumann, A., Laranjeiro, N., & Bernardino, J. (2018). An analysis of public rest web service apis. *IEEE Transactions on Services Computing*, 1. doi:10.1109/TSC.2018.2847344

Pautasso, C., Zimmermann, O., & Leymann, F. (2008). Restful web services vs. big web services: making the right architectural decision. *Proceedings of the 17th international conference on World Wide Web*. 10.1145/1367497.1367606

Richardson, L., & Ruby, S. (2008). *RESTful web services*. Sebastopol, CA: O'Reilly Media, Inc.

Santos, W. (2017). *531 reference APIs: GeoNames, Wikipedia and CrunchBase*. Retrieved from https://www.programmableweb.com/news/531-reference-apis-geonames-wikipedia-and-crunchbase/2013/07/31

Tihomirovs, J., & Grabis, J. (2016). Comparison of soap and rest based web services using software evaluation metrics. *Information Technology and Management Science*, *19*(1), 92–97. doi:10.1515/itms-2016-0017

Wagh, K., & Thool, R. (2012). A comparative study of soap vs rest web services provisioning techniques for mobile host. *Journal of Information Engineering and Applications*, *2*(5), 12–16.

Wasson, M. (2012). *Content negotiation in ASP.NET Web API*. Retrieved from https://docs.microsoft.com/en-us/aspnet/web-api/overview/formats-and-model-binding/content-negotiation

Winer, D. (2002). *Four years of XML-RPC*. Retrieved from http://scripting.com/davenet/2002/04/04/fourYearsOfXmlrpc.html

Xiao-Hong, L. (2014). Research and development of web of things system based on REST architecture. *2014 Fifth International Conference on Intelligent Systems Design and Engineering Applications*. 10.1109/ISDEA.2014.169

XML-RPC Working Group. (2003). *XML-RPC specification*. Retrieved from http://xmlrpc.scripting.com/spec.html#update3

Zhou, W., Chen, M., Wei, R., & Wang, C. (2019). *Systems and methods for building and providing polymorphic rest services for heterogeneous repositories*. Google Patents.

ADDITIONAL READING

Alarcon, R., Saffie, R., Bravo, N., & Cabello, J. (2015). *REST web service description for graph-based service discovery*. Paper presented at the International Conference on Web Engineering. 10.1007/978-3-319-19890-3_30

Allamaraju, S. (2010). *Restful web services cookbook: solutions for improving scalability and simplicity*. Sebastopol, CA: O'Reilly Media, Inc.

Aroraa, G., & Dash, T. (2018). *Building RESTful Web Services with. NET Core: Developing Distributed Web Services to Improve Scalability with. NET Core 2.0 and ASP. NET Core 2.0*. Packt Publishing Ltd.

Kobusińska, A., & Hsu, C.-H. (2018). Towards increasing reliability of clouds environments with restful web services. *Future Generation Computer Systems*, *87*, 502–513. doi:10.1016/j.future.2017.10.050

Lo Iacono, L., Nguyen, H. V., & Gorski, P. L. (2019). On the need for a general REST-Security framework. *Future Internet*, *11*(3), 56. doi:10.3390/fi11030056

Remier, M.-L. (2018). *Building RESTful Web Services with Java EE 8*. Packt Publishing Ltd.

Wilde, E., & Pautasso, C. (2011). *REST: from research to practice*. Springer Science & Business Media. doi:10.1007/978-1-4419-8303-9

Yellavula, N. (2017). *Building RESTful Web services with Go: Learn how to build powerful RESTful APIs with Golang that scale gracefully*. Packt Publishing Ltd.

KEY TERMS AND DEFINITIONS

AJAX (Asynchronous JavaScript and XML): A JavaScript technique that enables the client applications to communicate with a server asynchronously.

JSON (JavaScript Object Notation): A data exchange (or message) format that is used by JavaScript to represent the objects.

Payload: The actual, intended message which is located in request and response body when the data is transmitted through HTTP.

SOAP (Simple Object Access Protocol): An XML-based envelope or messaging protocol that is used to exchange information between the service requester and the web service.

URI (Uniform Resource Identifier): A string that identifies resources and includes the scheme (network protocol), host and path of the resource and may also include query parameters and a fragment.

WSDL (Web Services Description Language): An XML-based language that describes endpoints, bindings, interfaces, operations (web methods) and data types of a web service.

XML (Extensible Markup Language): A markup language or format that is used to present the data in a hierarchy of elements in accordance with a set of rules.

ENDNOTES

[1]   However, XML-RPC (XML-RPC, 2003) as a lightweight distributed computing solution has still been used recently (Gonzalo & Rakela, 2015; Santos, 2017).

[2]   Although they are far from being as popular as SOAP and REST (Gonzalo & Rakela, 2015; Santos, 2017), new web service architectural styles and protocols such as JSON-RPC, GraphQL and gRPC have been introduced in recent years.

JSON-RPC, introduced in 2010, is a stateless, lightweight RPC protocol and uses JSON instead of XML (JSON-RPC, 2013). GraphQL was designed in 2015 as a "better REST" which claims more flexibility and efficiency than REST (GraphQL, 2019). gRPC, developed by Google in 2015, is an open-source, high performance RPC framework (gRPC, 2019).

[3]   See Mehta (2014) for a more detailed illustration.

[4]   Microservices are lightweight, independent services (or units of development) that are developed to build individual software applications and run on HTTP in accordance with REST constraints (Jamshidi, Pahl, Mendonça, Lewis, & Tilkov, 2018).

[5]   In general, RESTful service calls which use GET method can be easily tested by browsers by writing the URI to the address bar of the browser. For other methods such as POST and PUT, there are many free computer programs such as Fiddler and Postman with which you can call the web method by specifying the HTTP method, URI and the payload.

Chapter 7
Measurement in Software Engineering:
The Importance of Software Metrics

Ruya Samli
Computer Engineering Department, Istanbul University, Turkey

Zeynep Behrin Güven Aydın
Software Engineering Department, Maltepe University, Turkey

Uğur Osman Yücel
Software Engineering Department, Maltepe University, Turkey

ABSTRACT

Measurement in software is a basic process in all parts of the software development life cycle because it helps to express the quality of a software. But in software engineering, measurement is difficult and not precise. However, researchers accept that any measure is better than zero measure. In this chapter, the software metrics are explained, and some software testing tools are introduced. The software metric sets of Chidamber and Kemerer Metric Set (CK Metric Set), MOOD Metric Set (Brito e Abreu Metric Set), QMOOD Metric Set (Bansiya and Davis Software Metric Set), Rosenberg and Hyatt Metric Set, Lorenz and Kidd Metric Set (L&K Metric Set) are explained. The software testing tools such as Understand, Sonargraph, Findbugs, Metrics, PMD, Coverlipse, Checkstyle, SDMetrics, and Coverity are introduced. Also, 17 literature studies are summarized.

DOI: 10.4018/978-1-7998-2142-7.ch007

INTRODUCTION

In real life, people need measuring objects in many situations. Thanks to measurement, they know how much money they have, their weight or current time. According to those measurements' results, they can plan their future. Software measurement is also similar to real life measurement process.

It is important for every step in the SDLC. Software developers can plan the future of project based on the measurement results. In software world, metrics allow software to be evaluated in many ways. These assessments help develop quality software (Ertemel, 2009). Many measurements have been proposed in the literature to capture and measure the structural quality of object-oriented code and design in particular. Software Metric Tools are the most basic measurement tools for measuring the quality of software.

In this chapter, first of all, five most popular object-oriented software metric sets (Chidamber & Kemerer Software Metric Set, MOOD Metric Set, QMOOD Metric Set, Rosenberg et al. Metric Set and Lorenz & Kidd Metric Set) are explained and secondly some software testing tools (Radar, QuickBugs, Bugtrack, ZeroDefect, Roundup, Abuky, Sonargraph, Understand, Findbugs, Metrics, PMD and Coverity) are examined.

BACKGROUND

In the literature, there are many studies that investigate software metrics in different software sets. Table 1 shows a summary about these studies.

As seen from the table, there are many studies about software metrics that handle different datasets, investigate various metric sets and use lots of methods.

OBJECT-ORIENTED METRIC SETS

Chidamber and Kemerer Metric Set (CK Metric Set)

- *Weighted Methods per Class (WMC):* This metric shows the complexities of all classes in a software. By using WMC, software development team can estimate their effort to develop those classes. Rather than use Cyclomatic Complexity they assigned to each method, a complexity of one making WMC is equal to the number of methods in the class (Chidamber & Kemerer, 1994; Virtual Machinery, 2019).

Table 1. A summary about software metric studies

Reference	Dataset	Metric Set	Methods
Briand et al., 1993	146 components of an ADA system (260,000 lines of code)	Library Unit Aggregation metrics, Compilation unit metrics	applied logistic regression, classification trees, OSR
Lanubile et al., 1995	27 academic projects in University of Bari	11 method level metrics which include Halstead, McCabe, and Henry and Kafura information flow metrics	component analysis, logistic regression, logical classification approaches, NN, holographic networks
Khoshgoftaar et al., 1997	13 million lines of code	Type-I, Type-II, and overall misclassification rates	NN and discriminant model
Ohlsson et al.,1998	Ericsson telecommunications system	Misclassification rate	PCA, applied discriminant analysis for classification
Menzies et al., 2004	public NASA datasets	method level metrics	LSR, model trees, ROCKY and Delphi detectors
Kanmani et al, 2004	Pondicherry Engineering College	64 metrics	GRNN
Koru& Liu, 2005	NASA datasets	class level metrics	J48, K-Star, and Random Forests
Challagulla et al., 2005	NASA datasets	level metrics	linear regression, SVR, NN, support vector logistic regression, Naive Bayes, IBL, J48, and 1-R techniques
Gyimothy et al., 2005	-.	object oriented metrics	logistic regression, linear regression, decision trees, NN
Hassan & Holt, 2005	6 open source projects	APA metrics	MFM, MRM, MFF, MRF
Zhou & Leung, 2006	NASA's KC1 dataset	Chidamber–Kemerer metrics	Logistic regression, Naive Bayes, Random Forests
Boetticher, 2006	NASA public datasets	Performance evluation metrics	J48 and naive bayes
Mertik et al., 2006	Nasa dataset	level metrics	C4.5, unprunned C4.5, multimethod, SVM
Bibi et al., 2008	Pekka dataset of Finland bank	Disk usage processor usage number of users document quality	Regression
Li & Reformat, 2007	JM1 dataset	level metrics and accuracy parameter	SimBoost
Pai & Dugan, 2007	NASA datasets	Chidamber–Kemerer metrics and lines of code metric	linear regression, Poisson regression, logic regression
Cukic & Ma, 2007	JM1 dataset	level metrics	-

where, OSR is Optimized Set Reduction, LSR is Linear Standard Regression, GRNN is General Regression Neural Networks, SVR is Support Vector Regression, NN is Neural Network, IBL is Instance Based Learning, MFM is Frequently Modified, MRM is Most Recently Modified, MFF is Most Frequently Fixed, MRF is Most Recently Fixed and PCA is Principal Component Analysis.

- *Depth of Inheritance Tree (DIT):* In trees, depth means the maximum length between a child node and the root (Chidamber & Kemerer, 1994). Inheritance tree shows the structure of classes. Root is the superclass and child nodes are the subclasses.
- *Number of Children (NOC):* This metric measures how classes are used to create another class (Chidamber & Kemerer, 1994). In other words, it is the number of classes derived from a class. Every class has its own NOC value.
- *Coupling Between Objects (CBO):* Coupling means that an object use property or message of an object which belongs to another class. This metric is the sum of objects like that.
- *Response For a Class (RFC):* This is the number of methods which will be executed when a message sent to a class by an object (Chidamber & Kemerer, 1994). If RFC increases, both testing and debugging processes will be more complex.
- *Lack of Cohesion in Methods (LCOM):* Cohesion metric examines how the methods of a class have relation with the others (Sandhu et al., 2005). High cohesion is always better than lower ones.

MOOD Metric Set (Brito e Abreu Metric Set)

- *Method Hiding Factor (MHF):* In the name of this metric, hiding means encapsulation (Abreu et al., 1996). Therefore, this metric examines how methods are encapsulated. The formulae of this metric is: MHF = 1 − (Visible Methods − (Total Number of Methods − 1))
- *Attribute Hiding Factor (AHF):* As it can be easily seen, this metric examines how attributes are encapsulated (Abreu et al., 1996). The formulae of this metric is: AHF = 1 − (Visible Attributes − (Total Number of Attributes − 1))
- *Method Inheritance Factor (MIF):* This metric is the ratio of inherited methods to the total number of methods (Abreu, 1995). Its range is between 0-100. It is better to be not too low or too high. MIF should get an optimal value. According to the creator of the MOOD who is Fernando Brito e Abreu, acceptable MIF values should be lower than 80% (Abreu et al., 1996). The formulae of this metric is: MIF = number of inherited methods / total number of methods
- *Attribute Inheritance Factor (AIF):* This metric is the ratio of inherited attributes to the total number of attributes (Briand et al., 1993). If a child class redefines it superclass' attribute, this attribute will be an inherited attribute. The formulae of this metric is: AIF = number of inherited attributes / total number of attributes.

- *Polymorphism Factor (POF):* This metric represents the actual number of possible different polymorphic situations (Abreu, 1995). Polymorphism Factor is the ratio of overrided methods to the maximum possible overrided methods. Its range is between 0-100. If POF is equalls to 100, all of the possible methods are overrided in derived classes. If POF is equals to 0, none of those methods are overrided.

- *Coupling Factor (COF):* This metric is the ratio of couplings between classes to the maximum possible number of couplings (Abreu et al., 1996). An example will be given here to understand what is coupling. There are two classes which are C1 and C2. If C1 calls C2's methods or accesses C2's variables, it can be said that C1 is coupled to C2. However, C2 is not coupled to C1. There is one way relationship between them. This metric's range is between 0-100.

QMOOD Metric Set (Bansiya and Davis Software Metric Set)

- *Average Number of Ancestors (ANA):* This metric is the number of classes among all paths from the root to all classes in a structure (Bansiya & Davis, 2002). This metric gives people an opinion about inheritance structure of the project.

- *Cohesion Among Methods of Class (CAM):* This metric can be calculated by using summation of the intersection of parameters a method with the maximum independent set of all parameter types in the class (Menzies et al., 2004). Its range is between 0-1. About this metric, maximum value is the best case and minimum value is the worst case.

- *Class Interface Size (CIS):* Class interface size is the number of public methods in a class (Bansiya & Davis, 2002).

- *Data Access Metric (DAM):* DAM is the ratio of private methods to the all methods (Goyal et al., 2014). Not only privates, but also protected methods will be counted while calculating DAM (Ohlsson et al., 1998). Its range is between 0-1. Higher DAM values are more desired.

- *Direct Class Coupling (DCC):* This is the number of classes which have relationship with another class (Bansiya & Davis, 2002). Relationship can be everything like derivation, message passing or attribute declarations and so on.

- *Measure of Aggregation (MOA):* This metric checks the data types (Bansiya & Davis, 2002). If data types are user defined classes, then value of MOA will increase (Goyal et al., 2014). In other words, MOA is the number of data declarations which has a user defined type.

- *Measure of Functional Abstraction (MFA):* This metric is the ratio of number of inherited methods to total number of methods. Its range is between 0-1.
- *Number of Methods (NOM):* This is the count of all methods in a class.
- *Rosenberg and Hyatt Metric Set*
- Rosenberg and Hyatt grouped the metrics as Traditional Metrics, Object-Oriented Specific Metrics and Inheritance metrics.
- *Cyclomatic Complexity (CC):* Cyclomatic Complexity is equal to number of decisions which means number of logical operators. Low cyclomatic complexity is always better (Rosenberg et al., 1997). The reason behind this is it is always difficult to test the codes with high CC. A basic example is given below.

```
void method()
{
        if(a == 1)
                x = 1;
        else
                x = 0;
}
```

The CC of this code is 2 because there are 2 different possible situations therefore there are 2 decisions.

- *Size:* Size can be measured in various ways including Lines of Code (LOC), the number of statements, number of blank lines and so on. (Rosenberg et al., 1997). Software engineers use the size to evaluate understandibility.
- *Comment Percentage (CP):* Comment Percentage is the ratio of total number of comments to the total number of lines except the blank lines. The SATC has found a comment percentage of around 30% (Rosenberg et al., 1997).
- *Weighted Methods Per Class (WMC):* WMC is also a member of CK Metric Set. As we mentioned above, Rather than use Cyclomatic Complexity they assigned each method a complexity of one making WMC is equal to the number of methods in the class (Chidamber & Kemerer, 1994; Virtual Machinery, 2019). This metric measures Understandability, Maintainability and Reusability (Rosenberg et al., 1997).
- *Response For a Class (RFC):* This metric is also belongs to the CK Metric Set. This metric looks at the combination of the complexity of a class through the number of methods and the amount of communication with other classes (Rosenberg et al., 1997). If RFC will increase, it will be harder to test and

debug. This metric affects Understandibility, Maintainability and Testability (Chidamber & Kemerer, 1994; Rosenberg et al., 1997).

- *Lack of Cohesion of Methods (LCOM):* As mentioned above, LCOM is member of CK Metric Set. This metric examines the methods' similiarities according to their attributes or data inputs. High cohesion is always better (Rosenberg et al., 1997). Classes with low cohesion should be divided into subclasses.
- *Coupling Between Objects (CBO):* CBO belongs to the CK Metric Set. According to Rosenberg and Hyatt, classes are coupled in three ways. First, when a message passed between objects, second, when a message declared in a class and used by another one, they are coupled. Third and the last one is Subclasses and Superclasses are coupled (Rosenberg et al., 1997). CBO is the number of other classes which is coupled to a class.
- *Depth of Inheritance Tree (DIT):* Depth is the maximum length from child nodes to the root node. More complex systems have deeper trees. However it will increase the reusability.
- *Number of Children (NOC):* This metric is the last one of Rosenberg & Hyatt Metric Set. NOC is the number of subclasses. The classes which have higher NOC value are more difficult to test (Rosenberg et al., 1997).

Lorenz and Kidd Metric Set (L&K Metric Set)

There are ten metrics in L&K Metric Set.

- *Number of Public Methods (PM):* As it can be understood from its name, this is the number of public methods. According to Lorenz and Kidd, this metric can be used to estimate the amount of work to develop a class (Lorenz & Kidd, 1994).
- *Number of Methods (NM):* This is the total number of Public, Private and Protected Methods defined.
- *Number of Public Variables Per Class (NPV):* This is the number of Public Variables per class. Lorenz and Kidd thought that if a class has more NPV than another class, this means that the class has more relationship with other classes (Goel et al., 2013).
- *Number of Variables Per Class (NV):* This metric counts all Public, Private and Protected Variables in the class.
- *Number of Methods Inherited by a Subclass (NMI):* This is the total number of inherited methods by a subclass.
- *Number of Methods Overridden by a Subclass (NMO):* This is the total number of methods overridden by subclasses. According to Lorenz and Kidd,

larger number of overridden methods indicates a design problem (Lorenz & Kidd, 1994).

- *Number of Methods Added by a Subclass (NMA):* According to L&K, the normal expectation for a subclass is that it will specialise or add methods to the superclass' objects (Lorenz & Kidd, 1994; Goel et al., 2013).
- *Average Method Size:* This is the physical size which means Lines Of Codes. While counting, comment lines and blank lines should be extracted from the total number of lines. Then, the total size will be divided into total number of methods for finding Average Method Size.
- *Number of Times a Class is Reused (NCR):* According to Goel and Bhatia, the definition of NCR is ambiguous (Goel et al., 2013). They assumed that NCR is the number of a class is referenced (reused) by other classes.
- *Number of Friends of a Class (NF):* This metric is the number of friends of the class. It can be calculated for each class. Friends allow encapsulation to be violated (Goel et al., 2013). For this reason, they should be used carefully.

SOFTWARE TESTING TOOLS

Understand

Understand is a static analysis tool focused on source code comprehension, metrics, and standard testing. It is designed to help maintain and understand large amounts of legacy or newly created source code. It provides a cross-platform, multi-language, maintenance-oriented IDE (Integrated Development Environment). The source code analyzed may include C, C++, C#, Objective C/Objective C++, Ada, Assembly, Visual Basic, COBOL, Fortran, Java, JOVIAL, Pascal/Delphi, PL/M, Python, VHDL and Web languages (PHP, HTML, CSS, JavaScript, and XML). It offers code navigation using a detailed cross-referencing, a syntax-colorizing "smart" editor, and a variety of graphical reverse engineering view (VandenBos, 2001).

Understand is a customisable IDE that enables static code analysis through an array of visuals, documentation, and metric tools (Scientific Toolworks, 2018). It was built to help software developers comprehend, maintain and document their source code. It enables code comprehension by providing flow charts of relationships and building a dictionary of variables and procedures from a provided source code (Dragomir, 2018).

In addition to functioning as an IDE, Understand provides tools for metrics and reports, standard testing, documentation, searching, graphing and code knowledge. It is capable of analyzing projects with millions of lines of code and works with code bases written in multiple languages (Adkins & Jones, 2018). Developed originally for Ada, it now supports development in several common programming languages (Loren & Johnson-Laird, 2018). Integration with the Eclipse development environment is also supported.

Understand has been used globally for government, commercial, and academic use. It is used in many different industries to both analyze and develop software. Specific uses include a variety of applications: code validation for embedded systems (Adkins & Jones, 2018), software litigation consulting (Loren & Johnson-Laird, 2018), reverse engineering and documentation (Richard, 2019) and source code change analysis (Phillips & Mok, 2019).

Sonargraph

Sonargraph is a powerful static code analyzer that allows people to monitor a software system for technical quality and enforce rules regarding software architecture, metrics and other aspects in all stages of the development process. The Sonargraph platform supports Java, C#, Python 3 and C/C++ out of the box and includes powerful features like a Groovy based scripting engine and a DSL (Domain Specific Language) to describe software architecture (Eshow, 2019). Sonargraph is a commercial tool for static code analysis of software written in Java, C#, C or C++. By parsing the source code it builds an in memory dependency and metrics model of the analyzed code. Then the model dependencies can be visualized graphically so that the user is able to understand the structure of the system. Moreover, the tool allows the definition of a logical architecture model (intended structure of the software) based on a domain specific language designed for software architecture. By comparing the logical model with the real dependency structure Sonargraph finds and list all architecture violations (deviations from the intended structure). Moreover, Sonargraph computes a wide range of software metrics that help the user to pinpoint problematic code sections and to estimate the overall technical quality of his project. It also helps with finding duplicated blocks of code, which are usually considered undesirable. A Groovy based scripting engine allows the user to compute user defined metrics and to create customized code checkers (Anonym, 2019a).

Findbugs

FindBugs is an open-source static code analyzer created by Bill Pugh and David Hovemeyer which detects possible bugs in Java programs (Grindstaff, 2019a; Grindstaff, 2019b). Potential errors are classified in four ranks: (i) scariest, (ii) scary, (iii) troubling and (iv) of concern. This is a hint to the developer about their possible impact or severity (Sprunck, 2019). FindBugs operates on Java bytecode, rather than source code. The software is distributed as a stand-alone GUI (Graphical User

Interface) application. There are also plug-ins available for Eclipse (SourgeForge, 2019a), NetBeans (Lahoda & Stashkova, 2019), IntelliJ IDEA (Anonym, 2019c; Anonym, 2019d; Kustemur, 2019) Gradle, Hudson, Maven (QA Plug, 2019), Bamboo (SourceForge, 2019a) and (Anonym, 2019e). Additional rule sets can be plugged in FindBugs to increase the set of checks performed. A successor to FindBugs, called SpotBugs, has been created. Findbugs is an open source tool for static code analysis of Java programs. It scans byte code for so called bug pattern to find defects and/ or suspicious code (Anonym, 2019f).

It is an open source static code analysis tool developed by the University of Maryland. By performing various analyzes on the existing Java code of the software, it can automatically find common software errors and design defects in a short time. FindBugs; Java, Netbeans, Jboss, such as the development of many popular programs are used effectively today.

Metrics

Metrics is another open source program developed as an extension to the Eclipse project. The Java program in the Eclipse development environment can run in an integrated format, automatically measuring many commonly used software metrics and reporting to the developer. Metrics such as the number of static functions, the depth of derivation, dependency, complexity of functions, and the number of abstraction are just a few of them. Metrics also has the ability to graphically show dependencies in the software. In this way, it is possible for the developers to analyze the dependencies in the software better visually (SourceForge, 2019b).

PMD

PMD is a static source code analyzer. It finds common programming flaws like unused variables, empty catch blocks, unnecessary object creation, and so on. It's mainly concerned with Java and Apex, but also supports JavaScript, Visualforce, PLSQL, Apache Velocity, XML and XSL. Additionally it includes CPD, the copy-paste-detector. CPD finds duplicated code in Java, C, C++, C#, Groovy, PHP, Ruby, Fortran, JavaScript, PLSQL, Apache Velocity, Scala, Objective C, Matlab, Python, Go, Swift and Salesforce.com Apex and Visualforce (Anonym, 2019g).

Coverlipse

Coverlipse is an open source Eclipse plug-in that examines the overlap relationship between implementation and software code and requirements and test cases. The program analyzes the overlap relationships between these three basic stages of software development, revealing gaps between them (SourceForge, 2019c).

Checkstyle

Checkstyle is a static code analysis tool used in software development for checking if Java source code complies with coding rules. The CheckStyle program is another open source software tool that deals with format rather than software structure. It helps developers work in accordance with code writing standards by performing format analysis on existing Java code. This software, where the institution can create its own writing standards, also has some generally accepted international writing standards (SourceForge, 2019).

SDMetrics

SDMetrics is a commercial program that can perform various visual and numerical analyzes on UML (Unified Modelling Language) design documents, not on code. By analyzing the design of the software before the design phase, ie the development phase, the program can reveal many nonconformities about dependency and complexity. Early detection at this stage can also be significant in terms of cost. SDMetrics is a software design quality measurement tool for the UML. It measures structural design properties such as coupling, size, and complexity of UML models. SDMetrics also checks design rules to automatically detect incomplete or incorrect design, and adherence to style guidelines such as circular dependencies or naming conventions (Anonym, 2019h).

Coverity

Coverity is a brand of software development products from Synopsys, consisting primarily of static code analysis tools and dynamic code analysis services. The tools enable engineers and security teams to find defects and security vulnerabilities in custom source code written in C, C++, Java, C#, JavaScript and more (Anonym, 2019i). SonarQube is a sophisticated quality assurance package with many source code measurements from anomaly numbers to traditional size and complexity measurements, similar to FindBugs or PMD.

SOLUTIONS AND RECOMMENDATIONS

In software process, there can be many different problems. Some of them are mentioned below:

- how can a software's size be measured?
- how can a software's security be measured?
- how can a software's deadline be estimated?
- how can a software's cost be estimated?
- how can a software's usability be improved?
- how can a software's complexity be calculated?

The number of these type of questions can be increased. The software metrics are the solutions of these questions. So the software metric subject is very important in software engineering concept and the authors of the chapter recommend that there must be more studies about software metrics.

FUTURE RESEARCH DIRECTIONS

The software metrics are getting more and more important in "software engineering" concept. As new software programming approaches come up, new software metric tools will come up too. In recent years, the number of literature studies about software metrics has been increased and in the future, it is expected that the number will increase more and more. Also, it can be easily said that to work about software metrics become a more valuable subject in the future.

CONCLUSION

Software metrics are the parameters that provide the comparison of software. So they are very important while estimating a software's deadline, cost and so on, Therefore a programmer need software metrics a lot. Because there is no definite rule for measuring software metrics, there are different metric sets and all of them mention about different properties of software. A programmer or a development team chose the most definite software metric set to their software.

This chapter mentions about the importance of software metrics with three points. First of all, the literature studies about software metrics are given. From this literature review, it is understood that there are different classes of software metrics and many different software types uses software metrics since 1990s. Secondly, the different software metric sets such as Chidamber & Kemerer Metric Set, MOOD Metric Set, QMOOD Metric Set, Rosenberg & Hyatt Metric Set and Lorenz & Kidd Metric Set are mentioned. There are other software metric sets in the literature but these are the most popular ones so the other sets are not mentioned inthe chapter. This part of the chapter tries to answer the question of a programmer "Which metric set I must use?". The last point which the chapter explains is software metric tools. A software metric tool is a way to measure software metric values.

By this chapter, software metrics, software metric sets and software metric tools are explained. The aim of the chapter can be said as "to mention the importance of software metrics in software engineering concept".

REFERENCES

Abreu, B. F., & Melo, W. (1996). Evaluating the impact of object-oriented design on software quality. *Proceedings of 3rd international software metrics symposium.*

Abreu, F. B. (1995). The MOOD Metrics Set. *Proceedings of workshop on Metrics – ECOOP.*

Adkins, F., & Jones, L. (2018). *Machine Assisted Semantic Understanding.* Retrieved from http://insurehub.org/sites/default/files/reports/FinalReport_MachineAssistedSemanticUnderstanding_Adkins_Jones.pdf

Anonym. (2019a). Retrieved from https://www.wikiwand.com/en/Sonargraph

Anonym. (2019b). Retrieved from https://code.google.com/archive/p/idea-findbugs/

Anonym. (2019c). Retrieved from https://code.google.com/archive/redirect/a/code.google.com/p/findbugs/

Anonym. (2019d). Retrieved from http://www.methodsandtools.com/tools/findbugs.php

Anonym. (2019e). Retrieved from https://pmd.github.io/latest/index.html/

Anonym. (2019f). Retrieved from https://www.sdmetrics.com/PRMar2011.html/

Anonym. (2019g). Retrieved from https://www.wikiwand.com/en/Coverity/

Bansiya, J., & Davis, C. G. (2002). A Hierarchical Model for Object-Oriented Design Quality Assessment. *IEEE Transactions on Software Engineering*, 28(1), 4–17. doi:10.1109/32.979986

Bibi, S., Tsoumakas, G., Stamelos, I., & Vlahvas, I. (2008). Regression via classification applied on software defect estimation. *Expert Systems with Applications*, *34*(3), 2091–2101. doi:10.1016/j.eswa.2007.02.012

Boetticher, G. (2006). *Improving credibility of machine learner models in software engineering. Advanced machine learner applications in software engineering.* Hershey, PA: Idea Group Publishing.

Briand, L., Basili, V., & Hetmanski, C. (1993). Developing interpretable models with optimized set reduction for identifying high risk software components. *IEEE Transactions on Software Engineering*, *19*(11), 1028–1044. doi:10.1109/32.256851

Challagulla, V. U., Bastani, F. B., Yen, I., & Paul, R. A. (2005). Empirical assessment of machine learning based software defect prediction techniques. *Proceedings of tenth IEEE international workshop on object-oriented real-time dependable systems*, 263–270. 10.1109/WORDS.2005.32

Chidamber, S. R., & Kemerer, C. F. (1994). A Metrics Suite for Object Oriented Design. *IEEE Transactions on Software Engineering*, *20*(6), 476–493. doi:10.1109/32.295895

Cukic, B., & Ma, Y. (2007). Predicting fault-proneness: Do we finally know how? In Reliability analysis of system failure data. Cambridge, UK: Academic Press.

Dragomir, M. (2018). *Understand.* Retrieved from www.softpedia.com

Ertemel, H. Ö. (2009). *Examination of quality criteria in object oriented software development* (MS dissertation). Yıldız Technical University, Institute of Science.

Eshow, M. (2019). *RTMA Source Code Change Analysis.* Retrieved https://en.wikipedia.org/wiki/Understand_(software)

Goel, M. B., & Bhatia, P. K. (2013). An Overview of Various Object Oriented Metrics. *International Journal of Information Technology & Systems*, *2*(1), 18–27.

Goyal, K. P., & Joshi, G. (2014). QMOOD metric sets to assess quality of Java program. *Proceedings of International Conference on Issues and Challenges in Intelligent Computing Techniques.* 10.1109/ICICICT.2014.6781337

GrindstaffC. (2019a). Retrieved from https://www.ibm.com/developerworks/java/library/j-findbug1/

GrindstaffC. (2019b). Retrieved from https://www.ibm.com/developerworks/java/library/j-findbug2/

Gyimothy, T., Ferenc, R., & Siket, I. (2005). Empirical validation of object-oriented metrics on open source software for fault prediction. *IEEE Transactions on Software Engineering*, *31*(10), 897–910. doi:10.1109/TSE.2005.112

Hassan, A. E., & Holt, R. C. (2005). The top ten list: Dynamic fault prediction. In *Proceedings of twenty-first IEEE international conference on software maintenance* (pp. 263–272). IEEE Computer Society. 10.1109/ICSM.2005.91

Kanmani, S., Uthariaraj, V. R., Sankaranarayanan, V., & Thambidurai, P. (2004). Object oriented software quality prediction using general regression neural networks. *SIGSOFT Software Engineering Notes*, *29*(5), 1–6. doi:10.1145/1022494.1022515

Khoshgoftaar, T. M., Allen, E. B., Hudepohl, J. P., & Aud, S. J. (1997). Application of neural networks to software quality modeling of a very large telecommunications system. *IEEE Transactions on Neural Networks*, *8*(4), 902–909. doi:10.1109/72.595888 PMID:18255693

Koru, A. G., & Liu, H. (2005). An investigation of the effect of module size on defect prediction using static measures. *Proceedings of workshop on predictor models in software engineering*, 1–5. 10.1145/1083165.1083172

KustemurA. (2019). Retrieved from https://alicankustemur.github.io/#/

LahodaJ.StashkovaA. (2019). Retrieved from https://netbeans.org/kb/docs/java/code-inspect.html/

Lanubile, F., Lonigro, A., & Visaggio, G. (1995). Comparing models for identifying fault-prone software components. In *Proceedings of Seventh international conference on software engineering and knowledge engineering* (pp. 312–319). Academic Press.

Li, Z., & Reformat, M. (2007). A practical method for the software fault-prediction. *Proceedings of IEEE international conference on information reuse and integration*, 659–666. 10.1109/IRI.2007.4296695

Loren, L., & Johnson-Laird, A. (2018). *Computer Software-Related Litigation*. Retrieved from https://papers.ssrn.com/sol3/papers.cfm?abstract_id=1969587

Lorenz, M., & Kidd, J. (1994). *Object-Oriented Software Metrics: A Practical Guide*. Englewood Cliffs, NJ: Prentice Hall.

Machinery, V. (2019). *The Chidamber and Kemerer Metrics*. Retrieved from http://www.virtualmachinery.com/sidebar3.htm

Menzies, T., DiStefano, J., Orrego, A., & Chapman, R. (2004). Assessing predictors of software defects. *Proceedings of predictive software models workshop*.

Mertik, M., Lenic, M., Stiglic, G., & Kokol, P. (2006). Estimating software quality with advanced data mining techniques. *Proceedings of international conference on software engineering advances*, 19. 10.1109/ICSEA.2006.261275

MojoHaus. (2019). Retrieved from https://gleclaire.github.io/findbugs-maven-plugin/

Ohlsson, N., Zhao, M., & Helander, M. (1998). Application of multivariate analysis for software fault prediction. *Software Quality Journal*, 7(1), 51–66. doi:10.1023/B:SQJO.0000042059.16470.f0

Pai, G. J., & Dugan, J. B. (2007). Empirical analysis of software fault content and fault proneness using Bayesian methods. *IEEE Transactions on Software Engineering*, 33(10), 675–686. doi:10.1109/TSE.2007.70722

Phillips, M., & Mok, A. (2019). *Spacecraft Flight Software Design Pattern Discovery*. Retrieved from https://en.wikipedia.org/wiki/Understand_(software)

PlugQ. A. (2019). Retrieved from https://qaplug.com/

Richard, B. (2019). *Source Code Analyzers as a Development Tool*. Retrieved from https://www.owasp.org/index.php/Source_Code_Analysis_Tools

Rosenberg, L. H., & Hyatt, L. E. (1997). Software quality metrics for object-oriented environments. *Crosstalk Journal*, 10(4), 1–6.

Sandhu, P., & Singh, H. (2005). A Critical Suggestive Evaluation of CK Metric. *Proceedings of Pacific Asia Conference on Information Systems*, 16.

Scientific Toolworks. (2018). *Understand User Guide Reference Manual*. Retrieved from https://scitools.com/documents/manuals/pdf/understand.pdf

SourceForge. (2019a). Retrieved from http://fb-contrib.sourceforge.net/

SourceForge. (2019b). Retrieved from http://metrics.sourceforge.net/

SourceForge. (2019c). Retrieved from http://coverlipse.sourceforge.net/index.php/

SourceForge. (2019d). Retrieved from https://checkstyle.sourceforge.io/index.html/

SourgeForge. (2019). Retrieved from http://findbugs.sourceforge.net/downloads.html

Sprunck, M. (2019). *Findbugs – Static Code Analysis of Java*. Retrieved from http://www.methodsandtools.com/tools/findbugs.php

VandenBos, G., Knapp, S., & Doe, J. (2001). *Role of reference elements in the selection of resources by psychology undergraduates*. Retrieved from http://jbr.org/articles.html

Zhou, Y., & Leung, H. (2006). Empirical analysis of object-oriented design metrics for predicting high and low severity faults. *IEEE Transactions on Software Engineering*, *32*(10), 771–789. doi:10.1109/TSE.2006.102

KEY TERM AND DEFINITIONS

Line of Code (LOC): Line of code (LOC) is a software metric used to measure the size of a computer program by counting the number of lines in the text of the program's source code.

Object-Oriented Programming (OOP): Object-oriented programming (OOP) is a programming paradigm based on the concept of "objects", which can contain data, in the form of fields (often known as attributes), and code, in the form of procedures (often known as methods).

Software Complexity: Software complexity is a way to describe a specific set of characteristics of a code. Software complexity is a natural byproduct of the functional complexity that the code is attempting to enable.

Software Development Life Cycle (SDLC): Software development life cycle (SDLC) is a process that produces software with the highest quality and lowest cost in the shortest time. SDLC includes a detailed plan for how to develop, alter, maintain, and replace a software system.

Software Metric: A software metric is a standard of measure of a degree to which a software system or process possesses some property.

Software Testing: Software testing is a process, to evaluate the functionality of a software application with an intent to find whether the developed software met the specified requirements or not and to identify the defects to ensure that the product is defect free in order to produce the quality product.

Software Testing Tool: Software testing tool is an automation, a program or another software that provides a quick and reliable software test.

Section 3
A Real–World Application on Internet of Things

Chapter 8
A Blood Bank Management System–Based Internet of Things and Machine Learning Technologies

Ahmed Mousa
Minia University, Egypt

Ahmed El-Sayed
Minia University, Egypt

Ali Khalifa
Minia University, Egypt

Marwa El-Nashar
Minia University, Egypt

Yousra Mancy Mancy
Minia University, Egypt

Mina Younan
Minia University, Egypt

Eman Younis
ⓘD https://orcid.org/0000-0003-2778-4231
Minia University, Egypt

ABSTRACT

Nearly all of the Egyptian hospitals are currently suffering from shortage in rare blood types (e.g., -AB, -B, +AB), which are needed to perform vital surgeries. This

DOI: 10.4018/978-1-7998-2142-7.ch008

leads them (hospitals or doctors) to ask patients' relatives to donate the amount of the required blood. The alternative is that they are forced to pay for the blood if the required type and amount is already available in these hospitals or the blood banks. The main idea of this work is solving problems related to the blood banks from collecting blood from donators to distributing blood bags for interested hospitals. This system is developed in order to enhance the management, performance, and the quality of services for the management of blood banks, which will be positively reflected on many patients in hospitals. This chapter targets undergraduate students, academic researchers, development engineers, and course designers and instructors.

INTRODUCTION

Humanity should be the main practice of all people towards others in order to live in peace. One of the best characteristics of humanity is to help save people's life. Modern and smart cities are evaluated by the healthcare level they provide, which is reflected on their production levels. The main problem in field of healthcare is to provide more accurate equipment and requirements for healing and saving human life, but what if the required equipment in already within our hands, do we offer them for helping patients to save their lives? The main equipment is the blood, which really save human life on earth. The main idea of this project is to encourage people to help themselves by being permanent donators and to help in managing the blood banks and hospitals.

The problem occurs when many patients in hospitals are in emergency situations and need blood urgently, but the hospital administration runs out of blood and they can't fully save the situation and in this way one's life becomes in danger. Most hospitals suffer from shortage in quantities of rare blood types (e.g., -AB, -B, +AB) to perform urgent surgeries, which leads hospital administration to ask patients' families to donate the required blood quantities or they are forced to pay if the required quantities are already available in these hospitals or blood banks. According to the health international organization, each country has to donate with percent at least (2:3) % from its population (World Health Organization, 2019).

Recently, the ministry of healthy focus has been on improving the management processes between blood banks and hospitals (The Ministry of Health and Population, 2016). The proposed idea of this project (*Point of Life*: *Blood Bank Management System (BBMS)*) is to tackle problems related to the blood banks for collecting blood bags from donators and distributing them for interested hospitals according to criticality of patients' cases. In addition to the lack of blood bags due to urgent patients requirements, the other problem that face blood banks and hospital administration could be summarized into the following points: (a) there were poor communication between hospitals and blood banks for reserving and delivering blood bags, (b) because blood bags are limited, hospital administration should set some criteria for reservation priorities, (c) blood banks have to select the most valuable places for starting their campaigns, (d) patients require urgent communication with donators. The proposed idea of the project concerns addressing and solving these problems in a way that encourages citizens to be permanent donators.

This chapter presents our software engineering and implementation details for an information system that serves Egyptian blood banks. This proposed system is called *Blood Bank Management System (BBMS)*. This system will give assistance for the blood banks, starting from collecting the blood from the donators to distributing the blood bags for interested hospitals. This system was developed in order to improve the management, performance and the quality of services for the management of blood banks, which will be reflected on the number of the served patients in the hospitals (Egyptian National Hospitals).

The chapter is organized according to the system development life cycle (SDLC) of the waterfall model as follows. The next section presents background, then the related work section surveys current applications and researches to clarify opportunities and new features of the proposed system. The subsequent two sections present system architecture and software engineering details, such as use-cases, system sequence diagram and so on. After the implementation and results details are discussed, conclusion and future work are finally presented.

Background

This section presents some knowledge concerning the Internet of Things (IoT) and Machine Learning (ML) that we need to enhance our system performance to achieve main goals and ideas to solve the above-mentioned problems.

Internet of Things

Internet of things (IoT) is a new technology, which provides information about things, devices, and environmental events on the Internet. A similar technology which is an extension to the IoT is the Web of Things (WoT) which visualizes sensed information on the web. But for building simple IoT application, what we need is to attach sensor or actuator to the thing that we need to inform about its states online. (Younan, Khattab and Bahgat, 2015; Younan, Khattab and Bahgat, 2017) . This process converts ordinary things into smart things (STh), such as shown in Figure 1. In the project we built simple IoT using GPS with the mobile application in order to track nearby campaigns such as discussed later in the implementation section.

Machine Learning

Machine learning (ML) technology enables machines to learn from the current inputs to assess or predict some situation. ML algorithms are classified into three main categories: supervised, unsupervised, and reinforcement learning. Algorithms examples of type supervised are: Support Vector Machines, neural networks, decision trees, K-nearest neighbors, naive Bayes, etc., and there are some algorithms of type unsupervised, such as K-means, Gaussian mixtures, hierarchical clustering, etc.

In our project we implement some aggregation functions in the first version - during studying machine learning fundamentals - in order to get best place, in which we get the highest quantities. In the next version we use some python libraries like pandas, skitlearn, numpy, matplotlib etc. to study current generated data sets to study the correlation between elements such as quantities, blood type, job, etc. more details are presented later in the chapter, system implementation section.

RELATED WORK

This section summarizes the current manual and most relevant software solutions relevant to this work.

Manual Solutions

Manual solutions in the Egyptian hospitals: are set of rules for managing the processes of getting the required quantities: (a) enforcing patients' families to donate for their patient directly, if they have the same blood type, or they donate and the hospital exchange this quantity with the required blood type, and (b) pay for the hospital if the required quantity and type is available.

Software Solutions

Current automatic software solutions partially solve the problem by increasing the possibility of finding donors.

1. Ahyaha (Mn Ahyaha | Blood Donation, 2019): a mobile application which enables its users to search about donors and call them.

Figure 1. From things to smart things (STh)

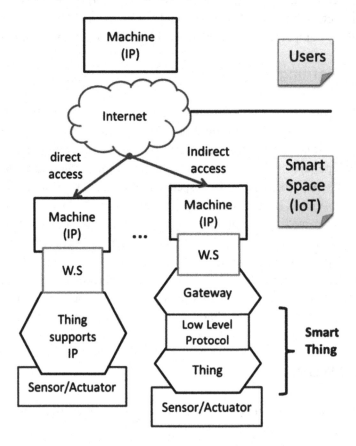

2.   Short message service (SMS) blood bank (Krishna and Nagaraju, 2016). The authors in the research paper propose an application which sends a short SMS for communicating blood bank, donors, and patients.

3.   The research work (Mahalle and Thorat, 2018) presents a smart blood bank system based on IoT for improving response time tacking benefits of cloud computing for connecting almost blood banks.

4.   GPS is used to create an e-Information about the donor and organization that are related to donating the blood (Mandale, et al., 2017). The main service is the communication between patients and blood bank centers.

5.   OneBlood (OneBlood, n.d.) is a mobile application that enables its users to search for places to donate, see health history, lookup for donation history.

6.   Blood Donation (BD) is a mobile application where user send request to all users who use this application and have the same blood type (written in their profile) (Mostafa, et. al, 2013).

7.   The application described in this chapter offers extra features to ease the donation process in the sub-system 'donator app'. The application includes properties such as adding friend, transfer points, donate for charity. It uses IoT to search nearby campaigns and displays some information about the current campaign.

Other applications for the same purpose of connecting donator with the patient could be downloaded from the app store:

8.   Inove Blood Donor, 2018 (Inove Blood Donor, n.d.)
9.   B POSITIVE - Blood Donation, 2018 (B POSITIVE - Blood Donation, n.d.)
10.   Donate Blood, 2019 (Donate Blood, n.d.)
11.   The Blood Donation Process, 2018 (The Blood Donation Process, n.d.)
12.   NHS blood donation –NHS blood donation, 2019 (Home–NHS blood donation, n.d.)

To sum up, these are examples of the current solutions for enhancing the process of blood donation but not limited. All of these applications are selected based on their relevance to the main problem that we target to solve. They offer sub-features which partially solve the problem. No one of them provide the ability to save blood to be available before the critical events occur, but the proposed system adds these extra features in addition to the common feature of connecting donators with patient. Additional feature which is the ability to select the best and the most relevant donators who are (family member, nearby friends, and charity donators as well), these features increase the availability of blood bags and increase the ability of saving lives.

The proposed solution in this chapter adds new features for encouraging donors and for predicting urgent events for helping to take the right action in the right time, where all patient needs are reserved automatically once doctors' examinations are finished. The proposed system takes benefits of the artificial intelligence and machine learning in addition to the cloud computing and IoT for solving problems of rare blood types. All of the systems described previously try to enhance the communication between patients and donators by announcing and communicating them using central database. This feature was expanded in our work to enhance the communication between blood banks as well.

Table 1 summarizes the main features compared to our application. From this table it is possible to infer that all the expected features that our system presents as discussed later. These comprehensive features are for managing blood collection and distribution between the blood banks and the hospitals for enabling donators to serve patients directly and themselves indirectly, where donation points are saved in their balances.

Table 1. Related work summary

Feature		Ahyaha	BD [10]	Smart BB Based On IoT [7]	BB using android [8]	SMS BB [6]	One Blood	Point of Lif
Target		D	D	D	D, BB	D	D, BB	D, BB, H
Request time		CE	CE	CE, NC	CE, NC	CE	NC	CE, NC
Donator communication	Online	✓	✓	✓	✓	✓		✓
	Offline						✓	✓
Availability of blood	Online	✓	✓	✓	✓	✓		✓
	Offline			✓			✓	✓
Distribution	Patient	✓	✓	✓	✓	✓		✓
	Hospital							✓
Organization with	BB			✓	✓	✓	✓	✓
	Hospital							✓
Donator Relation		hu	hu	hu	hu	hu	hu	fm, fr, hu
Donator benefits				✓	✓		✓	✓
Blood type								✓
Total Blood quantitiy		p	mp	mpc	mp	p	mp	mpc
Total points		6	7	13	12	8	9	22

Where: D: Donator, BB: Blood Bank, H: Hospital

Fm: family, fr: friend, hu: human

CE: Critical Event, NC: Nearby Campaign

p: one patient < mp: more-patients < mpc: more-patients continuously

Total points were calculated supposing that every feature = one point, and it is just for comparing the number of recommended services that every project has to support. The impact of a feature that enables patient find donator is less than the feature that enables patient find nearby family and friends as donators as well. In addition to 'find donator', or 'encourage donators to be permanent donators'. From this comparison, we found that our system excels all the existing software and presents promising solutions.

System Description

This section presents more detailed information about the process that the project development team did to extract the system requirements to provide the recommended services, all this information was reflected on the system description presented in this chapter.

Needs Assessment

In order to gather information about system requirements, we have to gain some official privileges from our faculty to visit different hospitals and blood banks. Thus, we prepared some documents and plans for getting recommended information about current processes and the problems facing these organizations in order to understand and infer opportunities that our project idea will be built up on. Team members usually meet every week to discuss current progress, new obstacles and risks, and to determine list of tasks that have to be accomplished before the next meeting, i.e., Periodical meetings assess accomplished tasks highlighting recommendations for the next period, a short plan may be created if it is required. By executing these plans, we could summarize main requirements recommended by these organizations (blood banks and hospitals) as follows:

Hospitals were recommended to:

1. Increase the availability of blood bags in real-time (from blood banks or donators).
2. Organize the delivery of the blood bags with hospitals in an easy and well managed way.
3. Faced problems: in some situations, surgeries' schedule cannot be managed due to the unavailability of the required blood bags.

Blood banks:

1. Organize the way of requesting the blood bags.
2. The difficulty of identifying when they have to save some blood bags on the shelf for urgent surgeries.
3. They complain from the low-level of the donation culture among people.

Other requirements are gathered using social media (questionnaires) for analyzing what donators need in order to be a partner in solving these problems. We found some notes from their answers, in brief, they are:

1. We don't know where the campaign is.
2. We already donate in urgent events if we know patients and, in all times, if they are near us or they are one of our family members.
3. Some of them need special persuasions for donate in most times it is available

Table 2. Milestones and outputs

Milestone	Output
1. Meeting Hospital and Blood bank Manager to discuss exact problems and to get more details about the recommended features.	Features list
2. Limit and discuss final service and features that our system should present to serve main goals.	Features report
3. Organize and put final system architecture	Design report
4. Design pages and forms (i.e., UI) for all sub-systems.	Design Prototype
5. Meeting Blood bank Manager for the second time to show him a prototype (design sequence)	Modifications List
6. Selecting basic services to start implementation in each sub-system in parallel. 7. Hospital registration – create donator profile –start campaign – add new donation – etc.	Task Report
8. Reorganize team members to work on each part according to their experience	Work Plan

All these notes were studied carefully to understand and infer what is behind each answer and comment such as explained in the following few sections. General milestones in brief are organized in Table 2:

Economical, Technical, and Logistical Constraints

Contingency and risk mitigation plan: Table 3 organizes risks according to main phases and system parts. Main phases are: (a) information gathering, (b) development, and (c) system operation. Main system parts are: (a) Blood Bank, (b) Hospital, (c) Donator, and (d) Campaign. Critical constraints are coloured with red. Table 4 shows different constraints and their associated managing rules.

Challenges Encountered and Lessons Learned

As mentioned previously in risk mitigation sub-section, during requirements gathering we needed to understand how the cooperation between hospitals and blood banks are held or established, what are roles of each employee in the blood bank, what are the main rules for distributing blood bags for patients, how blood banks help hospitals in critical issues, etc. we learned in this step that when we intend to develop systems for governmental organizations, we have to work and start meetings formally, i.e., by preparing the required recommendation letters. We have to prepare our questionnaires well to save employee time, so that we can gain their acceptance and cooperation.

Table 3. Risk analysis

Phase	Risk		Likelihood	System Part	How to avoid
	Title / State	Details			
Information gathering	**RS-01:** Main Problems. / Solved	In earlier phases in SDLC, we needed to speak to blood bank manager to gain the required information about current problems in collecting and distributing blood bags	Planning & analysis Phases	Software Engineering, System backbone	- We gained recommendation letters from our faculty to speak to hospital and blood bank mangers. - Also gained some privileges to speak to employees as well in order to gather the required information.
	RS-02: Encourage Donators. / Solved	Which features have to be added to our system in order to encourage donators to be permanent members	Planning & Operational phases		- Our system was proposed based on points idea, where everyone can save donated blood bags as points in his account (balance).
	RS-03: Expected Features / Solved	It is a critical risk to determine early basis and main features of the system (required and recommended facilities) that patients, donators, doctors, and employees need	Mainly in the earlier phases & in directly in development		- The team search for related works to study current solutions and identify most existing risks (i.e., Survey) - Write some posts on social media to analysis highlighted risks and expected features (i.e., Questionnaires). - Finally analysis and summarize results and answers to get final list of the expected features.
Development	**RS-04:** Hospital Requests / Solved	- How to receive requests on blood bags from hospitals? - Can hospitals' systems provide APIs? - What privileges that we need?	Design & Implementation	Hospital Part	By offering these questions on hospital managers (doctors), they prefer to send these requests using a separate system, thus team members suggested implementing sub-system as a web application to enable hospitals to register patients requests.
	RS-05: Managing points / Solved	Listing all constraints for managing patients under critical and urgent conditions.		Blood Bank Part	Studying all constrains as mentioned in **Error! Reference source not found.**
	RS-06: Centralized Database / Solved	Sharing data between different system parts	Implementation	All Parts	- In the prototype version we use firebase tool for sharing data. - But in the next version, data base will be hosted on special server.
	RS-07: Suggesting places / Solved	BB need to start new campaigns to fulfill shortage in blood bags		Blood Bank Part	- Implement some aggregation functions to get places with high total quantities - Implement ML algorithms
	RS-08: Study ML / Solved	Study machine learning fundamentals		Blood Bank Part	- Download some valuable books and study as a team with our supervisor
	RS-09: Study IoT	Buy some basic components to learn IoT, such as arduino,		Campaign and Donator	- Team work cooperate to buy some basic components - Download some valuable

Table 4. Points, constraints and proposed managing rule

No.	Constraint	Solution
1	If patient has enough points	- (Best Case): Just consume the required points form his own balance
2	If patient hasn't enough points	- System search for family members who have enough points ordered by relationship degree to automatically transfer points.
3	If patient has no profile	- Once hospital request was received, a profile was created to the patient and initiated with zero point in his balance. - System can transfer points immediately from the charity points to patient's balance in order to do urgent operations and surgeries, but the hospital was informed to add extra constraints to encourage family members to donate instead on the consumed points (not limited yet). - Add extra fields in the profile table to enable donator to manage his/her points between family use and charity use.

In system analysis phase it is preferable to relay on different methodologies like questionnaires, and Joint Application Development (JAD) sessions. Cooperation between team members in earlier phases comes provides more satisfactions during latest phases. Almost all of User Interfaces were modified due to added features and due to blood bank manger involvement. Thus, before starting implementation in almost services, we decided designing a prototype to gain initial acceptance from blood bank manager. We agreed to implement basic services in each sub-system in parallel at first to present backbone services for blood bank manager in later meetings.

Initial System Specification

System has to provide services of features that tackle many problems as indicated briefly:

- Solve the problem concerning the lack of blood quantities by making the blood available to improve the healthcare services.
- Find the right donors at the right time.
- Provide the full management system for patients who need blood.
- Live monitoring for blood types, current quantities, and recommendations from hospitals.
- People won't pay money to get the blood so they will save their money.
- There will be more blood bags in all hospitals (i.e., supporter live-events).
- Solve the problem of delaying, which happens when the patients need the blood
- Improves the confidence between the government and our system through enhancing medical sector of the Ministry of Health.

- Organize the distribution process of ambulances on all regions to avoid the problems like the ambulances were founded in regions don't have any blood donator or in regions suffer from lacking the blood type that has a greatest need, this solution save the time and efforts so the process become more organized.

Such features will build a new organized environment in the healthcare sector by enhancing performance of the blood bank systems, where its results will be reflected on healthcare services presented by the governmental hospitals. High functional description for main services that our system presents are as follows:

- **Search for Donors:** Enables patients search for near donors and call them.
- **Urgent Family Announcement:** Enables patients' family members know their status directly.
- Connect patients with donors.
- **Create Accounts for New Donors:** Donors can create their accounts and track their health states using reports that the system adds for them.
- Our system enhances the trust (between donors and ministry of health) by offering some medical help and advice for the donors.
- **Monitor and Analyze Blood Types:** All blood types and their current quantities are analyzed in the real-time to act best actions in the right time.
- Reserve certain blood type for certain surgery operation: hospitals can reserve blood for their patients according to hospital surgery schedule.
- The donator who has the largest number of points from his donations processes gets a special treatment from different sectors.

This application is recommended to enhance its performance by getting benefits of the latest technologies and science.

Final System Specification

Requirements Elicitation, Analysis, Prioritization and Change Management

By analyzing the current problems in the donation process using questionnaires and JAD sessions, we found that most people need to trust in the distribution process, and they can donate only for patients they know. The main goal of our system is to encourage donators to be permanent members in our system especially in urgent situations for serving the critical cases, which lead us to put some features like saving points in donator balance to save his/her family when some circumstances occur, and sending medical analysis report concerning their states.

Thus, features to encourage donators came in front of recommended features list. We think in the idea of saving blood bags for themselves and for their families to leverage trust level for donators. On the other side, for people who already has the culture of donation, we added another feature called 'Charity points', so that saved points could be used for serving urgent case (people haven't accounts and are in need). The common solution is to call donors in urgent cases. From this point we think to improve this process by collecting more blood bags and grouping people according to their choices to participate in our catchword *'sharing the blood for saving life flood'*. The proposed system supposes some rules to be executed in order to manage and organize the blood collection and distribution processes.

To sum up, during the analysis phase, our system was recommended to present solutions for the following problems, which recommends some modifications on the initial system requirements such as indicated in Table 5:

- Blood Shortage.
- Unbalancing among different BBs.
- Getting required blood bags on time, i.e., saving time consumed for getting need blood type and quantities.
- Obligating the patient relatives, the required amount of blood (patients or their families search for donors).
- Culture of donations depends on the trust between donors and BBs.
- Random distribution for campaigns.
- Difficulty of distributing blood types for patients.
- Surgeries in hospitals depend on the availability of blood (type, quantity)

Functional Requirements and Main Stakeholders

Patient is the first point of contact who gains the most valuable benefits of this system (saving his/her life). Also *Hospitals* are main stakeholders, where the system can improve quality of services they present. *Blood bank manager*, *Employees*, *donators*, and *doctors* are main system users; also they can act as donators to save their life and their family. Blood banks get a lot of benefits from system features. Main actors of our system are indicated in the following use-case diagram.

Figure 2 briefly highlights most of functional requirements as a list of services categorized by main users. But for more details, we summarized them in a form of use-case diagram to indicate which actor can access which feature.

Table 5. A list of changes and modifications made in system features

Previous Features	Current Features
Register patients' needs	*Hospital registration* was modified to register *criticality level* for patients' needs, so that our system can rank patients according to their states to fulfill their needs.
Inform family members to transfer points	*Enabling automatic point transfer* between family members once a critical or urgent issue has been occurred and notify extra donators if points are not enough.
Search for donators for urgent donation	*In addition to this process, allow to modify donator profile by setting criteria to manage his/her points:* for example if someone donated for many times and has extra points in his/her account he can put some of them for the charity use and save the other points for urgent family use.
Get list of requests and available quantities	*(Visual Analysis):* adding *extra charts* for the bank sub-system in order to present powerful monitoring for available blood bags in campaigns in the real-time.
Initiate campaigns manually	*Enable our system to analyze previous campaigns results* in order to predict new valuable presence places for donators considering current shortages in blood types.
(New Feature)	*Enable donators to track nearby campaigns (Using GPS)*
(New Feature)	*Automatic schedule surgeries in hospitals once requests are served*

Figure 2. Use-cases diagram

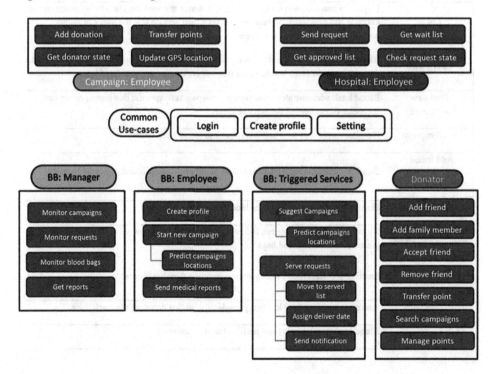

Table 6 presents a brief description for some selected common use-cases, while main such as, make donations, start new campaign, mange balance points, and manage patient request use cease are written in fully dressed format in Table 7.

System Sequence Diagram (SSD)

Figure 3, Figure 4, present SSD for some selected use cases to explain more details for the interactions between the actors of these use cases and the system.

Design Class Diagram (DCD)

Main classes are different actors (e.g., BB employee, donator, patient, and doctor) and main system parts (e.g., campaign, BB, hospital, donator-App); additional classes are such as (medical-report, request, donation, notification, friend, balance, blood bag), Figure 5 shows relationships between classes after filtering and summarization.

Table 6. A brief description for selected use-cases

Use cases	Description
Login	Login is a common service in system parts, where the user can login to the system using his code and password. System determines which service that the user can access according to his assigned privileges.
Check state	Blood bank employee checks if donator has an account to retrieve all required data in the donation process (e.g., last donation date) or create new account (profile).
Start new campaign	Blood bank administrator launches new campaigns to specific destination or suggested locations where needed donators be there.
Send requests	Hospital employees send patients request to blood bank system
Add friend / family member	Donator can add more friends or family members to share blood points with them.
Transfer points	Friends can share their points of blood bags in their balance
Monitor campaigns	Blood bank administrator can follow all of campaign to know all of its information like place, quantities of blood bags.
Sending medical reports	Sending medical reports to donators to improve their healthcare.
Update GBS	Campaigns update their location periodically, so that donators can track them.
Add new profile	Blood bank employee creates profiles for new donators.

Table 7. Main use-cases written in fully dressed format

Use Case Name	Donation process
Actor(S)Name	Campaign employee
Trigger	Create new process of donation in application
Precondition	Find process donation under way
Main success scenario	1. Employee enters his code and password (login). 2. Checks if donator has an account to retrieve all required data in the donation process (e.g., last donation date) Campaign employee enters donator's card id to check his state for donation. 3. add point to donator balance 4. The system tell the Campaign employee confirm from data is correct 5. End process of donation
Alternative Paths	*a. In case of system failure: -Notification should require from users to use the system at any time later. - Employee of blood bank restart the application 2.a he has to create new account (profile) for him 2.b Campaign employee enters donator's information (name, telephone number, age, etc). 3.a . If the system refuse to illustrate anything
Post condition	1. Registration is completed 2. The system must send report to blood banks. 3. Campaign balance increases by donation quantities 4. blood type quantities increases by one 5. Donator waits to receive medical reports. 6. BB manager view real-time donations
Use Case Name	Start new campaign
Actor(S)Name	BB: Employee
Trigger	Create new campaign
Precondition Main success scenario	BB: Employee should start day work 1. enter his code and his password (login). 2. launch new campaigns to specific destination. 3. Assign employees 4. confirm
Alternative Paths	*a. In system failure: -Notification should require from users to use the system at any time later. - BB: Employee should restart his pc. 2.a select from suggested locations where needed donators be there 2.b Campaign employee receive notification about place which go to it
Post condition	1. Registration is completed 2. Campaign was added to the schedule 3. Employees delivered messages about campaign details

Non- Functional Requirements

In order to build system that gains trust of its users, we determine the following features to be integrated in our system to enhance confidence level for our users:

- **Availability:** Main system requirement is the internet. In case of the Internet is unavailable, the system stores the data on local server until the connection is back then replicate data.

- **Security:** Server should be secured, and access privileges should be organized and assigned.
- Easy to use: because donators are normal users.
- **Reliable Communication Between System Part:** Because data sharing between hospitals, blood banks, and campaigns monitor real-time availability of blood bags.
- **Operational:** The system is designed to have a web-based and a mobile-based application. The user will need to download the application from Google play store.

Figure 3. System sequence diagram: create profile - add donation

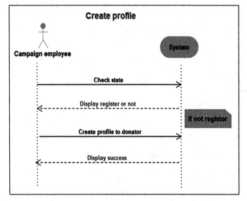
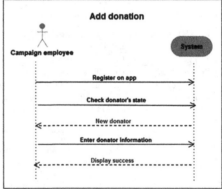

Figure 4. System sequence diagram: monitor blood bags -get report

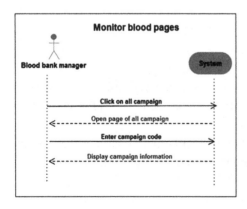
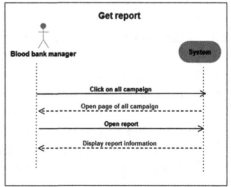

Figure 5. Point of life design class diagram

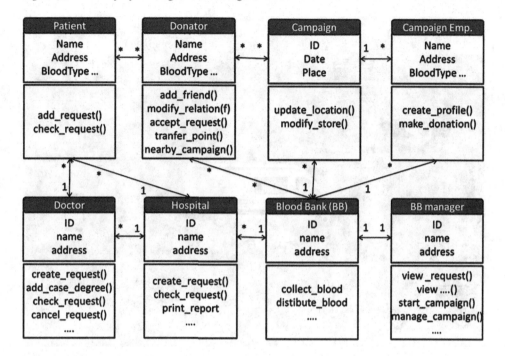

SYSTEM OVERVIEW

This section provides an overview of the proposed system. Main parts as mentioned earlier are: The first two main parts (i.e., organizations: Hospital, and Blood Bank), and the other two essential parts are donator and campaigns. Based on this organization, the following scenario clarifies how these parts cooperate to make donation processes easy and available in the real-time without any pressure.

Scenario

Suppose that someone did an accident and the ambulance carried him to the nearest hospital. The problem now is how to save that patient who needs blood transfusion for at least X blood bags. Thus the hospital communicates with the nearest blood bank, but unfortunately, there aren't available blood bags to save patient life. In that critical time, the patient is requested to inform his family (but how?), also to search for donators, but who is available now and who has the same blood type?

Figure 6 explains the above scenario and solution presented by our system. Where circle (1) is the hospital, a request was registered for the patient, now the BB receive

Figure 6. A scenario for declaring benefits of the IoT as a sub-system in our project

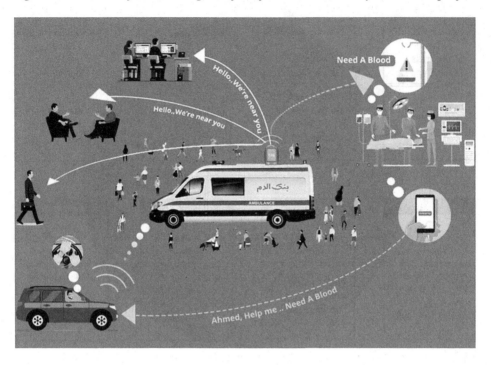

Figure 7. System Architecture: (a) Main Parts - (b) IoT model in our system

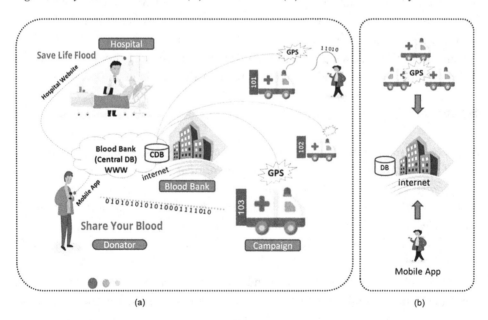

a new patient request, patient's family members and friends are informed with that accident and know that he was in need to blood bags such as shown in circle (2), friends now can transfer points from their balance and can search for nearby campaigns to donate (i.e., thanks to IoT technology). Circle (3) is the campaign car that is located in a place where most donators exist, circle (4), due to historical data analysis using aggregation functions and machine learning algorithms for prediction.

System Architecture

The following figure explains the main architecture of our system in more details, where the left part of Figure 7 explains how different parts of the system communicate and cooperate to serve patient and to help donator to present his service in an easy way.

Hardware Architecture

The proposed system has two versions due to some circumstances on the implementation costs and blood bank acceptance, current version uses simple components to integrate benefits of the IoT, such as shown in the left part of Figure 7. The figure indicates how the system implements the IoT module to integrate its benefits in the total benefits of the system to serve patients and donators. The next version, which is postponed for getting final acceptance, basis on integrating the IoT deeply in our system, for instance designing some type of wearable that add more smartness in the life for enabling patients more secure and personalized notifications.

Software Architecture

In this section we present the main services as a list of milestones indicating work progress and who are involved in each sub-system. Figure 8 lists of services that each sub-system presents, note that next step and final step was colored red in during interim report submission, but now these services are finished. The software main architecture of the proposed system could be categorized into main four parts as follows:

- **Part One (the Core of the Blood Bank System):** Which collect all data about campaigns, collected blood bags, patients' requests (recorded by hospitals), this part is being implemented as a web application, this part enable all doctors and employees in the bank to manage and do all required functions with more facilities.
- **Part Two (Hospitals):** This part of the system is being implemented as a web application, through which the hospital can request and record their need

Figure 8. Software architecture detailed by milestones, time schedule, and team members

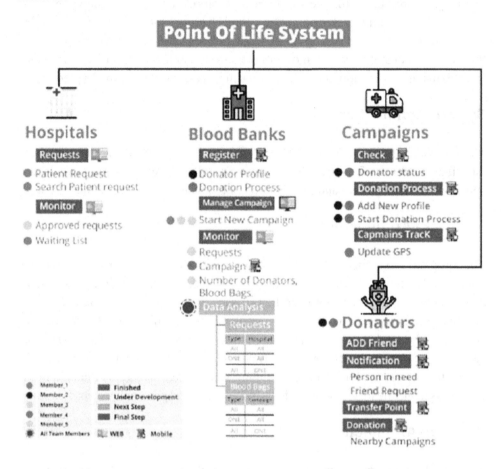

form the blood bags (i.e., record patient information and limit critical degree for every case).

- **Part Three (Donators):** This part is being implemented as a mobile application, which enables donators to follow and track current near campaigns, receive their medical analysis report, get notification about critical events concerning a member of their families, friends or any patient near them and need a help. Using this application, donators can transfer some of their points to other accounts so that patients in need to extra point can deliver the required blood bags.

- **Part Four (Campaign):** A mobile application is being implemented for campaigns so that employee can record new donation process creating profiles for new donators.

SYSTEM IMPLEMENTATION

This section discusses the implementation details declaring each stage to fulfill the main scenario listed above in system description. Next sub-section clarifies algorithms implemented in the project based on use-cases declared earlier. Then, the following sub-section explains user interfaces. IoT and ML explanations is given in the subsequent sub-section.

System Algorithms

In this section we explain a flowchart for serving patients requests. The full scenario starts when a patient entering the hospital. Firstly, the hospital registers a request for the patient to be sent to nearby blood bank, once BB receives the request, it checks if that patient has enough points or he needs to transfer some points from his family members and friends. Our system checks this state automatically and withdraws remaining points then informs his family and friends. In the case that they have no points it checks if there were a charity points available or not. Once points were withdrawn, his request will be moved to the served list to assign delivery date for receiving blood bags as indicated on the right-hand part in Figure 9.

This section presents in more details the user interfaces in each part and explains how each part presents the required use-cases mentioned earlier.

Hospital Sub-System

Using this part of the system, hospitals can login to the system (left part of Figure 10) to manage requests. The right part of Figure 10, the hospitals can view current requests grouped by their states. When doctor or employee press on the add request button a new window (see Figure 11) will open to fill all required details (patient id, blood type, quantity, level (i.e., criticality degree... etc.).

Blood Bank Sub-System

This part was implemented as web application. Employees login to the system to handle incoming patients' requests, and lunch new campaigns to collect blood bags from donor. Such as shown in Figure 12 users login to the system (see the left part of Figure 12) and manage all processes in blood bank, the right part of Figure 12 shows current blood statistics such as current requests, current shortage, and available quantities in blood bags and so on. Employee can lunch new campaigns as discussed before and select which destination campaign will be located according to the required need and availability of donors in that place (see Figure 13). This

Figure 9. Serving patients requests

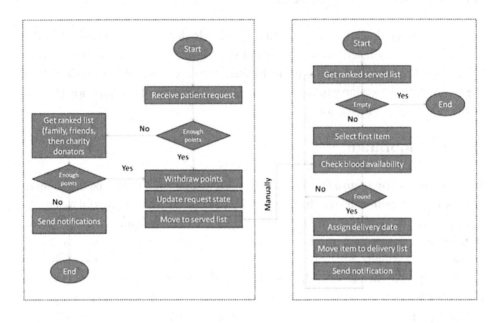

Figure 10. Hospital. (a) login to the system. - (b) view requests.

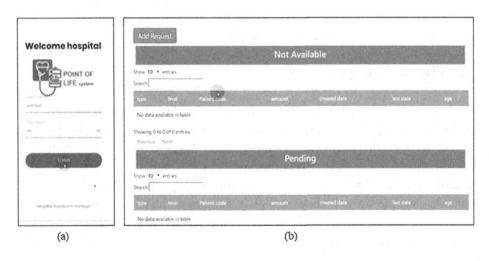

Figure 11. Hospital - add new request

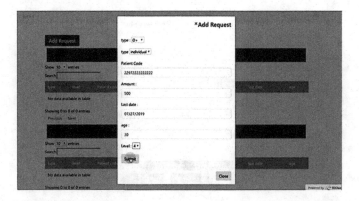

service was presented into versions as explained next, using simple aggregation functions and using machine learning.

Donator Sub-System

Donator mobile application (Figure 14) enables its users to add friend mange points for family and friend use or for charity use; also, they can search for nearby campaigns (IoT implementation), such as shown in the left part of Figure 14. After donation, BB sends medical analysis reports for them, they can save their report to be healthy archive. They can receive notifications concerning other friends.

Some snapshots are taken for more explanation in the implementation of this part as follows. Code behind add friend button is shown in Figure 15, which is divided into four parts after checking the value of the current state for the current user with the person who wants to authenticate him:

Figure 12. Blood Bank. (a) login screen. (b) general blood statistics.

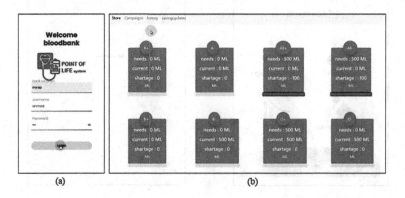

Figure 13. Blood Bank -new campaign registration

- If the current state value is equal to "not_friends" in this case, it allows the sender to send a friendship request to the other person. The id of both the sender and the receiver is stored in the (Request Friends) table and the current state is changed to "request_sent".
- If the value of current state is equal to "request_sent" in this case, the user can cancel the friendship request that sent, and then the id of both the sender and the receiver is deleted in the (Request Friends) table and the current state is changed to "not_friends".
- If the current state value is equal to "request_received" in this case, the user whose friendship request was sent may accept this friendship request or reject

Figure 14. Donator (a) main services. (b) search for nearby campaign service

it and then store the id of both sender and receiver in the (Friends) table and delete the id of both the sender and the receiver in the table (Friends Request) and change the current state to be equal to "friends."

- If the value of current state is equal to "friends" then the user can cancel the friendship between them and then delete the id of both the sender and the receiver in the (Friends) table and change the current state to be "not_friends".

In the following, code behind buttons are briefly explained.

- Manage points button: the left part of Figure 16 shows balance points, shared points and family points. This button has the possibility of distributing points to the family points or the shared points, as shown in the right part of Figure 16. The value of the points is reduced or increased according to the values that are entered in the family or the shared points. It is not possible to enter values greater than balance points.

- Near campaign button: Figure 17 retrieves latitude and longitude values for each vehicle where they are launched and follow the campaign that is near from the current location of the user. The current user location is obtained

Figure 15. Donator -code behind add friend button

```
if (!senderUserId.equals(receiverUserId)) {

    send_request.setOnClickListener((v) → {

            if (current_state.equals("not_friends")) {
                btn_requestPoints.setEnabled(false);
                sendRequestToDonator();
            }
            if (current_state.equals("request_sent")) {
                btn_requestPoints.setEnabled(false);

                cancelRequestToDonator();
            }
            if (current_state.equals("request_received")) {
                btn_requestPoints.setEnabled(false);

                acceptFriendRequest();
            }
            if (current_state.equals("friends")) {

                btn_requestPoints.setEnabled(true);
                unFriendThisPerson();
            }

    });
```

after displaying a dialog for allows permission to access the current location of the user. Next, the nearest vehicles are shown in the map. Then, the user can locate the appropriate location and can go to the nearest vehicles and donate.

- Viewing reports: Figure 18, in which the results of the medical reports of the donor after his donation are retrieved from the Firebase.

Campaigns Sub-System

A mobile application is being implemented for campaigns so that BB employee can record a new donation process creating profiles for new donators, also can get some information about current report, such as shown in Figure 19. For making a donation, empoyee firstly enter donator id and search if he has an account, if he has an account a profile and donation previlages appear such as shown in Figure 20.

Figure 16. Donator - Code behind manage points button

```
//get points and shared Points from firebase                              a
donatorPoints = dataSnapshot.child("points").getValue(Integer.class);
sharedPoints = dataSnapshot.child("sharedPoints").getValue(Integer.class);
family_points = dataSnapshot.child("familyPoints").getValue(Integer.class);

//show data on screen
edit_point_shared.setText(String.valueOf(sharedPoints));
edit_point_family.setText(String.valueOf(family_points));
value_YourPoint.setText(String.valueOf(donatorPoints));
```

```
btn_edit_shared.setOnClickListener(new View.OnClickListener() {          b
    @override
    public void onClick(View v) {
        if (btn_edit_shared.getText().toString().equals("Edit")) {...} else {...}
    }
});
btn_edit_family.setOnClickListener(new View.OnClickListener() {
    @override
    public void onClick(View v) {
        if (btn_edit_family.getText().toString().equals("Edit")) {...} else {...}
    }
});
```

Figure 17. Donator - code behind nearby campaign

```
private void getCampaignsLocations(final OnLoadingFinish onLoadingFinish) {

    onLoadingFinish.onStart();
    DatabaseReference rootRef = FirebaseDatabase.getInstance().getReference();
    final DatabaseReference campaignsRef = rootRef.child("campaigns");
    ValueEventListener valueEventListener = new ValueEventListener() {
        @Override
        public void onDataChange(DataSnapshot dataSnapshot) {
            for (DataSnapshot ds : dataSnapshot.getChildren()) {
                double latitude = ds.child("location").child("latitude").getValue(Double.class);
                double longitute = ds.child("location").child("longitude").getValue(Double.class);
                LatLng latLng = new LatLng(latitude, longitute);
                campaignsLocations.add(latLng);
            }
            onLoadingFinish.onSuccess();
        }
    }
}
```

Figure 18. Donator - code behind view report button

```
DonatorsRef.child(online_user_id).addValueEventListener(new ValueEventListener() {
    @Override
    public void onDataChange(@NonNull DataSnapshot dataSnapshot) {

        if (dataSnapshot.exists()) {

            if (dataSnapshot.hasChild( path: "ex1") & dataSnapshot.hasChild( path: "ex2") & dataSnapshot.hasChild( path: "ex3"))
                //get reports from firebase and check if it positive or not
                sugar = dataSnapshot.child("ex1").getValue(String.class);
                liver = dataSnapshot.child("ex2").getValue(String.class);
                virus = dataSnapshot.child("ex3").getValue(String.class);

                //show data on screen
                if (sugar.equals("+")) {
                    state_suger.setText("Positive");

                }
                if (liver.equals("+")) {
                    state_liver.setText("Positive");
                }

                if (virus.equals("+")) {
                    state_virus.setText("Positive");
                }
```

Machine learning algorithms (supervised learning) are used in the project for analyzing and classifying data (results from previous campaigns) in order to predict the most relevant and valuable places for starting new campaigns, which enables the proposed system to schedule new campaigns automatically considering current needs and shortage in blood types and quantities, such as shown in Figure 21. The implemented machine learning algorithms are regression for predicting the amount of blood that will be received and the SVM classification algorithm, which create a hyper-plane to distinguish between categories, which has been used for predicting the places of donations.

Taking benefits of the IoT and machine learning enhances performance of our proposed system where IoT enable donators to know about the nearby campaigns such as mentioned above (see Figure 7) and machine learning (ML) enable our system to

Figure 19. Campaign Login – services – current report

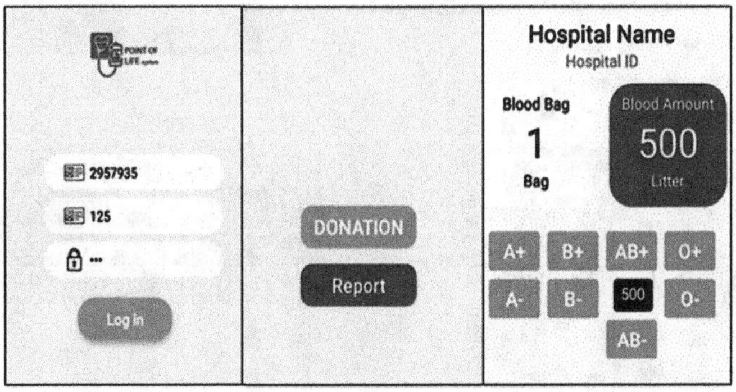

Figure 20. Campaign - make donation - get profile and privileges

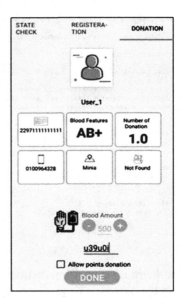

Figure 21. Point of life system analyzes collected data to predict new campaigns' places

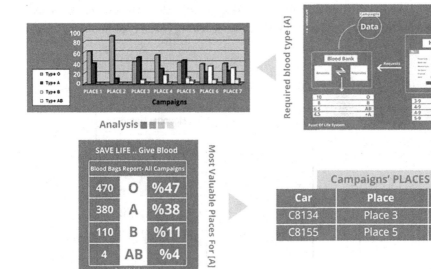

predict which place that campaign has to go to in order to get the required quantities and types. In addition to using machine learning our system can assess donation culture level, such as show in Figure 22, left part correlation matrix - generated by Python - indicates that job has the higher impact in the generated dataset. Figure 22 right part shows density distribution over each attribute. For example, from this figure, we infer that the higher donation processes were done by men and number of donators who donate two bags is higher than who donate one bag per time.

Campaign dataset was saved as a '.csv file' for executing ML algorithms and for data visualization to understand the main features that have impact on the blood donation or transfusion. The first step is to pre-process the data to be suitable for the

Figure 22. Blood Bank dataset (DS) - (a) Correlation Matrix– (b) density plot for DS attributes

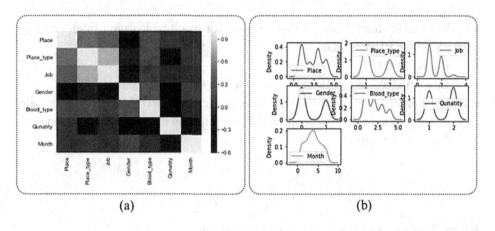

(a)   (b)

Figure 23. Load dataset after mapping fields

```
[34]:  # View first 10 rows
       from pandas import read_csv
       filename = "Blood_Bank_Year.csv"
       #names = ['Camp_id', 'Place', 'Place_type', 'Job', 'Gender', 'Blood_type', 'Qunatity', 'Month']
       data = read_csv(filename) #, names=names)
       peek = data.head(10)
       print(peek)
       print("------------------------------------------------------------------")
       # Dimentions
       shape = data.shape
       print(shape)
       print("------------------------------------------------------------------")
       types = data.dtypes
       print(types)

          Camp_id  Place  Place_type  Job  Gender  Blood_type  Qunatity  Month
       0     A100      1           1    1       0           1         1      1
       1     A100      1           1    1       0           1         2      1
       2     A100      1           1    1       0           1         2      1
       3     A100      1           1    1       0           1         2      1
       4     A100      1           1    2       0           1         2      1
       5     A100      1           1    1       0           1         2      1
       6     A100      1           1    1       0           1         2      1
       7     A100      1           1    1       0           1         2      1
       8     A100      1           1    1       0           2         2      1
```

machine learning algorithms by encoding values such as places into digits, blood types into digits, gender into binary, place type into digits, and month into digit.

The second step is to do some quantitative data analysis on quantities of each blood type, such as shown in Figure 23. Figure 24 shows some statistics such as mean, minimum, maximum, etc. for each attribute in the dataset.

The third step is to implement logistic regression in order select the best features' scores (ranking features based on their impact), such as shown in Figure 25. The fourth step is to split dataset into training and testing (Figure 26).

Hardware and Software Platforms

For blood banks and hospitals, the used hardware should have the specifications that can handle big data applications. Consequently, the development team planned to use massive storage capacity, GPUs and Multicore CPUs.

- Processor: -Intel® core™ i5-4200, and for machine learning Intel® core ™ i7-4790 CPU@3.60GHz.
- RAM: 6.00 GB
- Linux and Windows 10, 64-bit are used as Operating System
- For donator, the system is designed to include a web-based and a mobile-based application. The donator will need to download the application from Google Play Store.

Figure 24. Python statistics on campaign dataset

```
In [35]:  from pandas import set_option
          set_option('display.width', 100)
          set_option('precision', 3)
          description = data.describe()
          print(description)
          print("----------------------------------------------------------------")
          class_counts = data.groupby('Blood_type').size()
          print(class_counts)

                  Place  Place_type     Job  Gender  Blood_type  Qunatity     Month
          count 512.000     512.000 512.000 512.000     512.000   512.000   512.000
          mean    2.326       1.342   1.447   0.377       2.051     1.529     3.822
          std     1.142       0.475   0.564   0.485       1.064     0.500     1.815
          min     1.000       1.000   1.000   0.000       1.000     1.000     1.000
          25%     1.000       1.000   1.000   0.000       1.000     1.000     2.000
          50%     2.000       1.000   1.000   0.000       2.000     2.000     4.000
          75%     3.000       2.000   2.000   1.000       3.000     2.000     5.000
          max     4.000       2.000   3.000   1.000       4.000     2.000     7.000
          ----------------------------------------------------------------
          Blood_type
          1    209
          2    136
          3     99
          4     68
          dtype: int64
```

Development tools, languages, etc., utilized during the project are given in the following:

- NetBeans (Free), Android Studio (Free), Microsoft visual studios (with a license), Anaconda (Free), Tensorflow (Free), Microsoft office (free), visual paradigm (Free),
- Adobe xd (with a license).
- The team developed the mobile app with Android Studio that also needs at least Android 4.4.2.
- For machine learning, the development team used Python (Anconda and Pysharm) with machine learning packages such as skit-learn.
- For web developing, the development team used HTML5, CSS3, JQuery and JavaScript.

Figure 25. Logistic regression

```
In [89]:   # Feature Extraction with RFE
           from sklearn.feature_selection import RFE
           from sklearn.linear_model import LogisticRegression

           # feature extraction
           model = LogisticRegression()
           rfe = RFE(model, 3)
           fit = rfe.fit(X, Y)
           print("Num Features: ", fit.n_features_)
           print("Selected Features: ", fit.support_)
           print("Feature Ranking: ", fit.ranking_)

           # feature extraction
           from sklearn.ensemble import ExtraTreesClassifier
           model = ExtraTreesClassifier()
           model.fit(X, Y)
           print(model.feature_importances_)

           Num Features:  3
           Selected Features:  [ True False  True False  True False]
           Feature Ranking:  [1 2 1 3 1 4]
           [0.485 0.192 0.04  0.115 0.03  0.138]
```

Figure 26. Training and testing accuracy

```
names = ['Camp_id','Place','Place_type','Job','Gender','Blood_type','Qunatity','Month']
dataframe = read_csv(filename, names=names)
array = dataframe.values
X = array[:,1:7]
Y = array[:,3]
test_size = 0.33
seed = 7
X_train, X_test, Y_train, Y_test = train_test_split(X, Y, test_size=test_size,random_state=seed)
model = LogisticRegression()
model.fit(X_train, Y_train)
result = model.score(X_test, Y_test)
print("Accuracy: ",result*100.0,"%")

Accuracy:  95.26627218934911 %
```

CONCLUSION AND FUTURE WORK

The proposed system presents a mobile application and web application for collecting and distributing blood bags between blood banks and hospitals in order to enhance the healthcare sector taking benefits of new technologies such as the Internet of things (IoT) and machine learning. IoT affects our daily life, where it has been integrated in daily life objects and things to inform about their states and about their surrounding environment. Taking benefits of this technology in our proposed system could enhance and easy services presented to donators to interact with the system and participate as permanent donators.

Using the developed system, family members can help themselves when a critical issue occurs for any member. Once a critical notification has been delivered by family members (i.e., urgent notification concerns a family member), they automatically share their blood points and discover all nearby campaigns to donate, where campaigns cars host GPS devices and update their location in the real-time, such as shown in Figure 7, where patient was in a hospital and in need for blood bag, the point of life system can help him by informing his friends and family member, so that blood points were added to patient's account.

Taking benefits of machine learning implementations also enhance the smartness of our system, where the proposed system analyzes and classifies data (results from previous campaigns) in order to predict the most relevant and valuable places for starting new campaigns, i.e., scheduling new campaigns automatically considering current needs and shortage in blood types and quantities.

To sum up, outcome could be categorized based on main stakeholders such as follows:

The Hospital sub-system:

1. Gaining the required blood bags in an organized manner by registering requests with the required blood bags for every patient assigning his criticality degree.
2. Real-time monitoring for the availability of blood bags for certain request (i.e., patient).
3. Receive sufficiency-schedule for patients' requests to help hospital administrations in organizing surgeries and operations.

The Blood Bank and campaign sub-systems:

1. Monitor the campaigns and the availability of blood types and quantities in real-time.
2. Organize distribution process of the blood bags.

3. Increasing the availability of blood bags by encouraging donators, i.e., presenting to donators valuable feedback reports and notifications on their healthy and on their family.
4. Initiate campaigns in an easy way by selecting the valuable places for fulfilling patients' blood needs.
5. Real-time analysis for the donation processes done by all campaigns.

The Donator sub-system:

1. Increase maturity or culture level for donators to understand that they help themselves at first and their family as well by sharing their blood points from their accounts.
2. Increase charity cooperation especially in helping patients to save their life.
3. Remove obstacle for gaining urgent healthcare services that require blood donation in real-time.

The next version of our system can analyze settlement diseases to predict required blood quantities and types in the near future, for example the average number of children who suffer from 'the Mediterranean anemia' next year and percentage of each required blood type. Moreover, machine learning algorithms will be implemented for sending personalized notifications for certain donators in the right time. The next version can also classify and organize requests from hospitals based on the criticality of cases (i.e., ranking patients). Based on patients' information gathered from hospitals requests, our system can predict the required quantities and types of blood types in the near future. We plan to add extra features to improve the satisfaction level for donators, patients, blood banks, hospitals by studying current technologies that aid our implementation. IoT will be implemented deeply by designing special wearable devices that notify patients with vital measurements. Also it can call donators and inform family members and friends automatically.

REFERENCES

Ahyaha. (2019). Retrieved from https://play.google.com/store/apps/details?id=com.Ihsan.Ahyaha&hl=en_US

Brownlee, J. (2016). *Machine Learning Mastery With Python: Understand Your Data, Create Accurate Models and Work Projects End-to-End*. Academic Press.

Dell Emc. (2019). *Envision The Future: Point Of Life - A Smart System for Managing Donation in Blood Banks*. Retrieved from https://youtu.be/g3-C6aBD3Tw

Donate Blood. (2019). Retrieved from https://apps.apple.com/au/app/donate-blood/id1438603103

Inove Blood Donor. (2018). Retrieved from http://ow.ly/uJ2XT

Krishna, G. M., & Nagaraju, S. (2016). Design and implementation of short message service (SMS) based blood bank. In *International Conference on Inventive Computation Technologies (ICICT)*, Coimbatore, India.

Mahalle, R. R., & Thorat, S. S. (2018). Smart Blood Bank Based On IoT: A Review. *International Research Journal of Engineering and Technology*, 6(I), 1–3.

Mandale, M., Jagtap, P., Mhaske, P., Vidhate, S., & Patil, S. (2017). Implementation of Blood Donation Application using Android Smartphone. *International Journal of Advance Research, Ideas and Innovations in Technology*, 3(VI), 876–879.

Ministry of Health and Population. (2016). *National Blood Transfusion Services.* Retrieved from https://smc.gov.eg/hospitals.php?hospital_name=national_blood_transfusion_services

Mostafa, A.M., Youssef, A.E., & Alshorbagy, G. (2013). *A Framework for a Smart Social Blood Donation System Based on Mobile Cloud Computing*. Academic Press.

National Health Service, UK. (2019). *NHS blood donation*. Retrieved from https://www.blood.co.uk/

OneBlood. (2019). Retrieved from https://apps.apple.com/us/app/oneblood-donor-app/id1253115377

Segue Technologies, B. POSITIVE - Blood Donation. (2018). Retrieved from https://goo.gl/CUOr7I

The Blood Donation Process. (2018). Retrieved from https://play.google.com/store/apps/details?id=com.Blooddonation.smartapp

World Health Organization. (2019). *Who calls for increase in voluntary blood donors to save millions of lives.* Retrieved from https://www.who.int/ar/news-room/detail/23-08-1436-who-calls-for-increase-in-voluntary-blood-donors-to-save-millions-of-lives

Younan, M., Khattab, S., & Bahgat, R. (2015). Evaluation of an Integrated Testbed Environment for The Web of Things. *International Journal on Advances in Intelligent Systems*, 8(3-4).

Younan, M., Khattab, S., & Bahgat, R. (2017). A WoT Testbed for Research and Course Projects. In *Managing the Web of Things: Linking the Real World to the Web* (pp. 181–204). Elsevier. doi:10.1016/B978-0-12-809764-9.00008-1

KEY TERMS AND DEFINITIONS

Blood Bank: Is a place where blood donated by people is stored and distributed to hospitals whenever needed.

Blood Bank Management System: Is an information system to help blood banks in managing their work related to donators and hospitals.

Donator: A person who donates blood.

IOT: Is a set of technologies where different devices are connected throughout the internet.

Machine Learning: Is a collection of algorithms that learn from historical data.

SDLC: Is the system development life cycle, which refers to the steps undertaken to create and maintain an information system.

Software Engineering: Is the process of applying some engineering techniques in the process of software development.

APPENDIX 1

Project Plan

System development life cycle (SDLC) of this project is being implemented using combination of parallel development and prototype methodologies. Based on main parts of the system, Figure 27 shows system features and their progress in more details. Our team suggests assigning team leader for each part to be accomplished and revised well with our supervisor.

Campaign Dataset

Campaign dataset was saved in '.csv' format in order to be readable by python libraries (IDE: python – jupyter) (see Figure 28).

Project Presentation (Video Link)

A presentation for this project was recorded as a video and uploaded at YouTube under the following link https://youtu.be/g3-C6aBD3Tw (Point of Life - Presentation, 2019).

Figure 27. Detailed schedule of the second semester

System Part	Features	February				March				April				May				June			
		Week 1	Week 2	Week 3	Week 4	Week 5	Week 6	Week 7	Week 8	Week 9	Week 10	Week 11	Week 12	Week 13	Week 14	Week 15	Week 16	Week 17	Week 18	Week 19	Week 20
Part 1 (Blood bank system website)	system analysis																				
	Create new campaigns																				
	Follow campaigns (data collection)																				
	Manage reports																				
	Monitoring hospital requests																				
	Send donator notification																				
	Analyze blood bags																				
	Surgeon scheduling																				
	Predicting places of campaigns																				
	Number of donators transfer																				
	Data analysis (requests & blood bags)																				
Part 2 (Hospital system)	Hospital record need of blood bags (Patient requests)																				
	Hospital manage reports																				
	Approved request																				
	Waiting List																				
	Confirm scheduling (next version)																				
Part 3 (Donators mobile app)	Donators follow & track the current near campaigns																				
	Donators receive medical analysis reports																				
	Donators get notification about critical events																				
	Search & add friends																				
	donators take points because of his donation																				
	Donators can transfer some of their points to other accounts																				
	Receive suggested scheduling																				
Part 4 (Campaigns mobile app with car follower)	Car follower checks state of donators																				
	Car follower creates profile for new donators																				
	Car follower records new donation processes																				
	Car follower tracks maps by cars																				
	Assembling & testing																				
Final part	Finishing postponed enhancements and Retesting full system, writing final report ,and preparing discussion or defence presentation																				
	Intervals for other tasks									Interim report					Lab exam	Final exams					

Figure 28. Original dataset for campaigns in .csv format

Camp_id	Place	Place_type	Job	Gender	Blood_type	Qunatity	Month
A100	1	1	1	0	1	1	1
A100	1	1	1	0	1	2	1
A100	1	1	1	0	1	2	1
A100	1	1	1	0	1	2	1
A100	1	1	2	0	1	2	1
A100	1	1	1	0	1	2	1
A100	1	1	1	0	1	2	1
A100	1	1	1	0	1	2	1
A100	1	1	1	0	2	2	1
A100	1	1	1	0	3	2	1
A100	1	1	1	0	4	2	1
A100	1	1	2	0	2	2	1
A100	1	1	1	0	2	2	1
A100	1	1	1	0	2	2	1
A100	1	1	1	0	3	1	1
A100	1	1	1	1	3	1	1
A100	1	1	2	1	1	1	1
A100	1	1	1	1	1	1	1
A100	1	1	1	1	2	1	1
A100	1	1	1	1	2	2	1
A100	1	1	1	1	3	1	1
A100	1	1	1	1	3	1	1
A100	1	1	1	1	4	1	1
A100	1	1	1	1	4	1	1
A101	2	2	2	0	1	2	1
A101	2	2	2	0	2	2	1

Related Readings

To continue IGI Global's long-standing tradition of advancing innovation through emerging research, please find below a compiled list of recommended IGI Global book chapters and journal articles in the areas of crowdsourcing, software engineering, and probabilistic decision-making. These related readings will provide additional information and guidance to further enrich your knowledge and assist you with your own research.

Abramek, E. (2019). Maturity Profiles of Organizations for Social Media. In R. Lenart-Gansiniec (Ed.), *Crowdsourcing and Knowledge Management in Contemporary Business Environments* (pp. 134–145). Hershey, PA: IGI Global. doi:10.4018/978-1-5225-4200-1.ch007

Abu Talib, M. (2018). Towards Sustainable Development Through Open Source Software in the Arab World. In M. Khosrow-Pour, D.B.A. (Ed.), Optimizing Contemporary Application and Processes in Open Source Software (pp. 222-242). Hershey, PA: IGI Global. doi:10.4018/978-1-5225-5314-4.ch009

Adesola, A. P., & Olla, G. O. (2018). Unlocking the Unlimited Potentials of Koha OSS/ILS for Library House-Keeping Functions: A Global View. In M. Khosrow-Pour, D.B.A. (Ed.), Optimizing Contemporary Application and Processes in Open Source Software (pp. 124-163). Hershey, PA: IGI Global. doi:10.4018/978-1-5225-5314-4.ch006

Akber, A., Rizvi, S. S., Khan, M. W., Uddin, V., Hashmani, M. A., & Ahmad, J. (2019). Dimensions of Robust Security Testing in Global Software Engineering: A Systematic Review. In M. Rehman, A. Amin, A. Gilal, & M. Hashmani (Eds.), *Human Factors in Global Software Engineering* (pp. 252–272). Hershey, PA: IGI Global. doi:10.4018/978-1-5225-9448-2.ch010

Amrollahi, A., & Ahmadi, M. H. (2019). What Motivates the Crowd?: A Literature Review on Motivations for Crowdsourcing. In R. Lenart-Gansiniec (Ed.), *Crowdsourcing and Knowledge Management in Contemporary Business Environments* (pp. 103–133). Hershey, PA: IGI Global. doi:10.4018/978-1-5225-4200-1.ch006

Anchitaalagammai, J. V., Samayadurai, K., Murali, S., Padmadevi, S., & Shantha Lakshmi Revathy, J. (2019). Best Practices: Adopting Security Into the Software Development Process for IoT Applications. In D. Mala (Ed.), *Integrating the Internet of Things Into Software Engineering Practices* (pp. 146–159). Hershey, PA: IGI Global. doi:10.4018/978-1-5225-7790-4.ch007

Bhavsar, S. A., Pandit, B. Y., & Modi, K. J. (2019). Social Internet of Things. In D. Mala (Ed.), *Integrating the Internet of Things Into Software Engineering Practices* (pp. 199–218). Hershey, PA: IGI Global. doi:10.4018/978-1-5225-7790-4.ch010

Biswas, A., & De, A. K. (2019). *Multi-Objective Stochastic Programming in Fuzzy Environments* (pp. 1–420). Hershey, PA: IGI Global. doi:10.4018/978-1-5225-8301-1

Callaghan, C. W. (2017). The Probabilistic Innovation Field of Scientific Enquiry. *International Journal of Sociotechnology and Knowledge Development, 9*(2), 56–72. doi:10.4018/IJSKD.2017040104

Chhabra, D., & Sharma, I. (2018). Role of Attacker Capabilities in Risk Estimation and Mitigation. In R. Kumar, A. Tayal, & S. Kapil (Eds.), *Analyzing the Role of Risk Mitigation and Monitoring in Software Development* (pp. 244–255). Hershey, PA: IGI Global. doi:10.4018/978-1-5225-6029-6.ch015

Chitra, P., & Abirami, S. (2019). Smart Pollution Alert System Using Machine Learning. In D. Mala (Ed.), *Integrating the Internet of Things Into Software Engineering Practices* (pp. 219–235). Hershey, PA: IGI Global. doi:10.4018/978-1-5225-7790-4.ch011

Dorsey, M. D., & Raisinghani, M. S. (2019). IT Governance or IT Outsourcing: Is There a Clear Winner? In A. Mukherjee & A. Krishna (Eds.), *Interdisciplinary Approaches to Information Systems and Software Engineering* (pp. 19–32). Hershey, PA: IGI Global. doi:10.4018/978-1-5225-7784-3.ch002

Dua, R., Sharma, S., & Kumar, R. (2018). Risk Management Metrics. In R. Kumar, A. Tayal, & S. Kapil (Eds.), *Analyzing the Role of Risk Mitigation and Monitoring in Software Development* (pp. 21–33). Hershey, PA: IGI Global. doi:10.4018/978-1-5225-6029-6.ch002

Dua, R., Sharma, S., & Sharma, A. (2018). Software Vulnerability Management: How Intelligence Helps in Mitigating Software Vulnerabilities. In R. Kumar, A. Tayal, & S. Kapil (Eds.), *Analyzing the Role of Risk Mitigation and Monitoring in Software Development* (pp. 34–45). Hershey, PA: IGI Global. doi:10.4018/978-1-5225-6029-6.ch003

Fatema, K., Syeed, M. M., & Hammouda, I. (2018). Demography of Open Source Software Prediction Models and Techniques. In M. Khosrow-Pour, D.B.A. (Ed.), Optimizing Contemporary Application and Processes in Open Source Software(pp. 24-56). Hershey, PA: IGI Global. doi:10.4018/978-1-5225-5314-4.ch002

Ghafele, R., & Gibert, B. (2018). Open Growth: The Economic Impact of Open Source Software in the USA. In M. Khosrow-Pour, D.B.A. (Ed.), Optimizing Contemporary Application and Processes in Open Source Software (pp. 164-197). Hershey, PA: IGI Global. doi:10.4018/978-1-5225-5314-4.ch007

Gopikrishnan, S., & Priakanth, P. (2019). Web-Based IoT Application Development. In D. Mala (Ed.), *Integrating the Internet of Things Into Software Engineering Practices* (pp. 62–86). Hershey, PA: IGI Global. doi:10.4018/978-1-5225-7790-4.ch004

Guendouz, M., Amine, A., & Hamou, R. M. (2018). Open Source Projects Recommendation on GitHub. In M. Khosrow-Pour, D.B.A. (Ed.), Optimizing Contemporary Application and Processes in Open Source Software (pp. 86-101). Hershey, PA: IGI Global. doi:10.4018/978-1-5225-5314-4.ch004

Hashmani, M. A., Zaffar, M., & Ejaz, R. (2019). Scenario Based Test Case Generation Using Activity Diagram and Action Semantics. In M. Rehman, A. Amin, A. Gilal, & M. Hashmani (Eds.), *Human Factors in Global Software Engineering* (pp. 297–321). Hershey, PA: IGI Global. doi:10.4018/978-1-5225-9448-2.ch012

Jagannathan, J., & Anitha Elavarasi, S. (2019). Current Trends: Machine Learning and AI in IoT. In D. Mala (Ed.), *Integrating the Internet of Things Into Software Engineering Practices* (pp. 181–198). Hershey, PA: IGI Global. doi:10.4018/978-1-5225-7790-4.ch009

Jasmine, K. S. (2019). A New Process Model for IoT-Based Software Engineering. In D. Mala (Ed.), *Integrating the Internet of Things Into Software Engineering Practices* (pp. 1–13). Hershey, PA: IGI Global. doi:10.4018/978-1-5225-7790-4.ch001

Karthick, G. S., & Pankajavalli, P. B. (2019). Internet of Things Testing Framework, Automation, Challenges, Solutions and Practices: A Connected Approach for IoT Applications. In D. Mala (Ed.), *Integrating the Internet of Things Into Software Engineering Practices* (pp. 87–124). Hershey, PA: IGI Global. doi:10.4018/978-1-5225-7790-4.ch005

Kashyap, R. (2019). Big Data and Global Software Engineering. In M. Rehman, A. Amin, A. Gilal, & M. Hashmani (Eds.), *Human Factors in Global Software Engineering* (pp. 131–163). Hershey, PA: IGI Global. doi:10.4018/978-1-5225-9448-2.ch006

Kaur, J., & Kaur, R. (2018). Estimating Risks Related to Extended Enterprise Systems (EES). In R. Kumar, A. Tayal, & S. Kapil (Eds.), *Analyzing the Role of Risk Mitigation and Monitoring in Software Development* (pp. 118–135). Hershey, PA: IGI Global. doi:10.4018/978-1-5225-6029-6.ch008

Kaur, Y., & Singh, S. (2018). Risk Mitigation Planning, Implementation, and Progress Monitoring: Risk Mitigation. In R. Kumar, A. Tayal, & S. Kapil (Eds.), *Analyzing the Role of Risk Mitigation and Monitoring in Software Development* (pp. 1–20). Hershey, PA: IGI Global. doi:10.4018/978-1-5225-6029-6.ch001

Kavitha, S., Anchitaalagammai, J. V., Nirmala, S., & Murali, S. (2019). Current Trends in Integrating the Internet of Things Into Software Engineering Practices. In D. Mala (Ed.), *Integrating the Internet of Things Into Software Engineering Practices* (pp. 14–35). Hershey, PA: IGI Global. doi:10.4018/978-1-5225-7790-4.ch002

Köse, U. (2018). Optimization Scenarios for Open Source Software Used in E-Learning Activities. In M. Khosrow-Pour, D.B.A. (Ed.), Optimizing Contemporary Application and Processes in Open Source Software (pp. 102-123). Hershey, PA: IGI Global. doi:10.4018/978-1-5225-5314-4.ch005

Lal, S., Sardana, N., & Sureka, A. (2018). Logging Analysis and Prediction in Open Source Java Project. In M. Khosrow-Pour, D.B.A. (Ed.), Optimizing Contemporary Application and Processes in Open Source Software (pp. 57-85). Hershey, PA: IGI Global. doi:10.4018/978-1-5225-5314-4.ch003

Latif, A. M., Khan, K. M., & Duc, A. N. (2019). Software Cost Estimation and Capability Maturity Model in Context of Global Software Engineering. In M. Rehman, A. Amin, A. Gilal, & M. Hashmani (Eds.), *Human Factors in Global Software Engineering* (pp. 273–296). Hershey, PA: IGI Global. doi:10.4018/978-1-5225-9448-2.ch011

Lukyanenko, R., & Parsons, J. (2018). Beyond Micro-Tasks: Research Opportunities in Observational Crowdsourcing. *Journal of Database Management*, 29(1), 1–22. doi:10.4018/JDM.2018010101

Mala, D. (2019). IoT Functional Testing Using UML Use Case Diagrams: IoT in Testing. In D. Mala (Ed.), *Integrating the Internet of Things Into Software Engineering Practices* (pp. 125–145). Hershey, PA: IGI Global. doi:10.4018/978-1-5225-7790-4.ch006

Mansoor, M., Khan, M. W., Rizvi, S. S., Hashmani, M. A., & Zubair, M. (2019). Adaptation of Modern Agile Practices in Global Software Engineering. In M. Rehman, A. Amin, A. Gilal, & M. Hashmani (Eds.), *Human Factors in Global Software Engineering* (pp. 164–187). Hershey, PA: IGI Global. doi:10.4018/978-1-5225-9448-2.ch007

Memon, M. S. (2019). Techniques and Trends Towards Various Dimensions of Robust Security Testing in Global Software Engineering. In M. Rehman, A. Amin, A. Gilal, & M. Hashmani (Eds.), *Human Factors in Global Software Engineering* (pp. 219–251). Hershey, PA: IGI Global. doi:10.4018/978-1-5225-9448-2.ch009

Mukherjee, S., Bhattacharjee, A. K., & Deyasi, A. (2019). Project Teamwork Assessment and Success Rate Prediction Through Meta-Heuristic Algorithms. In A. Mukherjee & A. Krishna (Eds.), *Interdisciplinary Approaches to Information Systems and Software Engineering* (pp. 33–61). Hershey, PA: IGI Global. doi:10.4018/978-1-5225-7784-3.ch003

Nandy, A. (2019). Identification of Tectonic Activity and Fault Mechanism From Morphological Signatures. In A. Mukherjee & A. Krishna (Eds.), *Interdisciplinary Approaches to Information Systems and Software Engineering* (pp. 99–123). Hershey, PA: IGI Global. doi:10.4018/978-1-5225-7784-3.ch005

Omar, M., Rejab, M. M., & Ahmad, M. (2019). The Effect of Team Work Quality on Team Performance in Global Software Engineering. In M. Rehman, A. Amin, A. Gilal, & M. Hashmani (Eds.), *Human Factors in Global Software Engineering* (pp. 322–331). Hershey, PA: IGI Global. doi:10.4018/978-1-5225-9448-2.ch013

Onuchowska, A., & de Vreede, G. (2017). Disruption and Deception in Crowdsourcing. *International Journal of e-Collaboration*, 13(4), 23–41. doi:10.4018/IJeC.2017100102

Papadopoulou, C., & Giaoutzi, M. (2017). Crowdsourcing and Living Labs in Support of Smart Cities' Development. *International Journal of E-Planning Research*, 6(2), 22–38. doi:10.4018/IJEPR.2017040102

Patnaik, K. S., & Snigdh, I. (2019). Modelling and Designing of IoT Systems Using UML Diagrams: An Introduction. In D. Mala (Ed.), *Integrating the Internet of Things Into Software Engineering Practices* (pp. 36–61). Hershey, PA: IGI Global. doi:10.4018/978-1-5225-7790-4.ch003

Pawar, L., Kumar, R., & Sharma, A. (2018). Risks Analysis and Mitigation Technique in EDA Sector: VLSI Supply Chain. In R. Kumar, A. Tayal, & S. Kapil (Eds.), *Analyzing the Role of Risk Mitigation and Monitoring in Software Development* (pp. 256–265). Hershey, PA: IGI Global. doi:10.4018/978-1-5225-6029-6.ch016

Persaud, A., & O'Brien, S. (2017). Quality and Acceptance of Crowdsourced Translation of Web Content. *International Journal of Technology and Human Interaction*, *13*(1), 100–115. doi:10.4018/IJTHI.2017010106

Phung, V. D., & Hawryszkiewycz, I. (2019). Knowledge Sharing and Innovative Work Behavior: An Extension of Social Cognitive Theory. In R. Lenart-Gansiniec (Ed.), *Crowdsourcing and Knowledge Management in Contemporary Business Environments* (pp. 71–102). Hershey, PA: IGI Global. doi:10.4018/978-1-5225-4200-1.ch005

Priakanth, P., & Gopikrishnan, S. (2019). Machine Learning Techniques for Internet of Things. In D. Mala (Ed.), *Integrating the Internet of Things Into Software Engineering Practices* (pp. 160–180). Hershey, PA: IGI Global. doi:10.4018/978-1-5225-7790-4.ch008

Priyadarshi, A. (2019). Segmentation of Different Tissues of Brain From MR Image. In A. Mukherjee & A. Krishna (Eds.), *Interdisciplinary Approaches to Information Systems and Software Engineering* (pp. 142–180). Hershey, PA: IGI Global. doi:10.4018/978-1-5225-7784-3.ch007

Rath, M. (2019). Intelligent Information System for Academic Institutions: Using Big Data Analytic Approach. In A. Mukherjee & A. Krishna (Eds.), *Interdisciplinary Approaches to Information Systems and Software Engineering* (pp. 207–232). Hershey, PA: IGI Global. doi:10.4018/978-1-5225-7784-3.ch009

Realyvásquez, A., Maldonado-Macías, A. A., & Hernández-Escobedo, G. (2019). Software Development for Ergonomic Compatibility Assessment of Advanced Manufacturing Technology. In M. Rehman, A. Amin, A. Gilal, & M. Hashmani (Eds.), *Human Factors in Global Software Engineering* (pp. 50–83). Hershey, PA: IGI Global. doi:10.4018/978-1-5225-9448-2.ch003

Rjaibi, N., & Latifa Ben Arfa Rabai. (2018). New Classification of Security Requirements for Quantitative Risk Assessment. In R. Kumar, A. Tayal, & S. Kapil (Eds.), *Analyzing the Role of Risk Mitigation and Monitoring in Software Development* (pp. 100-117). Hershey, PA: IGI Global. doi:10.4018/978-1-5225-6029-6.ch007

Saini, M., & Chahal, K. K. (2018). A Systematic Review of Attributes and Techniques for Open Source Software Evolution Analysis. In M. Khosrow-Pour, D.B.A. (Ed.), Optimizing Contemporary Application and Processes in Open Source Software (pp. 1-23). Hershey, PA: IGI Global. doi:10.4018/978-1-5225-5314-4.ch001

Sen, K., & Ghosh, K. (2018). Designing Effective Crowdsourcing Systems for the Healthcare Industry. *International Journal of Public Health Management and Ethics*, *3*(2), 57–62. doi:10.4018/IJPHME.2018070104

Sen, K., & Ghosh, K. (2018). Incorporating Global Medical Knowledge to Solve Healthcare Problems: A Framework for a Crowdsourcing System. *International Journal of Healthcare Information Systems and Informatics*, *13*(1), 1–14. doi:10.4018/IJHISI.2018010101

Sharma, A., Pal, V., Ojha, N., & Bajaj, R. (2018). Risks Assessment in Designing Phase: Its Impacts and Issues. In R. Kumar, A. Tayal, & S. Kapil (Eds.), *Analyzing the Role of Risk Mitigation and Monitoring in Software Development* (pp. 46–60). Hershey, PA: IGI Global. doi:10.4018/978-1-5225-6029-6.ch004

Sharma, A., Pawar, L., & Kaur, M. (2018). Development and Enhancing of Software and Programming Products by Client Information Administration in Market. In R. Kumar, A. Tayal, & S. Kapil (Eds.), *Analyzing the Role of Risk Mitigation and Monitoring in Software Development* (pp. 150–187). Hershey, PA: IGI Global. doi:10.4018/978-1-5225-6029-6.ch010

Sharma, A. P., & Sharma, S. (2018). Risk Management in Web Development. In R. Kumar, A. Tayal, & S. Kapil (Eds.), *Analyzing the Role of Risk Mitigation and Monitoring in Software Development* (pp. 188–203). Hershey, PA: IGI Global. doi:10.4018/978-1-5225-6029-6.ch011

Sharma, I., & Chhabra, D. (2018). Meta-Heuristic Approach for Software Project Risk Schedule Analysis. In R. Kumar, A. Tayal, & S. Kapil (Eds.), *Analyzing the Role of Risk Mitigation and Monitoring in Software Development* (pp. 136–149). Hershey, PA: IGI Global. doi:10.4018/978-1-5225-6029-6.ch009

Sharma, S., & Dua, R. (2018). Gamification: An Effectual Learning Application for SE. In R. Kumar, A. Tayal, & S. Kapil (Eds.), *Analyzing the Role of Risk Mitigation and Monitoring in Software Development* (pp. 219–233). Hershey, PA: IGI Global. doi:10.4018/978-1-5225-6029-6.ch013

Sidhu, A. K., & Sehra, S. K. (2018). Use of Software Metrics to Improve the Quality of Software Projects Using Regression Testing. In R. Kumar, A. Tayal, & S. Kapil (Eds.), *Analyzing the Role of Risk Mitigation and Monitoring in Software Development* (pp. 204–218). Hershey, PA: IGI Global. doi:10.4018/978-1-5225-6029-6.ch012

Srao, B. K., Rai, H. S., & Mann, K. S. (2018). Why India Should Make It Compulsory to Go for BIM. In R. Kumar, A. Tayal, & S. Kapil (Eds.), *Analyzing the Role of Risk Mitigation and Monitoring in Software Development* (pp. 266–277). Hershey, PA: IGI Global. doi:10.4018/978-1-5225-6029-6.ch017

Srivastava, R. (2018). An Analysis on Risk Management and Risk in the Software Projects. In R. Kumar, A. Tayal, & S. Kapil (Eds.), *Analyzing the Role of Risk Mitigation and Monitoring in Software Development* (pp. 83–99). Hershey, PA: IGI Global. doi:10.4018/978-1-5225-6029-6.ch006

Srivastava, R., Verma, S. K., & Thukral, V. (2018). A New Approach for Reinforcement of Project DEMATEL-FMCDM-TODIM Fuzzy Approach. In R. Kumar, A. Tayal, & S. Kapil (Eds.), *Analyzing the Role of Risk Mitigation and Monitoring in Software Development* (pp. 234–243). Hershey, PA: IGI Global. doi:10.4018/978-1-5225-6029-6.ch014

Tolu, H. (2018). Strategy of Good Software Governance: FLOSS in the State of Turkey. In M. Khosrow-Pour, D.B.A. (Ed.), Optimizing Contemporary Application and Processes in Open Source Software (pp. 198-221). Hershey, PA: IGI Global. doi:10.4018/978-1-5225-5314-4.ch008

Trad, A. (2019). The Business Transformation Framework and Enterprise Architecture Framework for Managers in Business Innovation: Knowledge Management in Global Software Engineering (KMGSE). In M. Rehman, A. Amin, A. Gilal, & M. Hashmani (Eds.), *Human Factors in Global Software Engineering* (pp. 20–49). Hershey, PA: IGI Global. doi:10.4018/978-1-5225-9448-2.ch002

Vasanthapriyan, S. (2019). Knowledge Management Initiatives in Agile Software Development: A Literature Review. In M. Rehman, A. Amin, A. Gilal, & M. Hashmani (Eds.), *Human Factors in Global Software Engineering* (pp. 109–130). Hershey, PA: IGI Global. doi:10.4018/978-1-5225-9448-2.ch005

Vasanthapriyan, S. (2019). Knowledge Sharing Initiatives in Software Companies: A Mapping Study. In M. Rehman, A. Amin, A. Gilal, & M. Hashmani (Eds.), *Human Factors in Global Software Engineering* (pp. 84–108). Hershey, PA: IGI Global. doi:10.4018/978-1-5225-9448-2.ch004

Related Readings

Vasanthapriyan, S. (2019). Study of Employee Innovative Behavior in Sri Lankan Software Companies. In M. Rehman, A. Amin, A. Gilal, & M. Hashmani (Eds.), *Human Factors in Global Software Engineering* (pp. 188–218). Hershey, PA: IGI Global. doi:10.4018/978-1-5225-9448-2.ch008

Ziouvelou, X., & McGroarty, F. (2018). A Business Model Framework for Crowd-Driven IoT Ecosystems. *International Journal of Social Ecology and Sustainable Development*, 9(3), 14–33. doi:10.4018/IJSESD.2018070102

Zykov, S. V., Gromoff, A., & Kazantsev, N. S. (2019). *Software Engineering for Enterprise System Agility: Emerging Research and Opportunities* (pp. 1–218). Hershey, PA: IGI Global. doi:10.4018/978-1-5225-5589-6

About the Contributors

Zeynep Altan graduated from Istanbul Technical University as Mathematical Engineer. She completed her master studies at the Institute of Science and Technology System Analysis Department at Istanbul Technical University. She received her doctorate degree at Numerical Methods Program at Istanbul University. Until 2002, she taught at the Department of Computer Engineering at Istanbul University. Since 2013, she is the head of Software Engineering Department at Beykent University. Her research interests include software engineering, theory of computation and natural language processing. She has many studies published in several journals and conferences, and a lecture book on formal language and automata theory.

* * *

Muhammed Ali Aydin completed his B.S. in 1997-2001 in Computer Engineering at Istanbul University, M.Sc. in 2001-2005 in Computer Engineering at Istanbul Technical University and Ph.D. in 2005-2009 Computer Engineering at Istanbul University. His research interests are communication network protocols, network architecture, cryptography, information security and network security.

Serkan Ayvaz received his bachelors degree in Mathematics and Computer Science in 2006 from Bahcesehir University in Istanbul, Turkey. Later, he received his masters degree in Technology with specialization in Computer Technology from Kent State University in 2008. He completed his Ph.D. in Computer Science at Kent State University in 2015. He is currently an assistant professor of Computer Science at the Department of Software Engineering and serves as the coordinator of the Big Data Analytics and Management Graduate program at Bahcesehir University. He is a co-founder of Big Data center at Bahcesehir University and currently serves as vice director of the center. His research interests include Big Data Analytics and scalable knowledge discovery, Machine Learning, Semantic Searches, Semantic Web and its applications.

Birim Balci is a lecturer at the Department of Computer Engineering at Manisa Celal Bayar University. She had undergraduate and master degrees from Marmara University. She studied about Web-Based Distance Education area during her PhD at Ege University Science Institute, Computer Engineering Department and had a degree at the end of 2007. She worked in several major positions in the distance education. Her research interests include engineering education, e-learning, web-based learning. She has published many articles in conferences and journals, has written many book chapters in the related research fields.

Ethem Soner Celikkol is a professor at Beykent University Management Information Systems Department and head of Department of Management Information Systems. His research interests are algorithms and data structures, database management systems and management information systems.

Omer Cetin completed his PhD in computer engineering in 2015 on autonomous systems and parallel programming applications. He teaches courses on autonomous systems, image processing and parallel programming in undergraduate and graduate programs at different universities as assistant professor. He has numerous international articles and papers on autonomous path planning, real-time programming applications and he continues to carry out research activities in these fields.

José C. Delgado is an Associate Professor at the Computer Science and Engineering Department of the Instituto Superior Técnico (University of Lisbon), in Lisbon, Portugal, where he earned the Ph.D. degree in 1988. He lectures courses in the areas of Computer Architecture, Information Technology and Service Engineering. He has performed several management roles in his faculty, namely Director of the Taguspark campus, near Lisbon, and Coordinator of the B.Sc. and M.Sc. in Computer Science and Engineering at that campus. He has been the coordinator of and researcher in several international research projects. As an author, his publications include one book, 25 book chapters and more than 50 papers in international refereed conferences and journals.

Can Eyupoglu received the B.Sc. degree with high honor in Computer Engineering and Minor degree in Electronics Engineering from Istanbul Kultur University, Turkey in 2012, the M.Sc. and Ph.D. degrees with high honor in Computer Engineering from Istanbul University in 2014 and 2018, respectively. From 2013 to 2019, he was a Research Assistant with the Computer Engineering Department, Istanbul Commerce University. He is currently an Assistant Professor with the Computer Engineering Department, Turkish Air Force Academy, National Defense University, Istanbul, Turkey. His current research interest includes big data processing, big data privacy, bioinformatics, neural networks, natural language processing, and image processing.

Derya Yiltaş Kaplan completed her MSc and PhD degrees in computer engineering from Istanbul University, Istanbul, Turkey, in 2003 and 2007, respectively. She was a postdoctorate researcher at the North Carolina State University and received postdoctorate research scholarship from The Scientific and Technological Research Council of Turkey. She is now Associate Professor in the Department of Computer Engineering at Istanbul University-Cerrahpasa.

Adem Karahoca is currently a full-time professor in the Department of Computer Eng., Nisantasi University, Istanbul, Turkey. He received his B.Sc. degree in Mathematical Engineering from Istanbul Technical University, M.Sc. and Ph.D. degrees in Computer Engineering from Istanbul University. He has published 20 IT related books in Turkish and edited 4 IT related books in English. His research interests are data mining, fuzzy systems, information systems, business intelligence, computers in education, human computer interaction and big data.

Sefer Kurnaz graduated PhD at İstanbul University and specialized in Computer Science. He was the director of Aeronautics & Space Technologies Institute (ASTIN) in Turkish Air Force Academy, Istanbul. He worked at the 6 Allied Air Tactical Force (6ATAF) in NATO, İzmir as a chief of system support section. He retired from Turkish Air Force Command as colonel. He was the general chair of the Resent Advances in Space Technologies International Conference (RAST), Turkey until he has retired. He is an author of two books published in Turkey and United States of America. He has published over than 20 scientific papers.

Eyuphan Ozdemir is a Ph.D. candidate in Philosophy at the Victoria University of Wellington. He completed his Bachelor's in Computer Engineering at Trakya University followed by MSc in Computer Engineering at Beykent University, and MA in Philosophy at Bogazici University. He is specifically interested in web services and applications.

Yucel Batu Salman received his BS and MS degrees in Computer Engineering from Bahcesehir University, Istanbul, Turkey, in 2003 and 2005, respectively and his PhD in IT Convergence Design from Kyungsung University, Busan, Rep. of Korea, in 2010. Since 2010, he has been an assistant professor of Software Engineering at Bahcesehir University. He is currently the director of Graduate School of Natural and Applied Sciences at Bahcesehir University. His research interests include human computer interaction, big data analytics and computer vision.

Ruya Samlı has completed her MsC and PhD in Istanbul University, Computer Engineering Department in 2006 and 2011 respectively. She is working as an Assoc. Prof. Dr. in Istanbul University - Cerrahpasa, Computer Engineering Department. Her research areas are artificial intelligence, machine learning and software engineering. She has many SCI/SCI-E journal publications and book chapters about these subjects.

Ediz Saykol is an assistant professor in Computer Engineering Department, Beykent University since 2011. His research interests include video surveillance (abnormal event detection, human action recognition, visual privacy) and document/textual image processing. His contributions have been published in several journals and conferences, and his work has been cited more than 500 times.

Atinç Yilmaz completed his undergraduate and graduate educations in Computer Engineering Department. He received his PhD degree from Sakarya University Computer and Information Engineering Department. He has been an assistant professor of Computer Engineering Department at Beykent University since 2015. He is also the head of the Department of Computer Engineering (Turkish) and vice dean of the Faculty of Engineering and Architecture. His research interests include artificial intelligence, machine learning, data mining, and big data. The books on the subject artificial intelligence and deep learning are some of the books he has written at his research field.

Ugur Osman Yücel was born on 28 May 1994. He raised his hometown named Bilecik which is a small town in Turkey. In 2012, he started to study Software Engineering at Bahçeşehir University. After graduation, he started to work as Research Assistant at Maltepe University. Currently, he is a master student at Istanbul University - Cerrahpasa.

Jaroslaw Zelinski is an experienced Business & Information Systems Engineer, Independent Systems Researcher (my Academia.edu profile), Lecturer and Author. Over 20 years experience in business process modeling, data modeling, information engineering, requirements elicitation, software architecture design, systems integration, business analysis and extracting the business rules to base the business processes on. Also authoring supervising for implementation of designed systems and software. Work with the use of formal, scientific methodology and formal notation: in particular: BMM, BPMN, UML, SBVR.

Index

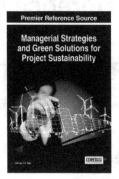

Printed in the United States
By Bookmasters